SIOUXSIE
AND
THE
BANSHEES

The
Early
Years

Laurence Hedges

SIOUXSIE
AND
THE
BANSHEES

*The
Early
Years*

Laurence Hedges

WYMER
PUBLISHING
Bedford, England

First published in 2023 by Wymer Publishing
Bedford, England www.wymerpublishing.co.uk Tel: 01234 326691
Wymer Publishing is a trading name of Wymer (UK) Ltd

Copyright © 2023 Laurence Hedges / Wymer Publishing.

Print edition (fully illustrated): **ISBN: 978-1-915246-24-0**

Edited by Jerry Bloom.

Printed and bound in Great Britain by
CMP, Dorset.

A catalogue record for this book is available from the British Library.

Typeset/Design by Andy Bishop / 1016 Sarpsborg
Cover design by 1016 Sarpsborg.
Front cover photo © Steve Emberton
All plate photos © Ray Stevenson

Contents

Prologue

There is a slight incongruity about writing this book. As a teenager, I was conflicted about which music I liked and was drawn towards. However, I can trace what I initially heard back to the early 1970s when, as a child, I remember my eldest brother playing along, note for note, with bands like Argent, Juicy Lucy and Family. The keyboard used by many blues-based rock bands formed in the late 1970s, which I was later to discover was the distinctive sound of a Hammond organ, featured regularly in this one room in our household of six. When my brother was out, I used to study the sleeves of albums in his collection and was thrilled by artwork of which I had no comprehension, such as 'Meddle' by Pink Floyd or 'Time and a word' by Yes. All seemed strange, scary and, looking back, a little clandestine: a portal into another, different world.

Also perhaps incongruously, the aforementioned brother was playing a baby grand piano that had been installed in his bedroom on the ground floor of a Victorian terraced house in Streatham in South West London: a bedroom where he had a phone, as it was the only room in the house with a phone socket, and an office desk with a slide-out tray that was rich with coinage I thought he had lovingly set aside for everyone to dip into. My eldest brother was also a DJ with a case full of compartmentalised 45rpm singles featuring everything from Motown, Eric Clapton, The Rolling Stones, Cream, The Who and The Beatles to the theme tune to 'Dr No', which he used to start every disco with for maximum dramatic effect. The mobile disco my brother ran was rather appositely named Pandora.

Fast forward several years and I arrive home from school, this time in a different house. As a family, we had moved from Streatham to Croydon when I was around eight years old. My memory is a little hazy as to why. However, my arrival home from secondary school — I must have been around 11 or 12 at the time — was greeted by another rich Hammond organ sound, this time by a different band: Deep Purple. Another older brother had bought their self-titled album, made in 1969, which uses a section of the descent into hell, in monochrome, of Hieronymus Bosch's 'Garden of Earthly Delights' 1490–1510 for the gatefold album sleeve. The Mk 1 incarnation of the band has been clumsily, and it would seem rather hastily, cut and pasted into the apocalyptic scene. The music itself is a fascinating, albeit discordant, hybrid of psychedelia, blues and, for good measure, one song ('April') replete with three movements including a folk-like section, an orchestral one and a rock one. This album was an inadvertent epiphany for the band, leading to the unceremonious sacking of both lead singer Rod Evans and bass guitarist Nick Simper. Along with 'Deep Purple', another purchase of my brother's, 'Ritchie Blackmore's Rainbow', released in 1975, was the catalyst in deciding my musical aesthetic for the next two to three years. I went to gigs at the Hammersmith Odeon, Croydon's Fairfield Halls and the Rainbow in Finsbury Park to see Motörhead, Black Sabbath, Uriah Heep, Gillan, Rainbow, Whitesnake and The Scorpions. I also relished all the support bands, some of which are still doing the rounds, including Girlschool, Magnum, Marseille and White Spirit. I was that teenager with the denim jacket, patchouli oil, myriad badges, patches and very crude embroidery.

Everything was about to change.

Chapter 1
Suburban (An)aesthetic

Neither punk, skinhead, ska aficionado, new romantic, soul boy/girl, metalhead or psychedelic, mushroom-guzzling pothead be…

Confusing…

In the episode 'Watership Alan' from the series 'I'm Alan Partridge' made between 1997 and 2002, Partridge's monthly Travel Tavern bill states '£8 miscellaneous services', which Partridge finds 'disconcertingly vague'; the crux of the storyline being that when the protagonist's 15-minute assignation with an adult cable channel is brought to light, he explains, disingenuously, that his interest was momentarily 'piqued' when he really wanted to watch 'Driving Miss Daisy' and not, in fact, 'Bangkok Chick Boys', but found the pay channels 'confusing.' Even though Partridge is in his mid to late forties in the series, his life is one of missed subtle social cues and protocols, stuck in a cultural time warp where 'Wings were only the band The Beatles could have been' and Britpop's nadir was UB40 and Def Leppard. It is as though, since his teenage years, Partridge has been unencumbered by any semblance of what might be called as 'taste.'

Although hilariously and beautifully observed, Partridge epitomises everything that is beige and soulless about the homogeneity of suburbs and suburban thinking; a seeming dystopia that The Banshees' nucleus of Susan Janet Ballion (Siouxsie Sioux — born 27 May 1957) and Steven John Bailey (Steve Severin — born 25 September 1955) hated with a passion and couldn't wait to escape.

Great(er) London

Allders department store coffee shop in Croydon's Whitgift Centre on a Saturday morning: this was where, as teenagers, we used to congregate. Our tribe. It felt so grown up at the time, almost sophisticated. In the late 1970s and 1980s, Croydon wasn't the suburban hinterland it is now. There were venues such as The Greyhound (now sadly defunct) where David Bowie played, supported by Roxy Music, Genesis (for all of 50p), Emerson Lake and Palmer, MC5 and Supertramp. Fairfield Halls boasted a stellar roll call of acts such as Pink Floyd, King Crimson, Kraftwerk, The Beatles, Morrissey and Canned Heat. Apparently, while a lavatory cleaner at the venue, Captain Sensible decided he was going pursue a career in music far more seriously after watching a T-Rex gig.

Beano's Record Store (1975–2010) was an Aladdin's cave of secondhand vinyl; with picture discs hanging from the ceiling on the ground floor. There was also Croydon College of Art, counting Malcolm McLaren and Jamie Reid among its alumni and Derek Boshier and Bridget Riley as tutors.

It was 1977 when I started secondary school. All my primary school mates had gone to local schools but, as a sort of guinea-pig experiment meets pin the tail on the donkey, my perfectly well-meaning parents hit on a school that was several miles away. A new school where my year group were the first intake. This was an experience I so despised almost instantaneously that, for several weeks, I would put on my school uniform, pack my school bag, eat breakfast and catch the bus to the Whitgift Centre, where I would just hang around until the school day ended, or opt for the 190 bus to Old Coulsdon, which felt like a trip to the countryside. My dislike of school manifested itself in physical illness. From that point onwards, as an 11-year-old, I sensed that I was going to need all the distractions available to get me through school.

Routemaster

Whether I decided to go to school or not, the Routemaster London bus, the one you could jump on or off at your leisure or peril, was my favoured mode of transport. Bus 119 from Thornton Heath to Bromley North Station took me to school. It is perhaps a more than serendipitous coincidence, not least for the purposes of this book, that Croydon and Bromley sit geographically side by side on the Greater London map. Greater London was an entity created by the London Government Act that came into being on 1 April 1965, replacing the administrative counties of Middlesex and London, including the City of London, where the London County Council had curtailed powers, and absorbing parts of Essex, Hertfordshire, Kent and Surrey.

'Bromley finally got what it deserved; it's turned into one big shopping mall.'[1] Bertie Marshall.

As a town, Bromley boasts a host of illustrious residents, a veritable who's who of the ground-breaking, seminal and influential including H.G. Wells, David Bowie, Charles Darwin, Billy Idol, Topper Headon, Haneif Kureishi and Richmal Crompton, to name a few. It is also home to the fictional Green Midget Cafe, the setting for the Monty Python 'Spam' sketch. Bromley, like with Croydon, at least cosmetically, is not deficient in culture; it has several theatres, including an outdoor amphitheatre, library and an annual festival of dance, comedy and drama. It has an abundance of shops to satiate the appetite of the most voracious consumer, including The Glades, a huge indoor shopping mall on several floors, replete with all the multi-national stores that can be found all over the world.

It is perhaps no surprise, or coincidence, that the final denouement of George Romero's 1978 seminal masterpiece 'Dawn of the Dead' is set in a mall and 'the group of survivors become victims of their own greed, having claimed the mall and do not want to share it. Even as the world is ending, their main concern is the spoil of all their riches in this massive resource-hoarding world they have shut themselves away in.'[2]

In an article entitled 'Grey Sky Modernists' published in June 2018, various aspects of Modernism and Brutalism are discussed, citing articles written in the Architectural Review in the 1950s appertaining to the infrastructural and aesthetic dichotomy of rebuilding and reimagining the many towns and cities decimated during the Second World War bombings, and the complex arguments between architectural ideologies including the Arts and Crafts movement and Brutalism.

Ian Nairn, who became Assistant Editor of the Architectural Review in 1954, made his name with the 'Outrage' issue of the journal, an incendiary attack, not against Modernism per se but against the 'sheer banality of British towns and cities', which had seen the 'steamrollering of all individuality of place to one uniform and mediocre pattern.' This statement now appears alarmingly prescient, nearly 70 years on, with towns and cities, nationwide, poorly designed, homogenised, under-funded and practically decimated.

Bromley Haphazard

Steve Severin lived in Archway until the age of 11 when he and his family moved to Bromley, recalling it 'was very green; I couldn't get over how green it was. There were parks everywhere. By that time, I already loved The Beatles and

The Rolling Stones. I remember having 'She Loves You' and really liking and wanting it, but the first record my parents bought me was 'Twist And Shout'.'³ Severin's mother was a seamstress by profession and his father ran the night picture desk at the *Daily Express*.

Severin, who also adopted the monikers of Steve Havoc and Steve Spunker during the time he was part of the Bromley Contingent, appropriated his name from the Velvet Underground 1967 song 'Venus In Furs', the Velvets having borrowed both song title and lyrics from the Austrian writer and journalist Leopold von Sacher-Masoch's novella published in 1870.

Part of an epic series Maosoch envisioned called 'Das Vermächtniß Kains' (Legacy of Cain), 'Venus in Furs' was part of 'Die Liebe' (Love), the first volume of the series. In the story, Severin von Kusiemski is completely infatuated with Wanda von Dunajew and he asks to be her slave, encouraging her to treat him in cumulatively more degrading ways. Wanda does not, at first, understand or grant the request, but after indulging Severin a little, finds the advantages of the method to be much to her liking, even embracing the idea, although at the same time she despises Severin for allowing her to do so. Severin describes his feelings during these experiences as 'suprasensuality'.

Travelling to Florence with Wanda, Severin adopts the generic Russian servant's name Gregor and becomes Wanda's servant. Subsequently, Wanda treats him brutally and recruits a trio of African women to dominate him. The term masochism is derived from Sacher-Masoch's name, much to the writer's chagrin. The parallels between Sacher-Masoch's story and the lyrical content of the Velvets' song are evident and certainly not lost on Steve Severin's developing penchant for filmic and literary imagery.

****

In interviews, Severin states that the 'Bromley Contingent' tag given to the group of friends, among them Siouxsie Sioux and Billy Idol, was something of a misnomer as Severin was the only member, excepting Berlin Bromley (Bertie Marshall) who is both dismissive and scornful of the label, who lived in Bromley and even he didn't feel any sense of belonging to the town, adding, 'We were really a group of people from all over south London, who clustered together because we liked the same things.'[4] Banshees' photographer Ray Stevenson also recollects, 'Siouxsie and Severin were never punks and I what I remember them being the most vocal about was that they weren't from Bromley. The Bromley Contingent Pistols' fans had a great style and Malcolm (McLaren) wanted to do a publication showing provincial kids how they could look, which, essentially meant shopping at his World's End shop. I lusted after the mohair sweaters but I was buying good cars for £100.'[5]

Siouxsie Sioux was born in Southwark but lived in the village of Chislehurst. Both Sioux and Severin give detailed and candid accounts of their formative and familial experiences growing up in the outer reaches of South London in Mark Paytress' comprehensive 'Siouxsie and The Banshees The Authorised Biography'. It is abundantly clear that neither future Banshee was interested in the tyranny and boredom of secondary education, although Severin 'had been very good at primary school, and the first years at secondary, where I had even won a school prize. But that all deteriorated when I was about fourteen. It was the usual — girls, drugs and music.'[6]

Both Sioux and Severin left school with a clutch of O-levels. Sioux's upbringing, at least cosmetically, was comfortably middle-class. When one scratches the surface, however, it is clear that Sioux's formative experiences as a child in Chislehurst resembled a hybrid of David Lynch's 'Blue Velvet' and Rene Magritte's 'Empire of Light' series of paintings from the 1940s to 1960s. Sioux's mother worked as an English/French bilingual secretary. Her father was a bacteriologist whose work included milking snakes for their serum. "I think that just because of the kind of family we were, there was definitely a sense of not feeling a part of the community, or of being neighbourly. I was very aware of us being very different. My father had a drink problem, which also sensitised that feeling."[7]

In the same interview, Sioux also states that "Where we lived was very residential, and our house seemed different. It wasn't red brick, to begin with — it was white stucco with a flat roof, and with trees. Everyone else had gardens with patios and neatly cut lawns, and we had these massive copper beech trees at the front, and a huge privet hedge. You couldn't look into our house. All the others were almost inviting you to look in — life in all its normality was being paraded. Which probably wasn't the case behind closed doors, but that was the perception."[8] In Bracewell's interview, Sioux also states her unassuaged hatred of the suburbs as "a yardstick for measuring how much we didn't fit in."[9]

Sioux has cited a whole raft of televisual and filmic experiences that captivated her imagination as a child, including her love of Indians in cowboy films, siding with them as the underdog and feeling that they were so much 'sexier'[10]; she was given a squaw outfit for her sixth birthday. There was also Doctor Who, especially episodes with the Daleks, which she found scary and captivating in equal measure. 'Julie Newman as Catwoman (from Batman) and The Avengers'[11] inspired Sioux to dress up, thinking Diana Rigg so 'sexy'.[12]

Sioux and her mother regularly went to the local cinema

to see Doris Day and Elvis Presley films. Early Disney films such as 'Snow White and the Seven Dwarfs' were a catalyst for Sioux's fascination with animation and she found the iconic shower scene in Pyscho, directed by Alfred Hitchcock, so disturbing that she remembers feeling worried when her mother told her she was going to buy a shower and always ensured she was out of the bathroom before the last vestiges of water had disappeared down the plughole. It is perhaps no surprise, in retrospect, considering the subsequent filmic allusions made throughout The Banshees' career, especially in 1988's 'Peepshow', that the future band name was inspired by the 1970 British horror film 'The Cry of the Banshee', whose title is loosely attributed to 'The Bell' by Edgar Allan Poe.

Featuring Vincent Price among the cast, the plot of the film, which is set in the 1500s, centres around the massacre of members of a witches coven at the behest of magistrate Lord Edward Whitman, who thus earns the revenge of their leader, Oona, who calls up a magical servant, a banshee (a female spirit in Gaelic folklore, whose appearance or wailing warns a family that one of them will soon die), to destroy Whitman's family. The film, the opening credits of which were animated by Terry Gilliam with his trademark surreal Monty Python style, is ostensibly a B movie and a deliciously perverse choice for a band that would, time and time again, eschew the obvious in favour of the unexpected and unpredictable.

As with many fruitful songwriting partnerships — Lennon and McCartney, Jagger and Richards, Morrissey and Marr — the initial bond of being captivated by the same musical genres was also the case for Sioux and Severin. The pair did not meet at a Sex Pistols gig, and certainly not the one at Ravensbourne College of Art in December 1975, the details of which were described by Sioux's sister and by a friend of Severin's. The excitement surrounding the gig had very little, or nothing, to do with set list or musical prowess; it was more about the attitude and exuberance of the band, in particular Johnny Rotten's confrontational, guarding and threatening attitude to the students attending the gig.

Sioux, who had adopted the pseudonym Candy Sue, and Severin first met at a sold-out Roxy Music show at Wembley Arena on 18 October 1975 during the 'Sirens' tour. It was, by all accounts, the same gig Vivienne Westwood attended, where discernibly vocal and outspoken, pointing directly at Bryan Ferry and shouting "You're disgusting, you're disgusting"[13] to such a disruptive extent that attempts were made by security to eject her from the gig. Simon Barker recalls: 'When Bryan Ferry came on, wearing army clothes or something, suddenly this woman with white hair and tight trousers and a big-shouldered jacket, jumped up and started shouting obscenities at him (Ferry).'[14]

Sioux recollects the event: "I was on my own, which wasn't unusual for me. I was quite independent. I didn't have people to go to gigs with, so I'd often trek off on my own. I got dressed in a purple and green outfit, with a huge fishtail-like bustle, got the bus to the train station, sat on the platform, perched myself in the train carriage and then traipsed across London. The dress must have been used in some vaudeville costume drama, but it seemed quite normal to me. I used to enjoy people staring at me and then me turning my nose up at them."[15]

For Severin's part, he recalls he "had a blond quiff, a tartan jacket, black drainpipes and platform shoes with white crepe soles and black patent leather uppers which had two stripes, Adidas-style. I think that's why Sioux said to me, "You look very sporty." Fashion was very important. It gave you a sense of belonging, of being outside of everything, and at the same time being with your own gang. I went with my friend Simon Barker."[16]

Sioux traces her initial formative encounters with music when, as a three year old in 1961, she heard John Leyton's 'Johnny Remember Me', stating that, "It had these amazing, ghostly backing vocals, a great melody, and it was about a dead girlfriend, basically."[17] The discovery of music, apparently profuse and stabilising in an otherwise mercurial household — her father's increasing alcoholism and surviving a sexual assault when Sioux was nine — was a means of both liberation and escape. A formative encounter was seeing David Bowie perform 'Starman' on Top of The Pops in 1972 when the fourteen-year-old Sioux was recovering from a bout of ulcerative colitis, exacerbated by the death of her father the same year from alcohol-related illness. Sioux has also cited her love of Motown, The Beatles, in particular the White Album, and The Rolling Stones.

Severin's musical tastes were far-reaching, including the Velvet Underground, Roxy Music, The Stooges, David Bowie, Can, Kraftwerk, Neu, Captain Beefheart, Steve Reich, Philip Glass, Gavin Bryars, Nino Rota and Bernard Hermann. His exposure to live music pre-dates that of Sioux, having seen David Bowie playing a gig in 1969, although she appears rather nonchalant about the experience, citing seeing Can play their first UK show at Brunel University in 1973 as more of a seminal moment; mesmerised by a two-hour set that saw every song seemingly segueing into the next.

With this initial alliance forged, Sioux and Severin started following the Sex Pistols everywhere: to their initial London gigs and then further afield, along with a group of similarly obsessed friends including Simon Barker, Bill Broad (Billy Idol), Debbie Juvenile (Wilson), Tracie O'Keefe, Sharon

Hayman, Bertie Marshall (Berlin Bromley), Susan Lucas (Soo Catwoman) and Simone Thomas (who played the violin in an early Banshees' incarnation).

The group, along with the Sex Pistols, also hung around the Malcolm McLaren and Vivienne Westwood co-owned SEX, a shop described as 'Specialists in rubberwear, glamour wear and stagewear'[18] in the King's Road that sold bespoke creations, including fetish and bondage wear that would become a staple of the punk "look."

The 'Bromley Contingent' term originated when music journalist Caroline Coon decided to write about the group of hardcore Pistols' fans instead of the group they were following, and first appeared in the UK music press after the Sex Pistols gig in Paris on 3 September 1976. It was much to Siouxsie's chagrin that she and her friends had been given this label on the entourage's return from Paris.

'I've just seen the English Stooges'[19] Simon Barker.
Sioux and Severin were not the first members of the Bromley Contingent to see the Pistols play live. Simon Barker relates how he unexpectedly saw the band at the gig at Ravensbourne College of Design and Communication on 9 December 1975: 'It was a Saturday night in Bromley and (as per usual) there was nothing else to do. There was a band called Fog on; we were just going for something to do, not to see them. It was 50p to get in. I got there and saw Malcolm (McLaren). I'd seen him in the shop (SEX) and I knew he'd managed the New York Dolls. We were big New York Dolls fans. I thought, "Wow, what's he doing here?" Then the Sex Pistols came on, and I just thought they were really brilliant. I was the only person clapping... All the students there were just going mad, shouting and crap... You could tell what they were trying to do, that sleazy rock 'n' roll... It had some style to it, even though it was so badly

played... Steve and (Sue) came afterwards and I told them about it.'[20]

Severin remembers being at the gig, arriving 'a bit late. I went to the bar and Simon went into the hall and saw the last song that the Pistols played. (He) just said, "I've seen the English Stooges."[21]

To give this late arrival some context, Sioux and Severin would regularly harangue, badger and cajole the unofficial Pistols HQ, SEX, to see when and where the Pistols would be playing, all too frequently arriving at venues to find the scheduled gigs had been cancelled.

There is a little bit of contention about the exact date Sioux and Severin first saw Sex Pistols play live. According to Severin, it was the first week in February 1976, a date that is hard to substantiate from any sources other than Clinton Heylin's conversation with Severin in 2006. However, two months after the gig they missed, Sioux and Severin returned to Ravensbourne College: 'This time Steve and Sue were down at the front (though Barker, mysteriously, was not).

The dressed-up Siouxsie even ran into an old school friend, Pete Long, and they exchanged "embarrassed greetings across the hippie/punk divide", or so writer Nigel Williamson recalled 26 years later, describing his own impressions of that wintry evening: 'A cold and cheerless Saturday night... (Shall we) spend the rest of the Saturday evening getting pointlessly drunk in Henekey's Wine Bar in Bromley High Street, or go the short distance to Ravensbourne College of Art to see an unknown band called the Sex Pistols? We opt for the latter... Within minutes we wished we'd stayed in the pub, for there is more future in getting mindlessly obliterated on Newcastle Brown than in listening to this racket. The Sex Pistols can barely play their instruments. Each tuneless thrash that passes for a song sounds the same as the one before. And while the spotty, under-nourished frontman knows how to sneer, he certainly doesn't know how to sing.'[22]

Sioux's memories of the gig include her recollections of 'Just a few students wandering about... Everybody kept their distance... (the Pistols) just played their music. Rotten didn't... really glare at anyone he did later. Glen was the loudest... He used to do backing vocals and he'd do them in tune! Who did he think he was? Ronnie Lane?'[23]

This evening was a catalyst for Sioux and Severin. Severin notes: 'We met them in the bar afterwards. We (already) knew Malcolm and Vivienne a little bit from going up to the shop, and Glen said, "We're playing the Marquee next week. Why don't you come along?"'[24]

Neither Sioux nor Severin were going to pass up this invitation: Severin remarks, 'After seeing the Pistols, I thought, "This is it; this is our mission." We went to see them everywhere. At last, we'd got a band who were playing everywhere and who we could really get into.'[25]

Chapter 2
The Rise and Fall of the 1970s

Musically, the 1970s is lauded as a 'golden' time for bands that were formed in the 1960s, some of whom, having relentlessly plied their trade the length and breadth of the country, and, in the case of UK groups, paid their dues at working men's clubs, were about to begin what would become their career zenith, playing ever-larger venues across the world, including 'enormadome' stadiums, and undertaking what were often punishing touring schedules, as well as recording albums while on tour at the corporate behest of the management and record label.

Everywhere one looked there was a glut of music. The Rolling Stones, Led Zeppelin and The Who were just getting into their stride; Jimi Hendrix had provided both blueprint and appetite for guitar acrobatics or what Pete Townsend refers to as 'Auto destructive art',[26] a term first coined by artist and activist Gustav Metzger in 1959, describing it as 'a desperate last-minute subversive political weapon against capitalism and consumerism.'[27] Retrospectively, the list of albums released in the early to mid-1970s reads like the stuff of fantasy, including 'What's Going On' by Marvin Gaye (1971), Pink Floyd's 'Dark Side of the Moon' (1973), 'Sticky Fingers' (1971) and 'Exile on Main Street' (1972) by The Rolling Stones, 'Ziggy Stardust and The Spiders From Mars' (1972) and 'Aladdin Sane' (1973) by David Bowie, 'Paranoid' (1970) by Black Sabbath, 'After the Goldrush' (1970) by Neil Young, 'Abraxas' (1970) by Santana, 'Catch a fire' (1973) by Bob Marley and the Wailers, 'L.A. Woman' (1970) by The Doors, 'Pink Moon' (1972) by Nick Drake and 'Raw Power' (1973) by Iggy Pop.

Such a rich seam of creative activity belies the global political and economic turmoil between 1973 and 1975. Among events in the US alone were the oil crisis of 1973, the steel crisis leading to the stock market crash of 1973–74, and the aftershock of an ill-conceived, insoluble war in Vietnam. Unemployment peaked at 9% in 1975. In the UK, GDP declined by around 3.9%, with a three-day week and inflation running at 20%. The miners rejected a pay rise of 13% by then prime minister Edward Heath, which was the catalyst for the 1974 general election, a Labour win but only the tiniest of margins.

The Labour government's inconsequential majority was decimated in 1977 as a result of by-election defeats, and James Callaghan formed a coalition with the Liberals to hang onto power. By this time, unemployment was at 1.5 million, a post-war high. Callaghan ruled out an election in September 1978 and, within weeks, a series of both private and public sector strikes began, which would be the catalyst for what became the Winter of Discontent, exacerbated yet further by being the coldest winter in 16 years. In March 1979, a vote of no confidence issued by Tory opposition leader Margaret Thatcher heralded the collapse of the Labour government and, with the election in May that year, the Tories returned to power.

During these years of political turmoil, one, 1976, would prove decisive in marking a shift in the cultural landscape, especially in terms of music. In 'Anarchy in the Year Zero',[28] author Clinton Heylin describes the concentration of activity centring around the Sex Pistols, The Clash and The Damned, the nucleus of punk bands before punk became commodified and commercialised.

Heylin argues that the Sex Pistols were so extraordinary because of the number of bands that were formed in their wake. To be a headline-grabbing phenomenon is only one part of the narrative; the other, and arguably most important part to the story, is how influential the Pistols were, and continue to be, inspiring a whole generation of bands including Nirvana and The Smiths. Heylin makes analogies between 1976 and 1966, both years where, musically, everything coalesced. Heylin argues that 'Psychedelia was pretty much dead and buried by the time 'Sgt. Pepper' came out; the year of psychedelia was 1966. All the interesting things that were going on — Pink Floyd, The Move, Tomorrow, Happenings — were all happening in 1966, not 1967. Well, punk is a bit like that really; once it becomes a cultural movement, once the tabloids think they know what punk is, it's over, because it has to be. Once any art movement becomes a public movement, it cannot retain its true self.'[29]

The stirrings of revolution and sea change that formed the DNA of punk can be traced pre-1976, at least in spirit, from the late 1960s in America, firstly with The Velvet Underground, then MC5, New York Dolls, Suicide, Iggy and The Stooges and Television, and later the Ramones, Patti Smith Group, Blondie and Talking Heads. The now defunct Bowery venue CBGBs in New York would prove a fertile breeding ground for what would become the American New Wave.

Chapter 3
The 100 Club

Serendipity

'I suppose looking back at it, it took some balls — not knowing what she was doing, or what we were doing, standing in the middle of the stage in front of, y'know, a pretty heavy audience, doing a song which wasn't even a song.'[30] Marco Pirroni on Siouxsie Sioux.

'I loved the bravery and the spirit of it. There was a diminished divide between audience and performer, and to have a member of the audience to be on stage was wonderful. I didn't think it was the beginning of the end for the band. I just thought, what a great one off. The next time they were on stage was a very different situation. They had rehearsed for one thing.'[31] Ray Stevenson.

The 100 Club started life as a live music venue in 1942. Originally called the Feldman Swing Club, in the 1940s it hosted acts such as Benny Goodman, Art Pepper, Johnny Dankworth, Ronnie Scott and Louis Armstrong. Remarkably, it is one of the only surviving independent music venues in London, outliving Borderline, Limelight, Zigzag, The Marquee, Dingwalls, Nashville Rooms, Rock Garden and Clarendon Ballroom.

The 100 Club, along with Ronnie Scott's (opened in 1959) in Frith Street, Soho, has weathered the storm of exorbitant rents, over-zealous property developers and homogenised, generic franchises, offering an eclectic and vibrant roster of live music including up-and-coming bands as well as major acts playing secret gigs or warm-up gigs before a major tour, including Queens Of The Stone Age, The Rolling Stones, Blur, Metallica, Toots And The Maytals, Paul McCartney, New York Dolls and Paul Weller.

The 100 Club maintains the magic, excitement and anticipation common to all great music venues. The austerity of the street-level entrance — grubby red canopy with '100 CLUB' in white writing and a 100 Club sign with an image of a pared-down but discernible trumpeter and glass double doors — belies the womb-like, red-walled subterranean space below ground level. There is a small stage, a bar and capacity for an audience of 350. Tickets for gigs invariably sell out very quickly and coming across a seemingly incongruous and unlikely combination, as I did, of John Paul Jones, Thurston Moore and Steve Noble, creating a two-hour wall of free form improvised, beautiful cacophonous music at the venue, was the metaphorical sought-after 'golden ticket'.

The venue is intimate without being claustrophobic and can be configured as a seated or standing space, depending on the gig, and allows for a studied appreciation of the music, conceivably a throwback to its jazz routes. The 100 Club has always been instrumental in promoting new music and this was certainly the case with punk, after 100 Club promoter Ron Watts saw Sex Pistols play a gig in Welwyn Garden City on 21 February 1976 and subsequently offered the band a residency to play every Tuesday in May of the same year. Sex Pistols were Sioux and Severin's epiphany and road to enlightenment, in much the same way as the Pistols were for many Manchester bands formed in the wake of the now iconic gig they played at the Lesser Free Trade Hall on 4 June 1976, among them Buzzcocks, Joy Division, The Smiths, New

Order, The Fall, Happy Mondays and Oasis, according to David Nolan, author of 'I Swear I Was There'.[32]

For two nights in September, The 100 Club hosted The Punk Rock Festival/100 Club Punk Special. On Monday 20 September, the bill included Sex Pistols, The Clash, Subway Sect and Siouxsie and The Banshees; on Tuesday 21 September, The Damned, Chris Spedding and the Vibrators, Buzzcocks and Stinky Toys (from France) played.

Myriad eyewitness accounts exist about this event, among which is journalist Caroline Coon's '1988 The New Wave Punk Rock Explosion.'[33] Published in 1982, Coon gives a detailed and insightful description of the sheer visceral excitement of the two-night festival, the first night of which saw a fledgling, under-rehearsed and hastily put together yet enthusiastic first incarnation of Siouxsie and The Banshees step onto the stage, the result of a last-minute cancellation by one of the bands on the bill.

Jack Whatley, in Far Out Magazine, describes the fortuitous event: 'Malcolm McLaren, Sex Pistols manager and chief PR mischief-maker, was told that one of the scheduled bands was being forced to drop out. A scramble for a new band ensued until one of the in-crowd that swarmed Vivienne Westwood's Kings Road store SEX on a daily basis came forward. That person was soon to be known as Siouxsie Sioux.'[34]

Replete with swagger and conviction, Sioux needed little persuading and, along with her musical soulmate Steve Severin, managed to enlist the services of guitarist Marco Pirroni, latterly of Adam and the Ants. The band were complete as a quartet when their final member joined on drums: the soon to be Sex Pistol John Beverley (Sid Vicious). Severin recalls: 'He said he had absolutely no ability. That sounded absolutely brilliant to us.'[35]

The new band's rather relaxed modus operandi before

their 100 Club debut was to meet for what they considered to be an important practice session: advisable, perhaps, under the circumstances. As Whately states: 'Considering most of the band members didn't know how to play any instrument, let alone the one they had in front of them, it (practising) was a smart idea.'[36]

The band booked time at Camden Lock's renowned rehearsal studio to plug their instruments in and see what would happen. 'Quickly after 10 minutes of thrashing around, Vicious allegedly called it quits on rehearsal time saying, "That's enough."'[37]

In the spirit of spontaneity, Sioux 'thought up the name Suzi & The Banshees the night before (the 100 Club gig), while looking for something that "sounded offensive but would get people confused."'[38]

The 100 Club event was not without its share of tumult, including when 'Sid Vicious threw a beer glass at one of the pillars and it shattered, blinding a girl'[39] during the second night. There was also the small matter of when 'The Clash planned to let Siouxsie and The Banshees use their equipment, but when their manager, Bernard Rhodes, saw Siouxsie wearing a swastika armband (which she refused to remove), they withdrew their consent.'[40]

With regard to that swastika, photographer Ray Stevenson 'didn't like it at all but thought that Siouxsie was using it to make a point that the emblem itself was no big deal.'[41] Rhodes also thought that Sioux 'wasn't aware of what she was letting herself in for. Our equipment is very distinctive, we've painted it luminous pink. If she used it, we too would be associated with the swastika. I felt she was mucking about with a loaded gun and we didn't want to have anything to do with it.'[42] To add to the frisson, Vicious was wearing 'a self-designed Belsen Babies T-shirt.'[43]

'That's a gleeful mockery of religion or any other fanaticism — for The Beatles or whatever. We're just spanners in the works of uniform progression.'[44] Siouxsie Sioux.

The Banshees' 20-minute set is the most extraordinary and direct statement of intent. In terms of actual performance, there was nothing else like it during the two-day event. Eyewitness Caroline Coon had been following the band and describes Siouxsie's appearance: 'She is nothing if not magnificent. Her short hair, which she sweeps in great waves over her head, is streaked with red, like flames. She'll wear black plastic non-existent bras, one mesh and one rubber stocking, suspender belts (various), all covered by a polka-dotted, transparent plastic mac.'[45]

Caroline Coon's account describes the musicians in the band: 'Two-tone Steve (his hair is black on top, white at the sides) was on a bass he picked up for the first time the night before. Sid Vicious, Johnny Rotten's friend, and inventor of the pogo dance, was on drums. He had one rehearsal. A mature gent called Marco (Pirroni) was lead guitarist.'[46]

Inner-circle accounts of the band's intended set list point to one 'standard' that was going to be the focal point of their performance: the John Barry, Leslie Bricusse and Anthony Newley written and composed 'Goldfinger'. The Velvet Underground's seventeen-and-a-half-minute 'Sister Ray' from their second album 'White Light/White Heat', released in 1967, was also mooted for The Banshees' set and it's conceivable that without the Velvet's one-take, improvised, sprawling and semi-extemporised jam as a musical cue, there would be no Siouxsie and The Banshees, such was their vital influence Sioux and Severin.

In an unexpected volte face, the band decided at the very last minute, in a radical act of extemporisation, to undertake a discordant version of the Lord's Prayer interspersed with 'Twist and Shout', 'Knockin' On Heaven's Door' and 'Deutschland, Deutschland Uber Alles'. One can also discern the inclusion of riffs from 'Smoke On The Water' and '(I can't get no) Satisfaction', '20th Century Boy' and 'Johnny B. Goode'. The 24-minute set is delivered with conviction, the constant being Vicious' metronomically repetitive 'minimal thud'.[47]

Coon describes the aural experience as a 'rough corrugation of sound, Siouxsie, with the grace of a redeemed ghoul, rifles the senses with an unnerving, screeching recitative.'[48] In Mark Paytress' 'Siouxsie and The Banshees The Authorised Biography', Severin recalls 'the first person that came up to The Banshees after their set was (future Banshees drummer) Kenny Morris. "That was fantastic", he said. "I want to be your drummer."[49]

Morris 'doesn't remember The Clash or the Pistols from that night. Siouxsie improvised the Lord's Prayer, throwing in bits from 'Deutschland, Deutschland, Uber Alles' and 'Twist And Shout', just putting everyone down. And Sid was amazing. He always gets knocked, but he played perfectly in time. It was wonderful. I told him his playing reminded me of Maureen Tucker, and he went all shy like a puppy and he whispered, "Oh, thanks very much." That was his first and only time on drums. He never touched them again after that.'[50]

This was also the night when Malcolm McLaren's assistant and Sex Pistols' roadie Nils Stevenson offered to manage the band. However, Severin took up the mantle of contrarian, and when the band left the club, he told an *Evening Standard* journalist that the band had 'split up, we'd been and gone and that was it.'[51]

With typical insouciance, Siouxsie recalls that when the band stopped playing she 'picked up my beer, got off the stage and walked through the audience',[52] an audience energised by the band's sheer exuberance, nerve and intrepidness. At the end of the set, with a nod from Pirroni to Vicious, Sid stopped pounding his drums and everything halted. The fervid reaction of the crowd was a signal of the success of this most improvised of gigs; the DIY dream realised. Sioux also remembers the encouragement heaped on the band after their debut, citing the number of women in the audience, including Palmolive, Viv Albertine and the rest of the Slits, Patti Paladin and Chrissie Hynde.

The murky and muffled recording of The Banshees' debut suggests that it was more akin to performance art and, even though the band's level of technical accomplishment as musicians, excepting Pirroni, is a more than a little rough and ready, one can sense the quartet's sheer, unabashed resolve and determination to make a long-lasting impression, crystallised by Siouxsie who 'wanted something apocalyptic to happen, like making people's guts fall out.'[53]

Post-100 Club

After the 100 Club gig, Marco Pirroni returned to his own band The Models, and Sid Vicious joined the short-lived Flowers of Romance, formed midway through 1976 by Jo Faull and Sarah Hall, the then girlfriends of Sex Pistols Steve Jones and Paul Cook respectively. Other notable members of the Flowers of Romance include founding member of The Clash and Public Image Limited Keith Levene, The Slits' Viv Albertine, and Palmolive, who was also in an early incarnation of The Slits as well as The Raincoats.

"I knew I had rhythm, I knew I had that"[54] Kenny Morris.

Kenny Morris, a close friend of Vicious, and like Sioux and Severin, with a penchant for Roxy Music, David Bowie and Marc Bolan, had also done a stint as the Flowers of Romance drummer, as well as previously playing what Morris remembers in a 2020 interview with John Robb[55] as a 'tin drum' in Adus Foxed, a band he formed with fellow St Ignatius' College, Enfield, pupil and future filmmaker John Maybury. Maybury's works include the 1998 Francis Bacon biopic 'Love is the Devil' starring Daniel Craig, Derek Jacobi and Tilda Swinton, and the 1990 video for 'Nothing Compares 2 U' by Sinead O'Connor.

Adus Foxed, which rehearsed at weekends in a Waltham Cross church hall, first saw Siouxsie at a gig at Screen on The Green in Islington on 29 August 1976, where Sex Pistols, Buzzcocks (their first London gig) and The Clash were playing. Morris's recollection of this meeting with Siouxsie was they "didn't speak"[56] but "made eye contact, let's say"[57] and "knew, absolutely knew, that something was going to happen between us. We had this lingering look. I was way at the back, and she was at the front with the Bromley Contingent and I thought, something is definitely going to happen between you and I, Sioux."[58]

However, it was at the inaugural gig at Roxy in Covent Garden, where Generation X[59] were playing, that Siouxsie asked Steve Severin to approach Morris to ask him if "he would be interested in playing with them (The Banshees)."[60]

Morris remembers that there was a "gig booked with the Flowers of Romance and Wayne County, somewhere, and I'm thinking, right, how am I going to do this. Steve (sic) Levine said "you can't do this or Sid is gonna fuckin' kill you. I said, alright, I'm trying to be in two or three places at once. He (Sid) won't allow it; no chance."[61]

As it transpired, the Flowers of Romance gig was cancelled and, subsequently, Sid got the call asking him to join Sex Pistols, which Morris points out he "knew he was going to do."[62] Keith Levine's prediction of physical harm to Morris, luckily, did not come to pass; instead, on Vicious's return from a Pistols-related trip to Berlin, his reaction was more disappointment at Morris joining The Banshees as, ironically, even though he played with The Banshees on their first ever live outing at the 100 Club, as Morris points out, Vicious was no great fan of The Banshees and it seems as though their close friendship dissipated from that moment.

The Grundy Incident

'Today' was an innocuous regional early-evening ITV regional news programme shown in the London area from 1968 to 1977. Presenters included Eamonn Andrews, synonymous with the long running 'This Is Your Life', also on ITV, and Bill Grundy. 'Today' also had the first Black television reporter and interviewer on television, Barbara Blake Hannah, unceremoniously sacked due to the volume of complaints about the colour of her skin.

On 1 December 1976, I, no doubt like many other viewers, was transfixed by one of the most memorable moments on terrestrial television.

The Sex Pistols' appearance on 'Today' — not their first televisual outing as they had appeared live playing 'Anarchy In The UK' on Granada TV's 'So It Goes' on 4 September 1976 — came about because of a last-minute cancellation by the band Queen and was a stroke of serendipitous luck and, as Malcolm saw it, a chance to promote the band whose debut single 'Anarchy In The UK' had been released a week previously.

The Bromley Contingent's Simon Barker got a call from Malcolm McLaren inviting Sioux, Severin, Barker and Simone Thomas to stand in the background while the Pistols were interviewed. Sioux thought it 'sounded too much fun to resist and hopped straight onto the train and went down to the studios.'[63]

Not everyone was enthusiastic about the Contingent's

presence, especially Glen Matlock who 'used to get a bit peeved that every time we did a TV show, we'd turn up and there would be the Bromley Contingent' again. I didn't know they would be on the Bill Grundy show. That was Malcolm's idea.'[64] Bromley Berlin (Bertie Marshall) thinks 'Malcolm had the notion of creating a scene with the Bromley Contingent, rather like Andy Warhol's Factory crowd.'[65]

By the time the live interview begins, the Pistols and the Bromley Contingent have both taken full advantage of the Green Room refreshment and are, as Sioux recalls, 'getting completely pissed.'[66] The lubricated guests are already winding up Bill Grundy, whose unwelcome and, by all accounts, licentious attention seems to be directed at Sioux.

On air, Grundy sets an antagonistic tone by asking the band about 'receiving £40,000 from a record company'[67] and whether that seemed to be slightly opposed to 'their anti-materialistic view of life?'[68] From that point onwards, when guitarist Steve Jones replies 'We've fuckin' spent it, ain't we'?[69], Grundy, launches into full goad mode, firstly eliciting the word 'shit'[70] from Johnny Rotten in relation to a question about Beethoven, Mozart, Bach and Brahms and subsequently, after what at first appears to be one of the more anodyne exchanges between Grundy and Sioux, the final denouement results in Grundy asking Sioux to 'meet afterwards, shall we'?[71]

This is the catalyst for what turns out to be the most memorable part of this entertaining yet disastrous (for Grundy) televisual event, eliciting Jones's 'You dirty sod. You dirty old man'![72], at which point, Grundy well and truly lights the blue touch paper when he remarks 'Well keep going, chief, keep going. Go on, you've got another five seconds. Say something outrageous.'[73]

Steve Jones after, being further provoked and patronised by Grundy, nonchalantly utters the now famous 'what a fuckin' rotter.'[74] After the interview, the Pistols, Sioux, Severin, Simone and Simon returned to the Green Room to take advantage of the remaining refreshments and, as Sioux recalls, 'They had all of these phones in there, so when people range up to complain about what they'd just seen, we picked up the phones, listened to them complain and told them to piss off. It was great fun.'[75]

Scapegoat
"It's all over, you've ruined everything."[76]

The Sex Pistols interview is significant because it happened at a time when punk, as a movement, was gathering momentum and music press column inches. Leading lights Buzzcocks, The Damned, and The Clash, along with the Pistols, were playing regular gigs and picking up a following that went beyond the cult or underground word-of-mouth parameters unwittingly set by the Bromley Contingent. Regular London 'punk' venues included The Nashville, Screen on The Green, 100 Club and The Greyhound in Croydon.

There are various accounts of Pistol's manager Malcolm McLaren's reaction to the 'Today' interview; one suggested that, in keeping with his puppet-master/Machiavellian persona, he was delighted by the incident. "I knew the moment the autocue lady threw up her hands and her bag, her make-up cascading through the air, that we had smashed the deception. It was live TV and the Sex Pistols were front-page."[77]

The account of another eyewitness, Steve Jones, suggests something markedly different: "He was terrified. He was shitting himself."[78] Those three minutes or so of live screentime generated a great deal of publicity for the Pistols over the ensuing days, including two consecutive Daily Mirror front pages, the first of which 'THE FILTH AND THE FURY' (Thursday 2 December 1976) has a verbatim transcription of the Grundy interview, along with a brief, sensationalist report of viewers kicking in their TV sets, and 200 viewer telephone complaints to the Daily Mirror.

The Friday 3 December headline 'OFF! OFF!' is accompanied by 'Siouxsie's a punk shocker' and published with two different photographs of Sioux, replete with bleached hair, striking black and white makeup, polka-dot bow and braces. One of the images has Sioux in an accentuated comedic frown, the other a grimace. Sioux remarks, "It was only after the Grundy show that people began to recognise us in the street. It didn't help that papers like the Daily Mirror were taking pictures of us and trying to turn it into one big scandal. They printed this grumpy photo of me with blonde hair, together with the headline 'Siouxsie's a punk shocker.' I hated that. It was like a handbook of how to be a punk: they drink brown ale and they spit. Total rubbish. It was the first time I realised we were fodder. Not again, thank you."[79]

It was around the time of the 'Today' programme, or even a few months earlier, that Sioux and Severin realised that the tabloids had got the bit firmly between their teeth regarding their view on the punk movement as a toxic concoction of threat to civilisation and freak show, rife with violence at gigs, many of which, especially in the case of the Pistols, were cancelled at least in part because of the salacious coverage by the media. It was time to disassociate themselves, if not from the movement as a whole, then from what they perceived as the tabloid version of punk: the ripped clothes, safety pins and other accoutrements, spitting at gigs and wholesale, homogenised packaging of a movement that was becoming commodified, marketed and sanitised for mass consumption and entertainment. Punk was certainly a distraction from the travails of the UK's increasingly high unemployment and financial crisis.

Sioux and Severin hated the suburbs for engendering a lack of imagination and group mentality: its deficit of ambition, its predictability, identikit housing and, most of all, the prospect of perpetual boredom. They sought emancipation from the miasma of sameness that punk was becoming and could see the writing on the wall when Sioux saw the Pistols play a second gig at The Screen On the Green in Islington on 5 September 1976, remarking, 'I thought to myself "It's all over." They were just another rock 'n' roll band and the sparkle of unpredictability had gone. They'd become just a package. The worst bit was when audiences started turning up with safety pins and lightbulbs hanging from their ears. The whole thing had gone completely tabloid.'[80]

On 15 December 1976, Severin attended a Sex Pistols gig at Notre Dame Hall in London's Leicester Square, where he had his own punk-related epiphany: 'For me, it all ended with that performance. The band were great but it was the audience that put me off. By this time there were, like, 300 people at the gigs. The Notre Dame show is the gig you see footage of most often because it was one of the few that was actually filmed. Every time it's shown you see all these people pogoing at the front. I remember thinking "Where did all these oiks come from? Where were they six months ago? And why are they acting like complete bozos at the front of the stage, spitting and all that nonsense"?'[81]

Severin thinks it was The Damned that started 'the gobbing thing'[82] by spitting at their audience. 'Pogoing and spitting just became part of the ritual for all of those jumping on the punk bandwagon, and I didn't want anything to do with that. It was horrible.'[83] Severin had never seen the media latch onto, and subsequently hijack and caricature, anything newsworthy with such ferocity and thinks that even though Malcolm McLaren might not have necessarily been at the helm in masterminding the feeding frenzy, he was at least responsible for its facilitation.

The ITV 'London Weekend Show', a capital-centric weekly arts and culture television programme presented by journalist Janet Street Porter, broadcast from 1975 to 1979, aired an episode dedicated solely to Punk Rock on 28 November 1976 that offers a timely snapshot of where punk was when the Pistols' 'Anarchy in the UK' was released two days earlier.

It centres around Street Porter's coverage of a Pistol's gig at the Notre Dame Hall, Soho. As well as interviewing the Sex Pistols and The Clash, Street Porter also talks to Sioux and Severin, assembled with other members of the Bromley Contingent in a London café. The conversations with the two future Banshees seem to confirm their focus not so much on the music or anything ideologically specific, instead preferring the creation of an unwritten manifesto to flush out the old guard, as Severin puts it, 'destroying everything that's gone before us.'[84]

Siouxsie speaks to Street Porter about her 100 Club experience, exuding impish confidence, revelling in the moment as leader, an instigator, biding her time, watching and observing. The Clash come across as furrowed-browed, earnest critics of what the band perceive as an increasingly inequitable, oppressed and broken society, posited through the lens of Joe Strummer's polemical lyrics and Ramones / MC5-esque urgency of the music. The Sex Pistols portray a dysfunctional, sarcastic, nihilistic dynamic, railing against boredom, hippies and bands like The Rolling Stones who had become, Lydon argues, less of a band and 'more of a business.'[85]

The five-month hiatus between the seminal 100 Club gig on 20 September 1976 and their performance at The Red

Deer pub in Croydon on 24 February 1977 saw The Banshees rehearse with newly drafted members Dixon on drums, of whom Marco Pirroni says 'Dixon looked like a shop dummy, completely perfect, glamorously, fabulously weird'[86], and 'he wasn't a punk; he was a clothes fetishist,'[87] and PT Fenton on guitar. Sioux points out that their membership was solely predicated on the fact that 'they both had their own gear.'[88] After a few attenuated and not entirely satisfactory rehearsals, Sioux and Severin realised that Dixon wasn't working out as a drummer, hence the acquisition of Kenny Morris as his replacement.

The Red Deer gig saw The Banshees supporting Johnny Thunders and The Heartbreakers. In the 2020 John Robb interview, Kenny Morris remembers that he and Banshees manager Nils Stevenson didn't exactly hit it off when Morris was having difficulty setting his kit up for the gig and Stevenson said, "well you're the fucking drummer aren't you"?[89] Morris took an "instant disliking"[90] to Stevenson from that point. Morris also recalls his plan to follow Sioux's staccato voice, playing right up to it and omitting all his cymbals in preparation for the gig, aping his drumming idol Mo Tucker.

Sioux recalls the 20-minute set opening and closing with the theme tune to 'Captain Scarlet', which subsequently became a live staple and the band's 'most popular song'[91] at the time. Sioux was inspired by Captain Scarlet being a "plastic man",[92] as well as loving the theme music from all Gerry Anderson's series. At that time, the band had a repertoire of around five songs, including the Severin-penned 'Scrapheap' and 'Psychic'. Morris recalls playing more songs at the gig, around nine or ten in total, a memory in line with Severin's, which is entirely feasible, considering the band recorded a rehearsal demo on 12 March 1977 at in a small studio at Track Records on Carnaby Street, to generate some interest in the band.

Track Records had signed The Heartbreakers, and Nils was on a retainer there. Track was founded in 1966 by Chris Stamp and Kit Lambert, former managers of The Who. The listing from what is almost certainly the earliest known studio (rough demo) recording of the band included 'Captain Scarlet', 'Scrapheap', 'Psychic', 'Bad Shape' and 'Love In A Void' and an unfinished version of 'The Lord's Prayer'. The Red Deer setlist would have also included an early regular staple of the band's live offering: T. Rex's '20th Century Boy'.

The Track sessions represent a time in early 1977 when Sioux and Severin decided that they would form a proper band. They had learnt enough through observing their default mentors the Sex Pistols' modus operandi to explore all the avenues available to them. In order to do this, there were key considerations, especially learning to play their instruments properly and write songs so they could play gigs, as well as finding the right band members; the latter a recurring and turbulent motif in the band's 20-year history.

Ceci n'est pas une guitar

No sooner was drummer Kenny Morris recruited into The Banshees than guitarist Peter Fenton was booted out. Never one to pull any punches, especially about the musicality, haircut, sleeping habits or sartorial deficits of Banshees' guitarists, there were two straws breaking the camel's back as far as Sioux was concerned; one of them pertained to Fenton's orange guitar lead which, Sioux points out 'really annoyed me.'[93] The other was Fenton 'was a real rock guitarist, always trying to put guitar licks into songs and pulling funny faces when he played. We spent most of our time trying to make him forget what he had learned.'[94]

Fenton's playing was certainly a far cry from the sound

Sioux and Severin were looking for: a drone redolent of The Velvet Underground. Fenton's tenure lasted about three months, from February to May 1977. Listening to live cassette tape versions of 'Love in a Void' and 'The Lord's Prayer' from a gig at the Vortex in London, objectively, one can hear why Fenton's tenure was so short lived. The playing sounds little more than perfunctory and at loggerheads with the sheer energy and urgency audible in the performances of Sioux, Severin and Morris. Ray Stevenson comments 'Pete Fenton wasn't a bad guitarist. It was just that there was no character in his playing and then John McKay came along and brought character and after that they became a good band.'[95]

The Sioux, Severin, Morris and Fenton line-up can be seen playing 'Love in a Void' in the 1978 Derek Jarman-directed film 'Jubilee'; a cameo that neither Sioux nor Severin were particularly enamoured of, subsequently refusing to let their music be used on the vinyl soundtrack to the film. The slightly more polished Track session demo, as can be heard on 'Psychic', also, both literally and metaphorically, amplifies Fenton's shortcomings as a guitarist. 'The Scream' producer Steve Lillywhite remarks 'He (Fenton) was a mediocre guitarist and that was the worst thing.'[96] And while the band were never going to be looking for trained, seasoned virtuoso musicians — Sioux is on record as hating anything resembling a guitar solo, or at least the way Fenton played one — whoever joined the band had to both sound and look right and, ostensibly, be prepared to be a Banshee.

John McKay

'McKay helped to give The Banshees their 'look'.'[97] Ray Stevenson.

John McKay came into The Banshees' frame through Morris's close friendship with John Maybury. In 1976, Morris was a Fine Art and Graphic Design student at Camberwell College of Arts, and Maybury a Fine Art student at St Albans College of Art, where John McKay was also studying. Morris and Maybury, in addition to attending their respective courses, were working on Derek Jarman's 'Jubilee' as production design assistants, earning £60 per week. Maybury told Morris that McKay, described by Severin as a 'tall, black-haired bloke who he'd seen skulking around the college not talking to anybody,'[98] played guitar (apparently, he had an acoustic guitar in the art studio at St Albans College, by all accounts spending more time playing David Bowie songs than painting).

Maybury suggested McKay as a possible replacement for Pete Fenton and subsequently invited Morris to an end-of-year exhibition at St Albans to meet McKay, but McKay was nowhere in sight. McKay made his Banshees' debut at the newly opened Vortex Club on Wardour Street in London on 11 July 1977. McKay understood the palette of colours Sioux and Severin wanted him to paint with, and it was clear, at least initially, that McKay shared their sonic vision in creating an original, evocative soundscape that would encompass the melange of musical and filmic references driving the band forward into unchartered territory.

A year is a long time in music...

By the time McKay had joined Siouxsie and The Banshees, there had been key events in establishing punk as a bone fide movement that could no longer be ignored or marginalised. Most of the old guard in the music press were yet to be convinced as to its musical content but there were palpable stirrings, with punk being written about in favourable terms by *Melody Maker's* Caroline Coon, and *Sounds'* John Ingham, the latter of whom, as well as being the first journalist to interview the Sex Pistols, wrote the first reviews of The Damned and The Clash gigs.

The Sex Pistols were still leading the charge and much of their continued momentum can be attributed to the two (now legendary) Lesser Free Trade Hall gigs in Manchester on 4 June and 20 July 1976, the first of which was made possible by former Bolton Institute of Technology students Howard Devoto and Pete Shelley.

A 17-year-old Steven Morrissey, New York Dolls fanatic and future founder member of The Smiths, penned a letter in praise of the Sex Pistols, comparing them to the New York Dolls, David Bowie and Iggy Pop, which was published in NME on 16 June 1976. Having travelled from Manchester to see the band play at High Wycombe College on 20 February 1976, Devoto and Shelley were so awestruck by the Pistols' performance that they became instrumental in promoting and selling tickets for the 4 June Manchester gig and wasted no time at all, subsequently, in forming Buzzcocks, the Pistol's support act, at the second Lesser Trade Hall gig on 20 July. Buzzcocks released 'Spiral Scratch', a four-track EP on 29 January 1977, on the New Hormones independent record label, founded by Buzzcocks manager Richard Boon.

Joe Strummer had retired his band the 101'ers, with almost immediate effect and, by all accounts, evangelical fervour, at least in his mind, after watching the Pistols' as the 101'ers support band on 4 April 1976 at The Nashville. He went on to form (The) Clash with Mick Jones, Paul Simonon, Keith Levene and Terry Chimes. The band, after playing 30 gigs, were signed to CBS Records on 25 January 1977 and released 'White Riot' on 18 March 1977 and 'Remote Control' on 13 May 1977.

The Damned continued to plough their gigging furrow

after their initial outing, supporting Sex Pistols on 6 July at the 100 Club, and had released the single 'New Rose' on 22 October 1976 and the 'Damned Damned Damned' album on 18 February, after signing to the Stiff Record label, established in August 1976.

The punk firmament was also assisted by a young television presenter, Tony Wilson, future mastermind behind the Hacienda club in Manchester and Factory Records impresario. He had managed to persuade Granada Television's 'So it Goes' producer Chris Pie, to give the Pistols' their first outing on television, playing 'Anarchy In The UK', broadcast on 4 September 1976.

The Sex Pistols, however, even though they continued to generate excitement, started to have mixed fortunes. The 25-date UK 'Anarchy In The U.K. Tour' from 12 December to 26 December 1976, with Sex Pistols headlining and supported by The Damned, The Clash, Johny Thunders and The Heartbreakers and the New York Dolls, was cancelled except for seven dates.

By 13 May 1977, the Pistols were on their third consecutive record contract, having been signed to EMI on 8 October 1976, ('Anarchy In The UK', the only single on EMI, was released on 26 November) only to be unceremoniously dropped in January 1977 (EMI still honoured the much-publicised £40,000 recording contract) after the Grundy interview on 1 December, as well as some adverse publicity surrounding Rotten's alleged behaviour at Heathrow airport on 4 January 1977, en route to playing a couple of gigs in Holland.

They were subsequently signed by A&M Records on 10 March 1977 with much fanfare and publicity, with a 'mock-up' contract-signing outside Buckingham Palace to coincide with the release of the 'God Save The Queen' single and Queen

Elizabeth II's Silver Jubilee year. After a two-month tenure with A&M, the band were sacked again and were headhunted by Virgin Records and signed with the label on 13 May 1977, the honoured A&M contract leaving the band £75,000 richer. 'Pretty Vacant' was released as a single on 2 July 1977. After ongoing arguments with Johnny Rotten, Glen Matlock left Sex Pistols in February to be replaced by Sid Vicious.

In the midst of what was becoming, for good and bad, a feeding frenzy, especially where the Pistols were concerned, The Banshees continued to hone their craft, embarking on a 54-date tour. On their itinerary were regular London venues such as The Vortex, Nashville and Roxy Clubs, already established as punk 'staples', as well as gigs at the Rainbow Theatre, the Music Machine, and the Roundhouse. Venturing further afield, the 1977 tour also took in a variety of venues in Birmingham, Nottingham, Edinburgh, Manchester, Stafford, Coventry, Plymouth, Leicester, Liverpool, Cardiff, Sheffield, Colwyn Bay, Brighton, Leeds and Middlesborough. There were two gigs in Paris and one in Amsterdam.

Despite this promising gigging schedule for a band on its first outing, venturing beyond the environs of London, The Banshees weren't entirely untouched by the legacy of controversy and negative press that had dogged The Sex Pistols, leading to a vastly pared down number of gigs for the Anarchy In The U.K. tour in 1976.

As Sioux remarks, being 'banned from a lot of London venues like the Marquee without ever having played there, because they didn't want anything controversial. They wanted to promote bands like Dr Feelgood and Eddie and the Hot Rods. But when we played up north, sometimes it would be like civil war. They told us to fuck off back to London.'[99] Severin also attests to the audiences' antagonism: 'You could guarantee that at just about every gig there would be a fight by the end of the third song. Someone would try to drag Siouxsie into the audience. She'd kick them, Kenny would jump over his drum kit and pile in, and it would all go off. And we were constantly being spat at. They were fairly intense experiences. I didn't get involved in the fights myself, although I did whack a few people with my bass. You could get a nice swing with it.'[100]

The Banshees took to the road with a staple of around 12 songs, although how many of these songs they actually played varied from venue to venue. The setlist included 'Helter Skelter' (Beatles cover), 'Make Up to Break Up', 'Mirage', 'Scrapheap', 'Psychic', '20th Century Boy' (T Rex cover), 'Mittageisen' 'Carcass', 'Love in a Void', 'The Lord's Prayer', 'Suburban Relapse', 'Bad Shape' and 'Captain Scarlet' (theme tune).

Style meets Substance

'Almost instantly, I discovered what a drug performing was'[101] Siouxsie Sioux.

I am watching footage of a Banshees' Manchester (Elizabethan Hall) gig, which they played on 15 December 1977 when the band are on the last leg of their tour. The footage was broadcast on the Tony Wilson-presented Granada programme 'So It Goes' on Sunday 27 December. The band play two songs: 'Make up to break up' and 'Mittageisen'. The venue is sweatbox and sardine packed, the audience stretching from the back of the venue all the way to the front.

With barely room for them to move, the audience jump up and down in syncopation to the pulsing, tom-tom drumming of Kenny Morris, looking like actor Jack Wild's twin: spiky black hair, angelic, wearing a sleeveless striped shirt, pounding his drum kit as though endeavouring to summon some primordial deity or spirit. The angle of the footage dictates that, excepting his guitar, (a semi-acoustic Hagström Viking, apparently), John McKay, stage left, can be heard but not seen. It is abundantly clear why he was welcomed into the Banshee fold. The guitar sound exudes warmth, texture and depth, characterising the metallic angularity that was to become associated with his unique and influential playing. Crescendos and diminuendos follow the tenor and pattern of the music at every twist and turn. McKay isn't just playing guitar; he is creating a polychromatic, cinematic soundscape.

Steve Severin is clearly in his element, exuding confidence, dressed in a diaphanous pink shirt and red, loose-fitting 'peg' trousers. His pale, almost white make up, coupled with rouged cheeks and bleached hair (Severin is the only blond in an otherwise raven-haired ensemble) creates a look that is part Pierot, part Frank-N-Furter. His bass playing is tight, precise and, especially on 'Mittageisen', menacing, as it aligns perfectly with Morris's drumming and McKay's guitar playing. Severin delights in every musical twist and turn as he moves in time to the rhythm of the music being made.

And then Siouxsie. Completely immersed in both moment and music, dressed in a SEX 'breasts' t-shirt, black PVC shorts ('mainly to be able to move around. I move to the music; the music is the most important thing. That's what makes me look that way, it's very cold and blue'[102]), fishnet stockings, studded wristband, thigh-length patent-vinyl bondage-style stiletto boots. Her striking, pale, face make up is given depth and emphasis through her rouged cheeks, Egyptian-esque made-up eyes and bright red lipstick. Sioux's black hair is short, with a semblance of spikiness on top. She commands the stage and is indomitable, stalwart and commanding. She stands, holding and leaning into the microphone stand, her elevation above the audience suggesting deification, with all eyes on her.nThis 'dominatrix' image is redolent of an anecdote from Bertie

Marshall recalling how he and Sioux, out of sheer boredom, with conceivably more than a little Situationism thrown into the mix for good measure, decided what a blast it would be if Sioux were to put Marshall on a lead and walk him like a dog, on all fours, to Cherry's Wine Bar in Bromley South: 'We crossed the road to the bar, outside I put on the choke chain and lead and got down on all fours and started wagging my tail. S.S. (Siouxsie) lifted her head imperiously and we sauntered in. It was a Friday evening, and the bar was getting busy. At first no one noticed, and we walked to the centre of the room; a few people looked, nudged their friends; we arrived at an empty table in the middle of the room. S.S. sat down and I jumped up on a chair, my tongue lolling out, panting.'[103]

This is no re-run of the 100 Club gig 15 months previously. Cumulatively, the band have become tighter and are beginning to hone their craft. The Manchester show isn't gob free and one can discern missiles of spit being directed towards the band, one white fleck clearly visible on Sioux's right, perfectly made up, eyebrow. Not that this bothers the singer at all; she and the rest of the band, chemically buoyed up or otherwise, are occupying their own transcendent stratosphere, playing for themselves, looking and sounding as though they are from a different time and dimension. They look great and sound great.

'Make Up To Break Up'

'Make up to break up' and 'Mittageisen' are indicative of a band that may share much of punk's DNA regarding the agitprop impetus to do something, make something happen, but this is no musical carbon copy of Sex Pistols, The Clash, Buzzcocks, The Damned or raft of new bands springing up tagged as punk, many of whom were seeking transmogrification or redemption when they realised how superfluously redundant or out of touch their music was in light of the Pistols' sheer shock, awe and increasing competence as a live ensemble.

There were also The Ramones from New York, formed in 1974 and considered to be the first punk band, whose first two UK (sold-out) gigs at the Roundhouse on 4 July and Dingwalls on 5 July 1976 had been the catalyst for The Clash (especially) and The Damned to play at increasingly 'breakneck' speed. They had a repertoire of (mainly two-minute) songs straightforward enough for future Sex Pistol bassist Sid Vicious to learn by heart. Siouxsie and The Banshees 'Make up to break up' was one of three demoed songs to be recorded at Riverside Studios, Hammersmith, along with 'Captain Scarlet' and 'Psychic' on 12–14 June 1977, encompassing and embracing the pop music Sioux so dearly loved.

However, this is no 'easy listening' pop song, and although it may have elements of Glam and Motown, Roxy Music, The Glitter Band, T. Rex and The Shirelles, Sioux's lyrics are the musical equivalent of the visceral 'ear scene' in Quentin Tarantino's 1992 film 'Reservoir Dogs', where Michael Madsen (Mr Blond) has tied Marvin Nash, a kidnapped policeman from the aftermath of a failed jewellery heist, to a chair in the middle of a warehouse, taped his mouth and then proceeds to taunt him, dancing around him and cutting his ear off to the jaunty 'Stuck in the middle with you' by Stealers Wheel.

Of the 'Make up to break up' lyrics, Sioux remarks that the inspiration came from 'Devil's Rain… a cheapo cash-in movie on the same lines as the Exorcist etc. An actress called Ida Lupino (beautiful name) was in it — Ernest Borgnine was the Devil and William Shatner, the guy from Star Trek, was the hero. The film was about this rain that melted people — their faces went like putty and if you squeezed their eyeballs all pus came oozing out.'[104] The iron fist in the Velvet Underground glove.

It is perhaps worth mentioning, although the similarities might be immediately dismissed as either tenuous or obvious, given the bandwidth and latitude of the 'four piece' ensemble structure including vocal, drums, bass and guitar employed by the Sex Pistols, The Damned and Ramones (pedantry excludes Buzzcocks and The Clash with two guitarists), The Damned's 'New Rose' and 'Make up to break up' are not entirely dissimilar, structurally, although, and this can be discerned more readily on the studio version of The Banshees' song which makes an appearance on the 2005 remastered version of 'The Scream', there is a tongue in cheek playfulness. Neither song takes itself too seriously, especially considering the trashy B movie references Sioux alludes to. This is more 'Carry On'[105] than 'Carrie'[106]; Sioux more Bette Davies' Baby Jane Hudson[107] than Cruella de Vil, and Dave Vanian more 'The Munsters'[108] Grandpa than Max Schrek's Count Orlok in 'Nosferatu'[109]

Of The Banshees' initial forays into making early demos, both at Track Records and Riverside Studios, the emotively and powerfully titled 'Mittageisen' (midday iron) is the only song that made the cut on the first album 'The Scream', released in 1978. The initial impetus for the song was Morris's driving, powerful drumbeat. There is a menacing minor chord interplay between McKay's guitar and Severin's base. Sioux's vocal is jumpy, fragmented and serrated and follows the '*sturm und drang*' pattern of all three instruments. The song is direct and almost militaristic in its sparseness. This is the sound of metal. Less poppy than 'Make up to break up', the audience has little to dance to; instead, they are transfixed and mesmerised by Sioux's every move as she wrings every last vocal inflection and nuance out of the lyrics, dedicated to 1920s and 1930s photomontage artist John Heartfield.

The original title for the song was 'Letter to John Heartfield'. A native Berliner, Heartfield's parents were political activists and socialists. Heartfield joined the Communist Party during the Weimar years and became a member of the Berlin Club Dada, where he associated with other members such as Erwin Piscator, Bertolt Brecht and Hannah Höch.

The specificities of the song allude to a piece by Heartfield made on 19 December 1935 in response to a propaganda speech by German Reich Marshall Hermann Goering (1893–1946) in defence of Germany's expenditure on arms. 'Hurrah, die Butter ist Alle!' (Hurrah, the butter is finished) with the caption underneath 'Goering in seiner Hamburger Rede: "Era hat stets ein Reich stark gemacht, Butter und Schmalz haben höchstens ein Volk fett Gemacht" (Goering in his Hamburg speech: "Ore (iron) has always made an empire strong, butter and lard have made a people fat at most." Hurrah, die Butter ist Alle! (English: Hurray, the Butter is All Gone!) was published on the front page of the AIZ 'Arbeiter-Illustrierte-Zeitung' (Workers' Illustrated Magazine) in 1935.

The monochromatic, small-scale work lampoons the machinations of propaganda, showing a domestic interior of a German family of five at a dinner table eating a 'feast' of metal objects including iron weights and various bicycle parts including chain, frame and handlebars. A portrait of Hitler hangs on the wall and the wallpaper is emblazoned with repeated swastikas. The baby gnaws on an executioner's axe replete with swastika motif and the grandmother tucks into a coal shovel, while the family dog licks a huge nut and bolt. Sioux saw it as 'A warning song. The whole propaganda of the Nazis at that time was very dangerous and it could easily creep its way in without there being all the hysteria of killing the Jews. Their whole propaganda could easily fit in today. Not being able to get away from the commands of the day, not being able to escape, the idea of having cameras in your room and having people watching you…'[110]

Being on the road not only gave the band a chance to hone their craft but was also an opportunity to write new songs. Steve Severin records, 'We stayed in a B&B in Tynemouth that night (having played a gig in Newcastle the previous evening). I walked out to the cliffs overlooking the North Sea, where I began the lyric for 'Voice'." I'd been reading Baudelaire's 'Hashish, Wine and Opium', in which he talks about seeing sound and hearing colours, and I'd recently seen one of Roger Corman's Edgar Allan Poe adaptations, 'The Haunted Palace'. Siouxsie and I were really into Poe at the time and I wanted to try and recreate that "suffocating" motif he used so often.'[111]

'Pure' was also written in transit, during the brief European sojourn when the band played four nights in Paris and one night Amsterdam, where they supported The Clash. It may have proved, along with catching an Iggy Pop gig (The Banshees were really into 'The Idiot' at the time) in a red and white circus tent, a high point of the jaunt which, by all accounts, brought to light the reality that the band were ostensibly living hand to mouth, subsisting on the occasional burger when Nils Stevenson dipped his hand in his pocket and gave the band a tenner, and a lot of booze, then the band's main drug of choice. There was a lot of speed around at the time, fairly profusely among punk bands, which is perhaps no surprise considering the high-octane, 90-mile-per-hour live performances.

The Banshees, however, didn't succumb to the allure of one drug that was beginning to seep into the punk scene: heroin. This wasn't the case with Johnny Thunders And The Heartbreakers, who were into that 'whole smack thing'.[112] Severin cites this as a reason why The Banshees' manager

Nils Stevenson wanted to keep The Heartbreakers in-situ as he wasn't only 'seduced'[113] by the band's image and music but also by their stash of 'Chinese Rock'.

Peel Sessions

'We did two early John Peel sessions. When the first one went out (5 December 1977), it was a huge thrill hearing ourselves for the first time. That we still didn't have a record deal made it even stranger. Peel and (his producer) John Walters, were always very supportive.'[114] Siouxsie Sioux.

After working in America undertaking stints as a travelling insurance salesman and writing programmes for IBM computer punch cards, and latterly at four radio stations: Dallas-located WRR (AM), KLIF (as the official Beatles correspondent due to Peel's Liverpool connection, having been born in Wirral), KOMA in Oklahoma City until 1965, Peel finally moved to KMEN in San Bernardino in California.

Returning to England in early 1967, Peel DJ'd for offshore pirate radio station Radio London with a midnight to 2am slot, gradually metamorphosing into The Perfumed Garden, described as a 'slightly esoteric community of late-night listeners.'[115]

Peel was one of the principal broadcasters to play 'underground' genres of music such as psychedelic and progressive rock on UK radio. Peel's late-night Radio One show ran from 1967 to 2004 and the DJ became acknowledged as a champion of new music, more often than not breaking new bands that otherwise would not have garnered any exposure, especially from mainstream daytime radio.

Peel Sessions usually comprised four songs, pre-recorded at the BBC Maida Vale studios, which were aired during his 10pm to midnight programme. Peel's radio show playlist would be interspersed with each of the four songs for the duration of the show and, over the 37 years of broadcasting, included, among myriad others', Jimi Hendrix, Pink Floyd, Joan Armatrading, Nirvana, Bauhaus, The Kinks, Cocteau Twins, X-Ray Specs, Chumbawamba, Ivor Cutler, Viv Stanshall, The Damned, Stiff Little Fingers, Buzzcocks, The Smiths, The Raincoats, The Cure, Killing Joke, Steel Pulse, Spiritualised, The Fall, The Jesus and Mary Chain, Sonic Youth, Suicide, Blur, Super Furry Animals, Napalm Death, Scritti Politi and The Flaming Lips.

Peel became known for his laid back, sardonic delivery and there was something beautifully clandestine and thrilling about his programmes with its sense of anticipation about what was going to be played next. There was danger, rebellion and the relief of finding another world where one could escape, often under the bed covers, from the Stepford tyranny of regular bland and anodyne chart music fodder. Peel embraced every facet of punk and New Wave, including a fledgling Siouxsie And The Banshees.

The Banshees recorded five John Peel sessions between 1977 and 1986. The first session, recorded on 29 November 1977 and broadcast on 5 December 1977, included 'Love In A Void', 'Mirage', 'Mittageisen' and 'Suburban Relapse'.

'There are aspects of early Banshees that are pretty well set in stone for their whole career, sound wise' John Robb.[116]

When this first Peel Session was recorded, The Banshees were 47 dates into their first 54-date tour and had become a cohesive, tight unit, as can be seen in the 'So It Goes' Manchester footage from the same month. The 20 minutes of improvised, glorious, untethered extemporisation at the 100 Club gig 14 months earlier had turned into a repertoire of thoughtful, well-crafted songs replete with verses, choruses and discernible beginnings and endings.

It is probably a bit too reductive to suggest that 'Love In A Void', written during the short-lived Fenton line-up, reflects the band's more nihilistic sensibilities and penchant for touching raw nerve-endings, but the lyrics suggest a disdain for anything disingenuous or fake. The result is an anti-love song of sorts. An early incarnation of the song included the line 'Too many Jews, for my liking', which, compounded with Sioux's penchant for wearing a swastika armband during Banshees' early performances was, even by Sioux's light-blue-touchpaper sensibilities, perhaps a lyric too far and too provocative, and was subsequently changed to 'Too many bigots for my liking.'

Sioux was sensitive and intelligent enough to understand the incendiary and emotive power of the swastika, and how the symbol was subsequently adopted by the skinhead movement during the late 1970s and early 1980s, as one skinhead faction increasingly aligned itself with far-right movements such as the National Front and British Movement.

With regard to her flirtation with the swastika, Sioux maintains that 'Certain people in the press who should have known better had taken it in the wrong way and had shown it as us supporting that. And it was damaging to us. Also, I saw no reason to wear it anymore as it was being taken for granted, too, that shock tactic was being used as a decoration and a fashion.'[117]

The Peel Session version of the word is rather more difficult to discern, sounding like 'wags' which is entirely feasible if one translates the word as meaning 'old fashioned' or 'outmoded.'

'Love In A Void'

The song is a two-and-a-half-minute, high-octane stomp; the aggressive, pounding instrumentation entirely in keeping with the barbed, abnegating 'everything is fake and idiotic' lyrics. McKay's urgent, crashing, feedback-strewn guitar introduction is swiftly followed by Morris and Severin's pounding rhythm section as Sioux joins the fray, veritably spitting the lyrics out. It is this sound of every member of The Banshees at the fore, with everyone playing a lead role, which makes the 'attack' of the song so exciting, so compelling.

'I think you get anxious if you think that people are taking what you are saying and doing as rules to live by. We've always tried to not let it come across that way.'[118] Siouxsie Sioux

'Mirage'

A song that takes its lead from 'the idea of blindness and screens rather than taking it down to TV. It's about walls, screens, inhibitions, inabilities, expressing oneself in public'[119] according to Kenny Morris, while Sioux described it as alluding to 'people seeing us and taking what we do superficially.'[120]

The lyrics to 'Mirage' could be said to mirror Sioux's mistrust, not only of adults, due to her traumatic formative experiences, but also of ideologies, be it the politics of the far right or far left, and what she perceived as 'lazy' journalism, especially in the music press and the tabloid press, the latter of whose "reporting" Sioux had experience, having been splashed over the front page of the Daily Mirror with the headline 'Siouxsie's a punk shocker' in the wake of 'Grundygate' on 1 December 1976, when she had been subjected to the leering and lechery of Grundy himself.

The song is also part prophetic warning of the dangers of believing what one is fed through partisan media. 'Mirage' is a paean to the experiential: the importance of first-hand evidence and scratching the surface rather than being anaesthetised through the indolence of convenient truths or lies.

The song also touches on the prevalent archaic attitudes towards women in the music industry in the 1970s, which saw them objectified and side-lined as genteel backing singers or pretty dancing girls.

'Us girls never stood in front of a mirror posing as if we had a guitar because we had no role models. So, when Patti Smith came along, it was huge. She was groundbreakingly different.'[121] Viv Albertine.

'The emergence of punk in the late 1970s signalled a major change for women in music. The ethos of punk was that anyone could form a band, perform and write their own songs, even if they had no skill or prior experience of doing so.'[122] Viv Albertine, in her superb autobiography 'Clothes, Clothes, Clothes. Music, Music, Music. Boys, Boys, Boys.' touches on the normalisation of being perpetually hassled and harangued for the double whammy of being female and standing out from the crowd because of the clothes she chose to wear.

Albertine recounts an instance when she and Clash guitarist Mick Jones were on their way to the Hammersmith Odeon and were confronted by a group of skinheads: 'One of the skinheads swears at us, the rest gather behind him, a sea of bobbing baldies. Mick stays calm. He's used to this kind of thing. The swearer gets more aggressive, taking the piss out of Mick's clothes. Then he turns to me and hisses, "Next time I see you I'm gonna *fuck* you." Every day something happens like this, or is likely to happen.'[123]

Sioux, and her contemporaries The Slits (all-female band until a certain Peter Edward Clarke AKA 'Budgie' joined in 1979) and Poly Styrene (X-Ray Spex) didn't exactly have a surfeit of 'current' female role models or musicians on whom to base their modus operandi; there was no instruction manual about what do if you were spat at or verbally abused in the street, or the most effective riposte to "show us your tits" when doing a gig.

Patti Smith, considered by Sioux to be (excepting Nico) 'the first real female writer in rock,'[124] having released the seminal 'Horses' album in September 1975, was the closest Sioux and her contemporaries had to a role model; not just the music, which was both pivotal and seminal for the punk movement, but also the album cover, a black and white photograph, taken by Robert Mapplethorpe, of Smith wearing a suit. 'The outfit is something which does elevate the shot. Smith looks every bit the punk-crooner she'd show she was on 'Horses'. Complete with braces that mean business and the steely gaze of a determined soul and an emboldened spirit. "I flung my jacket over my shoulder, Frank Sinatra style. I was full of references. He was full of light and shadow."[125]

Smith overruled changes her record label Arista wanted to make to 'soften' the image, which was completely different from other female recording artists at the time. Smith's 'unapologetic androgyny predates a time when that was *en vogue* or even an available option for women and represents a seminal moment in the reversal of the female gaze.'[126]

Smith's uncompromising attitude towards making music strengthened both Viv Albertine's and, in Sioux's case 'cast iron', resolve to be the ones in control and not at the beck and call of music industry puppeteers.

As a teenager, I was obsessed with the now virtually impossible to come by 'Once Upon A Time/The Singles' album, released on 4 December 1981. This is a retrospective of Banshees' singles, several of which weren't available on the first four albums: 'The Scream' (1978), 'Join Hands' (1979), 'Kaleidoscope' (1980) and 'Juju' (1981). The album is remarkably cohesive, ostensibly charting the musical trajectory of the band over a three-year period.

'Mirage', track two of the ten songs featured on 'Once Upon A Time' and the second song from the 1977 Peel session, signposts a band with far more than punk on their collective minds. From the opening swirling guitar riff, again ferociously accompanied by Morris's all or nothing drumming, following Sioux's vocal, enhanced by overdubbing to accentuate the potency of her acerbic, alliterative delivery at every twist and turn, punctuated with Morris's dramatic and highly effective use of the high hat and Severin's steady, resolute, pounding bass guitar, serving the music rather than being virtuoso flash. It is two or so minutes of dark sonic psychodrama that would become intertwined and synonymous with a band intent on pushing the boundaries of experimentation.

'Mittageisen' takes full advantage of the Maida Vale studio setting. The sound possesses an enveloping warmth, with a cohesive sonic landscape redolent of 'The Scream'. Kenny Morris's drums are overdubbed to create a more menacing, echoing effect, as though he is playing with two drumsticks in each hand. John McKay's guitar cuts like a knife, reflecting the sheer, venomous contempt in John Heartfield's diminutive but potent photomontage 'Hurrah, die Butter ist Alle!' There are inflexions of Patti Smith's 'Horses' in Sioux's vocal delivery, a bilious but fulsomely beautiful assault. In fact, as with the entire 1977 Peel Session, and without wishing to be reduced to unnecessary 'rock' platitudes, this is clearly the sound of a band locked in with each other as though nothing else either matters or exists.

'Suburban Relapse'
'It's committing a crime under the stresses of everyday life. Being so confused and... I don't know how anyone can be a judge, an actual one in court.'[127] Siouxsie Sioux on 'Suburban Relapse'.

'In her immaculate kitchen she said, "Yes, I've changed. I realised I was being awfully sloppy and self-indulgent. It's no disgrace to be a good homemaker. I've decided to do my job conscientiously, the way Dave does his, and to be more careful about my appearance. Are you sure you don't want a sandwich?"[128] Ira Levin 'The Stepford Wives' 1972.

Sioux and Severin were never enamoured of living in the suburbs: Chiselhurst and Bromley respectively. They pretty much hated everything about it: the drabness, lack of imagination, greyness, homogeneity and stultifying suffocation encountered on a daily basis. It was the antithesis of the energising, exciting, frisson-filled environs of Soho's Club Louise or Kensington's Sombreros that were frequented by Sioux, Severin and assorted members of the Bromley Contingent.

For a 15-year-old Bertie Marshall (Berlin Bromley), as a means of escape from habitual boredom, 'Bromley became Berlin in the 1930s. I wanted to worship and fall in love with a sailor, I eventually did. I was already thieving and drugs were a playground, a holiday in the head, from the horror of being an only child, in the numbing isolation of the suburbs.'[129]

The tenor of 'Suburban Relapse' is the hybridisation of tabloid headline, soap opera and Hitchcockian voyeurism. Severin is fascinated with 'true stories (the ones tucked away in the newspapers) and other people's experiences. I love to watch — that's a hangover from a crippling shyness as a child/youth. Touring brought me out of myself — gave me the framework to express but my natural habitat is essentially a voyeuristic one.'[130]

Sioux also recounts the salacious journalism of 'people doing the weirdest things, like this bloke who put his leg on the railway line because he wanted to claim more as a war hero. And the woman who wheeled around a chopped-up body in a pram. It's all there, in The Sun every day.'[131]

It has the hallmarks of a kitchen sink drama with the addition of a violent denouement; the curiosity or fantasy about what happens behind the net curtains of those seemingly innocuous, tidy Victorian terraced houses. There are also parallels between 'Suburban Relapse' and aspects of David Lynch's film 'Blue Velvet'; the wholesome belying what lies hidden in the shadows.

The opening sequence to Lynch's 1986 masterpiece starring Isabella Rossellini, Kyle MacLachlan and Dennis Hopper, juxtaposes the clapperboard, rose-covered picket fence middle-American idyll replete with its neighbourhood fire truck, manicured front lawns, children's crossing guard and perpetually blue sky, with a knick-knack-laden, dark domestic sitting-room inhabited by a seemingly disenfranchised seated woman, coffee in hand, watching a black and white film on television, just as a gun comes into shot and fills the screen.

The shot then switches to what one might assume is her partner, spraying a worn bit of front lawn with a hose. Sensing that the hose has snagged (we the viewers are privy to the loose connection between hose and outdoor water tap), the user pulls it but then suddenly reaches to his neck and falls to the ground in paroxysms of agony, still with hose in hand, water now uncontrollably spraying into the air as a small dog climbs onto his stomach to take advantage of the water jet and a small child comes into shot across the yard.

The camera then returns to a slowed-down shot of the dog wrestling with the water and then into a grass thicket where, embedded in the soil, a frenzied and audible colony of beetles can be seen. The final shot is of a large, badly painted 1950s billboard of a woman waving and the slogan 'Welcome to Lumberton'.

'Suburban Relapse' has been described as both 'Hitchcockian' and 'Lynchian' with its atmosphere of something ominous lurking around the corner, suggesting a suburban dystopia where someone, ordinarily rational, has simply had as much as they can take of the humdrum: the endless, thankless cycle of cooking, cleaning and domestic subjugation. The 'should I' thought becomes deed, but the genius of the lyric, as with the shower scene in the film 'Psycho' that so affected Sioux when she was a child, where we see the veiled knife behind the shower curtain, witness the look of horror on Janet Leigh's face, hear the cacophonous scraping of violin strings and see the blood as it cascades, mixed with water, down the plughole — but as for the lacerations themselves, well, we can only imagine...

The song is one of the first instances where, lyrically, Sioux creates a sort of filmic vignette or psychodrama. Although not an overtly autobiographical description of her formative experiences of suburbia, the lyric is part catharsis in its suburban allusion and is also not without humour, albeit of the darker variety. Musically and lyrically, it isn't a million miles away from The Beatles' 'Maxwell's Silver Hammer', a song that begins with a date between Joan (a paraphysical science hobbyist) and Maxwell (Edison) (a medical student), which is over before it has even begun when 'Band, bang Maxwell's silver hammer / Came down upon her head,'[132] and ends with a further two murders by Maxwell. The music is jauntily upbeat, akin to an oompah singalong. The storytelling in 'Maxwell's Silver Hammer', as with 'Suburban Relapse' melds credible fact with fiction, a sort of inverse 1970s' situation comedy.

Although it might be somewhat a leap of faith to imagine Ria Parkinson, the dissatisfied middle-class housewife and mother in the late 1970s' sitcom 'Butterflies',[133] doing anything more drastic than scattering post-breakfast toast and cornflakes debris around the dining room to the accompaniment of Tomaso Albinoni's 'Adagio in D Minor for strings and organ', there is the real-life story of Sally Challen who, after serving breakfast to her husband of 31 years 'took a hammer and hit him more than 20 times. In case he was still breathing, she stuffed a tea towel into his mouth, before wrapping him in some old curtains. Challen wrote a note that said, "I love you, Sally" and placed it on Richard's body. Then she washed the dishes and drove back to the home she shared with their son, David.'[134]

Musically, 'Suburban Relapse' is a three-and-a-half-minute slice of menacing drama that shares all the hallmarks of the work of Bernard Hermann, one of Severin's favourite film composers. The beginning of the song builds to a twisted crescendo with the stereophonic attack of John McKay's guitar playing, which has been distorted and sped up in the studio mix; a crashing assault accompanied by the austere minimalism of Steve Severin's bass. Both guitar and bass are then joined by Kenny Morris's thumping drums and Siouxsie Sioux piles straight in with the opening (literally killer) lyric 'I'm sorry that I hit you but my string snapped.'

The delivery is far from remorseful but rather the justification of a repressed character who has lost all control for their momentary (re)lapse of reason. The song is singularly unafraid to explore the spaces in between the notes, which adds to the overall melodrama and theatricality. Guitar, bass and drums act as metaphorical bludgeons, speeding up as the song reaches its exhausting climax, spiralling into paroxysms of insanity. The song begins as it ends, shuddering to a halt with Sioux's cry of 'Relapse' before the curtain comes down.

The John Peel broadcast coincided with some timely interest from the music press, with Sioux making the front cover of Sounds on 3 December 1977. Under the title 'New

Musick', which was part of a feature on Pere Ubu and Devo, the band discuss a myriad of topics, and particularly why, at the time, they had not been signed by a major record label. Sioux surmises, 'They're (record labels) so ignorant. Look at all these arseholes that are signed up, that's proof. I consider it a compliment in a way, but — I just don't know why…'[135]

Sioux articulately expounds on her reasoning for this myopia, remarking 'We'll do it on our own terms. We're not gonna water down things to make it acceptable to the people who sit behind desks. It does matter, because we want to get across to a lot of people. But we'll continue to such a degree that no-one can ignore us. For a band that hasn't been signed we've had an incredible amount of publicity. That's why we're doing this interview, to get across…'[136]

There is also the principle of not wanting to compromise or be compromised. Siouxsie and The Banshees certainly weren't going to kowtow to any lazy idea of what they should and shouldn't be, Sioux proving 'as likely to take shit as I am to flog my typewriter for a new frock. Maybe that's why she hasn't got a record deal.'[137] The not taking of 'shit' was proving to be a Sioux tenet, albeit an unwritten one. One instance of this is when the Banshees played a gig at one of the major London venues, the Rainbow Theatre, on 20 October 1977. This was also an important show for the band as it was likely to attract press and A&R men from record companies, although Nils Stevenson knew that the band would be more than likely to 'insult them from the stage.'[138]

The gig, supporting Johnny Thunders and the Heartbreakers, turned into a brawl when there was a complaint about the manhandling of audience members by rather overzealous security guards. Both Sioux and Kenny Morris took umbrage at this and (along with 999 drummer Pablo LaBritain) were rather 'outspoken' about what they construed as maltreatment (Sioux never had any compunction about kicking or punching anyone — audience member or security guard — if they were getting out of hand).

Sounds journalist Derek Johnson writes that Sioux, Morris and LeBritain 'were arrested, detained overnight at Holloway Road Police Station, and subsequently fined for obstruction. Eyewitness reports suggest that — after the incident leading the arrests — they were treated very brusquely by the police. It's alleged that Siouxsie was made to walk barefoot down the street in the rain, and Morris had his head banged against the side of the police van. After a night in the cells, the three musicians were each fined £20 — and as LaBritain did not have the money with him, he was further detained until the fine was paid.'[139]

'SIGN THE BANSHEES — DO IT NOW'[140]

'I suggested that we started our own record label: 'Banshee Records' but Nils was insistent that it had to be a major label. If it had been my choice, I would have refused to record Hong Kong Garden. It was wrong.'[141] Ray Stevenson.

The travails, twists and turns leading to the signing of Siouxsie and The Banshees to Polydor Records on 9 June 1978 was in stark contrast to the momentum of press coverage the band had garnered on the back of the 1977 tour. With the front cover of Sounds and the Peel Session, both in December, under the collective Banshees' belt, surely it was only a matter of time before they would be snapped up by a major label?

The 'Sign The Banshees — Do It Now' slogan has taken on folkloric status, with the band themselves being the named authors of the statement. Steve Severin seemed to set the record straight by remarking 'I think it was our roadie Les that did that. He had blond hair and a leather jacket with "Siouxsie" marked out in studs... He didn't just scrawl it, he chiselled it — right into the wall by the door of the CBS building.'[142]

Essentially, and this is the crux of the issue, The Banshees were simply not going to agree unless the minutiae of the small print was as they wanted it to be. If The Banshees had been perhaps a little more laissez faire, they would have already been immortalised in vinyl on the 'Jubilee' soundtrack in 1977. They said no.

They had a long list of contract-signing near misses, and perhaps lucky escapes. The Banshees were within a hair's breadth of signing to Anchor Records, established in 1974 and part of America's ABC Records, when Anchor decided they 'weren't rock and roll enough.'[143]

With EMI, they were close enough to a deal smell the evaporating alcohol on the Banda copier, with record executive John Darnley mustard keen on the idea, but, in a sudden volte face, Darnley had orders from above to back out, with the perfunctory explanation, 'We've had second thoughts.'[144]

The relationship with RCA was a brief flirtation rather than anything of potential substance, with the company citing a lack of compatibility between The Banshees and other acts on their roster.

Chrysalis Records also showed willing but changed their minds on the basis that their A&R man knew they would sell records but stated that 'no one here likes them.'[145]

They came close with big-hitters Atlantic Records until Atlantic A&R man Dave Dee, formerly of Dave Dee, Dozy, Beaky, Mick & Tich, refused them a deal on the basis that punk had 'finished.' Perhaps a little premature, considering Atlantic had also turned down the Sex Pistols.

Negotiations with CBS never got further than Banshees' manager Nils Stevenson cajoling their A&R men into buying him drinks and subsequently mistaking a top CBS person for a

Soho Square cleaner. Perhaps not the best way to make friends and influence people.

Arista Records disliked the name of the band and refused to see the band play, and Decca seemed to believe that Siouxsie and The Banshees would be only too delighted to accept their offer of 5% royalties and a £2000 advance. They weren't.

Astounded by these industry choppy waters, Nils Stevenson wondered what the real problem was. To his mind, record companies were there to fulfil demand, but he was beginning to have the unerring sense that this wasn't the case, stating at the time 'We draw more than any other unsigned band and more than 90% of the signed ones. But we've got this far and we're not giving up. For the first nine months we had no gear at all. We had to borrow it off our support acts. We'd tell them the truck with our gear in had broken down in a town fifty miles away. We even played Holland and Paris without any gear.'[146]

There was also the association with punk, one the band were keen to disassociate from. Sioux was never one for labels, anyway. The Sex Pistols' demise on 14 January 1978, after a disastrous US tour, was the catalyst for promoters to get cold feet about The Banshees, just as they were beginning to build up a full head of steam and draw large crowds, citing them as old-fashioned and lacking credibility. No matter how hard Nils Stevenson tried, barring the aftermath of the Rainbow gig on 20 October 1977 where Siouxsie Sioux and Kenny Morris spent the night in the cells of Holloway Road police station, the band could not even get arrested. Until…

'I can remember going into work and seeing the wall outside sprayed with the words "Sign The Banshees." I knew that somebody would have to do it, and it was (Head of A&R) Alan Black who went out on a limb. I think the graffiti on the wall helped considerably…'[147] George McManus, Head of

Marketing, Polydor Records.

On 9 June 1978 Siouxsie and The Banshees signed to Polydor Records. Established in 1946 and boasting a roster today of a diversity of artists such as Celeste, Madonna, Elbow, Billy Eilish, Yungblud, The Rolling Stones and Abba, Polydor had the insight to embrace all of the aspects of the band's principled integrity: their vision and dogged insistence they should have the latitude to be able to make decisions about the music they wanted to make and the way in which it should be presented and marketed.

Ostensibly, Polydor was keen to sign Siouxsie and The Banshees for all the reasons that the other major record labels had shunned them. However, never one to lavish a bouquet of roses without the knowledge that the recipient's finger might be pricked by a thorn, after the band were signed there was a meet and greet for them at a London hotel, and when the Dutch Managing Director of Polydor told Sioux, 'It's so great to have you here. I was going to sign you when you did 'The Lord's Prayer'[148], according to George McManus, Sioux's reply was 'Why the fuck didn't you'?[149]

'Hong Kong Garden'

'I knew that if I got the hit single, if I could get a single that they wanted, that they thought was good enough to be released, then it would be a hit; and having a hit is a game changer.'[150] Producer Steve Lillywhite.

'We weren't gagging for celebrity — we were a gang producing a sound we loved. We were ready to embrace success to promote what we felt was the best group in the world. We were excited — this was our first step out of the crucible of revolution into the treacherous world of the mainstream! We were going overground…'[151] John McKay.

'Hong Kong Garden' became a feature of Siouxsie and The Banshees' live set after debuting at the Barton Hill Youth Club in Bristol on 28 January 1978. The first studio outing for the song can be heard as one of four songs, including 'Overground', 'Carcass' and 'Helter Skelter'[152] that Siouxsie and The Banshees recorded for their second John Peel Session on 2 February 1978, two months after stepping into the BBC Maida Vale studios for the first time.

Again, the playing exudes confidence and there is the addition of Hammer Horror meets Velvet Underground organ playing by John McKay on 'Overground'. Nothing too sophisticated: several sustained notes, yet enough to propel The Banshees' musical metier into the realms of experimentation and intrigue. There is also a nod to Siouxsie Sioux's beloved The Beatles' 'White Album' with the inclusion of 'Helter Skelter', which had already become a regular feature of the band's live set.

The band thought that 'Hong Kong Garden' should be the band's first single as it was poppy and discernibly different from the other songs written to date.

The origins of 'Hong Kong Garden' are in guitarist John McKay's experimentation with a song with the working title 'People Phobia'. 'I first picked out the opening bars of Hong Kong Garden on an electronic xylophone in the Maida Vale Peel studio. I played it with the wrong end of the beater and the xylophone switched off, to achieve the right sound.'[153]

Steve Severin recalls that 'Hong Kong Garden' had happened in the same way as all their early songs: 'McKay would present the beginning of a chord sequence and would work around it, shape it, arrange it. Adding an Oriental feel with xylophone and the gong at the end seemed dead obvious.'[154]

The lyrics of the song allude to Sioux's experience of a

'Chinese restaurant in Chislehurst called The Hong Kong Garden. Me and my friend were really upset that we used to go there and like, occasionally, when the skinheads would turn up it would turn really ugly. These gits would go in en masse and just terrorise these Chinese people who were working there. We'd try and say "Leave them alone", you know. It was a kind of tribute.'[155]

Peel Session aside, the first demo for the song was made at Olympic Studios in Barnes in London on 6 June 1978. Sioux critiqued this first recording of the song as 'atrocious',[156] mainly the result of the band not having any particular producer in mind, except perhaps Severin's heroes John Cale and Brian Eno, whom, as the bass guitarist none too decorously describes, had 'temporarily lost their minds'[157] and were 'off working with Ultravox and Sham 69.'[158]

Nils Stevenson subsequently hired American producer Bruce Albertine, whose repertoire was mainly in the area of soul music, not, to all intents and purposes, the best match for a band whose imperative for a guitarist was channelling the bastard son of Bernard Hermann and Sterling Morrison.

A more suitable fit for 'Hong Kong Garden', Stevenson suggested, might be Steve Lillywhite, who at the time was working on Johnny Thunder's first solo album 'So Alone'. Before this, Lillywhite had produced (with the assistance of Brian Eno) the eponymously titled 'Ultravox' album, released on 25 February 1977. Lillywhite's trajectory as a producer started in 1972 when he worked as a tape operator for Polygram Records. The role of the tape operator or tape op was essentially an assistant recording engineer, trimming audio tape, setting up microphones and microphone stands, and, if they were deemed trustworthy enough, they would be charged with pressing one of the panoply of buttons now and again on the control desk.

Lillywhite describes his serendipitous encounter with Nils Stevenson and production of 'Hong Kong Garden,' and subsequently The Scream: 'I've caught a lot of artists when they're really firing... There was a great tailwind with Siouxsie and The Banshees. I've told the story a few times about how I got the job, but I was very lucky that my roommate at the time, Michael Beal, knew a guy called Johnny Thunders, who was in the New York Dolls. Johnny moved to England and had a band called The Heartbreakers, and they released an album called 'LAMF' (like a motherfucker), and the general consensus was that they were a great band, but the sound of the album wasn't good. I became friends with Johnny... So, and I can't imagine myself being this confident, when Jonny wanted a solo album, I seem to remember saying, "I can make that album better than the last album you did with your band."

So, he got this manager, a wonderful Irish guy called BP Fallon. Fallon had been Mark Bolan's press officer; he was from a previous generation, a wonderful leprechaun-type guy, a lovely man. He had all the connections; he got together the Sex Pistols, and Phil Lynott, and Stevie Marriott, all to come and play on Johnny Thunders' Record. We were in there recording Johnny's album, when Neil Stevenson... who was hanging around with Johnny (he knew that crowd)... came to the studio, and liked the sound of this one song I'd done called 'You can't put your arms around a memory', which is a fantastic song by Johnny Thunders. And he (Stevenson) said: "We've just recorded our first single. Now maybe you know who the producer was, but it was some American guy, and the band didn't like how it had turned out"; and because the band had waited for a record deal where they could have artistic control, if they didn't like the version this guy had recorded, they didn't want it released — they had complete creative control. So, Neil said to me: "Steve, we've recorded our single, but the band don't like it. I like how this sounds; would you like to do our single?'"[159]

Lillywhite knew that if he could record the band as they thought they should sound and get a single that the band would be 100% invested in, good enough to be released as a single, then it would be a hit. As Lillywhite remarks, 'Having a hit is a game changer, so I was looking for a hit. I'd had records by Johnny Thunders and Ultravox, but I'd never had a hit.'[160]

Recording and mixing the single took place in the basement of The Fallout Shelter, at the rear of 22 St Peter's Square in Hammersmith. Lillywhite describes the sound they were able to create as "nice, and tight, and poppy."[161]

Siouxsie Sioux recalls hearing her voice for the first time with the addition of multi-tracking as a 'revelation. When we heard the finished version of 'Hong Kong Garden' I was astounded. I couldn't believe it was us.'[162] Of the song's production, Sioux remarks 'Steve Lillywhite brought a lot of space and lightness, with that undercurrent of the band behind it pummelling away.'[163]

Kenny Morris, whose drums were recorded separately for 'Hong Kong Garden', with the cymbals added subsequently (a Lillywhite trademark), recounts that 'There were four people in a band who could not be more compatible, who were absolutely perfect — the four of us. I thought at the time that our best song was 'Love In A Void' and that it should be the first single, but our manager decided on 'Hong Kong Garden' because the very first few seconds that you hear on the radio or driving in a car, you're hooked straight away.'[164]

Ever the contrarian, Sioux maintains that the far less poppy and commercially accessible B-side 'Voices' would have been the A-side of the single, showcasing the more 'extreme side of the band.'[165] Both Sioux and Severin were big fans of Roxy Music at their most experimental, especially where non-album tracks were concerned. Sioux also recounts that the song was apparently 'A favourite amongst publicans in Liverpool. Put on 'Voices' at drinking-up time and you would instantly clear the bar!'[166]

'Voices' was inspired by two of Severin's favourite literary works: the poem 'The Haunted Palace' by Edgar Allan Poe and the book 'On Wine and Hashish' by Charles Baudelaire, both of which explore the inner recesses of the mind and the outer reaches of the imagination, accelerated, aided and abetted by hashish, opium and alcohol.

'Voices' starts as a jaunty, poppy instrumental, grinding to a halt 42 seconds in, with John McKay's angular, flange-distorted, menacing guitar playing and Sioux's voice, replete with haunting delay, the sole instruments for the remainder of the song, which, both musically and lyrically, is powerfully evocative of being alone with one's thoughts, whether substance enhanced or otherwise, either trapped in a nightmare of Poe-like imagined ghouls and demons, or cushioned by the plush velvet Baudelairian hashish enlightenment 'when an exquisite sensibility is no longer tortured by sick nerves.'[167]

'Voices'

'Voices' was the only song the band were able to salvage from the Olympic Studio session with Bruce Albertine and was subsequently successfully remixed by Steve Lillywhite.

With both A and B sides in the can, there was then the question of a suitable image for the single. At the time, Polydor had its own in-house design team, which Severin recalls being a 'bit of a struggle.'[168] Art Director Jill Mumford recalls that 'The Banshees bought the image in... My partner (Philip Sheffield) at the time was a silk-screen printer and I had the idea of making promotional posters from the image with the lettering. He printed some ten, maybe fifteen, original posters.

These were all given to people who would promote the record. From one of those posters, I made a limited edition giclee poster a few years back. I had had quite a lot of interest in the artwork I produced from fans from that time, when I produced lots of covers and had sold quite a few artworks to private collectors. Siouxsie and The Banshees didn't have copyright over the image as it was very old. The lettering was done by my old college tutor Sid Day from Hornsey College of Art.'[169]

The cover image that Jill Mumford used is a photograph, taken in the late 1800s, of Cuban actor Rose Lemoine, thought to be the model for 'Gibson Girl', the epitome of the feminine ideal of physical attractiveness as portrayed by the pen and ink illustrations of artist Charles Dana Gibson during a 20-year period spanning the late nineteenth and early twentieth centuries in the United States.

The 'physical ideal' in the instance of the cover of 'Hong Kong Garden', slightly antithetical to Gibson's aesthetic as Lemoine is depicted stretching a piece of cloth over her face, akin to artist Rene Magritte's painting 'The Lovers' (1928).

Bearing in mind Sioux and Severin's penchant for the macabre, especially the trashier B-movie end of the spectrum, it cannot have escaped their notice that the image was used for cartoonist and illustrator Charles Addams' (creator of the Addams Family cartoon 'Dear Dead Days' published in 1959, a collection of P.T. Barnum-like circus freakshow oddities.[170]

Before the single was released on 18 August 1978, the band recorded a promotional video with director Clive Richardson on 16 August. In the video, although unaccustomed to miming, the band look like seasoned professionals. Sioux dances with strutting, abandoned, confident ebullience, at one point throwing the microphone stand over. John McKay, the epitome of nonchalant cool, stands almost motionless, looking like an early incarnation of Radiohead's Jonny Greenwood.

Steve Severin is also resolutely cool, although one can discern the emanation of joy, the affirmation that this is the moment he and Sioux had been striving for, and all without any hint of duplicitous corporate compromise.

Kenny Morris completes the ensemble, wearing a sleeveless shirt, raven-black hair spiked up, his drumkit completed by a slightly incongruous gong that wouldn't have looked out of place behind the kits of Keith Moon, John Bonham, Roger Taylor or Neil Peart, although one senses that might not have been intentional; especially as far as Sioux was concerned, railing against every aspect of 'Spinal Tap'[171] rock excess. However, considering the East Asian and South-East Asian provenance of the gong, it is, in this instance, entirely apposite as 'Hong Kong Garden' ends with a bang, not a whimper, heralded by the gong's majestic crash.

This is no perfunctory, 'going through the motions' performance; it is, instead, a statement of intent. All four members of the band look stunning, almost film star like, with cheekbones as sharply defined and sculpted as the two minutes and 52 seconds of 'Hong Kong Garden's perfect pop.

The promo, filmed three years before the arrival of MTV, is shot like an animated monochromatic photographic negative, broken up with colourised close ups of Sioux, with the occasional cameo appearance from The Banshees.' Hong Kong Garden' first charted in the UK on 26 August 1978 at number 49 and peaked at number 7 on 10 September 1978, after spending ten weeks in the top 75.

Music press reviews of 'Hong Kong Garden' were positive, mentioning Siouxsie and The Banshees' originality and lack of compromise, the NME describing it as 'A bright, vivid narrative, something like snapshots from the window of a speeding Japanese train, power charged by the most original, intoxicating guitar playing I heard in a long, long time. Would you believe it's going to be played on Radio One?'[172]

Record Mirror thought the single 'Accessibility incarnated... I love every second — from John McKay's flurried chording to Steven Severin's pounding bass to Kenny Morris's bruising drums to Siouxsie's cockney intonations. The first love song to a Chinese restaurant?'[173] While Sounds made 'Hong Kong Garden' its Single of the Week, remarking that the single was 'One inspirational beacon in the mind-numbing darkness... I hardly expected Siouxsie and her Banshees to prove my musical salvation, what with all the 'Ice Queen' reputation and atonal bash and thrash that they're supposed to go in for, but this was a revelation. Goddammit, here was I expecting a screeching, torturous din, and instead this is New Wave starkness and chop suey frivolity, the main theme being tapped out in charming Chinese chimes ... catchy, original arrangement coupled with an irresistible sing-along chorus.'[174]

Melody Maker reported, 'They hate the press and seem to reserve especial vitriol for those that champion them (at whatever juncture)... I guess making them single of the week will increase my chances of being fly-swatted... Now all the elements have individually improved and come together with remarkable effect. The song is strident and powerful with tantalising oriental guitar riffs plus words and vocals that are the result of anger, disdain and isolation... It might even be a hit.'[175]

Subtextually, there is some suggestion of the first single, although universally well received by the UK music press, proving a little too bamboozling for its critics, both in terms of the band's cumulative skill as musicians but also how Siouxsie and The Banshees belied, and indeed, railed against, categorisation.

Can this be the same band that took to the 100 Club stage almost two years previously, on 20 September 1976,[176] after scant, and by all accounts, ramshackle rehearsal, and played a 20-minute sonic assault of improvised, extemporised, Situationist, Sister Ray-esque clangour? The intervening time had allowed the band to hone their craft, learn to play their instruments, gig solidly, write and air new songs, and, one suspects, strengthen their resolve to not give too much of a damn about what fanfares and clarion calls were forthcoming from the music press.

Chapter 4
'The Scream'

Buoyed by the success of the recording of 'Hong Kong Garden', Siouxsie and The Banshees and Steve Lillywhite booked one week of studio time at RAK Studios, 2-48 Charlbert Street, St John's Wood, in August 1978, almost immediately after recording the A-side of the single.

Lillywhite remarks that 'Mickie Most had a studio in St John's Wood. You could see the road from the control room, and there we could set the drums up. Because it was an old wooden schoolhouse, it was a lot more reverb-y. So, I set the drums up in the back, and I could use compression to suck some of the room sound in, so that was much more of a crazy sonic landscape. I wasn't 100 percent convinced by the sound of the Fallout Shelter but understood what Kenny was doing at that point, and I thought, I want to make these drums more rumbly, and more roomy. The room that they were being recorded in at the Fallout Shelter didn't have that lively ambience.'[177]

Lillywhite remembers the experience of working with the band as one of collaboration rather than being a Machievellian ringmaster. He singles out McKay's musicality, 'doing this guitar playing, which is almost like crying in some places, enabled everyone in the band to up their game to an amazing standard; it was so emotive… And all of us followed the greatness, Sue (sic) as well. Not only her singing, but her performances were really great, even when she was slightly out of tune; it doesn't matter because it has this wonderful chorus-y sort of sound. There are some singers who, when they're out of tune, don't sound very good, but for some reason, Sue in those days sounded fantastic when it was like that. I'm not saying that like "ooh, Sue sung out of tune", it doesn't matter — it sounded good. People get too small-minded, like things HAVE to be this way or HAVE to be that way — no! What it was, was something so expansive and so great that it transcended the need to be anything like that.'[178]

Asked whether the band wished to emulate or sound like another band, Lillywhite, quick as a flash, replies 'No — we never did that back then! That is an invention of the Internet age. The ability to reference every single fucking record that's ever been made is one of the reasons music is not so good. If anyone in the studio had anything that sounded a bit like someone else, we'd change it: it would be called out, and we'd be like "oh shit — we can't do that because it sounds like someone else." Now it's: "it sounds like that? Fucking great, that was a hit, I'll change a chord".'[179]

'Pure'
'That song wasn't written — it just happened'[180] Steve Severin.

The origins of 'Pure' can be traced back, according to Severin, to when the band embarked on their short European jaunt in 1977: a soundcheck before a gig in Paris. It is a haunting soundscape, a melange of sonically unexpected instrumental interruptions channelling the compositional discord of Oliver Messiaen, Bernard Hermann and Arnold Schoenberg and conceivably the most unexpected, theatrical and tense opening track of any album made in the late 1970s.

A song that treads a fine line between cohering and tipping

over into the realms of mania. It shares much of its DNA with Hong Kong Garden's B-side 'Voices', the two songs being more or less contemporaneous. John McKay's 'screaming' guitar refrain, along with Steve Severin's minimal bass, Kenny Morris's pagan, ritualistic and shamanistic drumming and Sioux's multi-tracked haunting banshee wail, all collude to create an overpowering siren's call. Steve Lillywhite remarks: 'It's so tense, and so emotive. For those first three songs, I'm completely in this world. I had a job as an A&R guy once, and my boss said "when you're looking to sign someone, you have to ask yourself "do I want to be in their world?", and when I hear those first three songs on that album, I want to be in their world — a world of mystery, a world of absolute magic, which I don't get with a lot of records; they're all either squeaky clean or too untogether. But this makes me want to be in the world of Siouxsie and The Banshees. And that sounds like an obvious thing to say, but how many artists inspire that feeling, of wanting to be in their world? Not many.'[181]

'Jigsaw Feeling'
'It's when your limbs won't do what your brain wants them to. You're so confused that you can't co-ordinate your limbs to do something positive, and you just twist yourself in knots.'[182] Siouxsie Sioux.

With the heavy theatre curtain lifted to reveal the magnitude of the proscenium in its full glory, Siouxise and The Banshees unleash the glorious maelstrom of 'Jigsaw Feeling'. The song builds, whisper to scream-like; John McKay playing a single scorching, repetitive note, joined by the minimal two-note menace of Steve Severin's bass guitar and the rhythmic punctuation of Kenny Morris's drumbeat.

The song explodes into full effect when Sioux joins the fray, the swooping timbre of her voice completes the ensemble and as John Robb in a rare interview with Kenny Morris remarks: 'There's a perfect symmetry in the classic four. Everyone's playing the lead line at the same time, and it's very difficult to do — but there it was being done instinctively.'[183]

Sioux's lyrics allude to an almost out-of-body experience, akin to Radiohead's paean to the madness of superstardom in the wake of 1997's 'OK Computer', 'How to disappear completely (and never return)' from Kid A, released in 2000.

'Jigsaw Feeling' also references the complexities of inhabiting the same body until death and living in one's head, as well as incorporating Lewis Carroll's 'Alice Through the Looking Glass' allusions: 'One day I'm feeling total, / The next I'm split in two, / My eyes are doing somersaults, / Staring at my shoe.'[184] There is, indeed, a sense of heroism in the song: four outsiders against the rest of the world, leading a forthright sonic charge. The song has all the prepossessing compositional elements of any intoxicating work of art and, even though Sioux would later acerbically refer to John McKay and Kenny Morris as 'The two arty ones'[185] the day the drummer and guitarist scarpered from the band after what can only be described as a disastrous 'Join Hands' album signing at The Other Record Store in Aberdeen, in truth, all four members of the band were, unwittingly or otherwise, artists.

All understood, and were complicit in, the making of alchemically transcendent tumult, more Francisco De Goya's series of 'Black Paintings' (1819–23) than Pierre August Renoir's 'Dance at the Moulin Galette' (1876). 'Jigsaw Feeling' burns bright and with such dervish intensity that, after a final attack of drumming, it pitters out along with retroceding guitar and drums; a bright conflagration spent and exhausted.

'Overground'

'It was written at a time when we were all getting desperate for a contract... and it's really to do with why we wanted a major record deal.'[186] Steve Severin.

Again, this is a song that builds from the quietude of a repetitive guitar refrain, accompanied by gentle, unassuming bass playing, subsequently joined by Sioux's melancholic refrain of the first verse, referring to a sort of existential limbo, clearly alluding to the travails of, as Steve Severin remarks, being 'desperate for a contract' but being fearful of the compromise this might entail.

Kenny Morris's drumming is an almost militaristic rejoinder when it joins voice, guitar and bass; the overall effect is akin to a multi-layered flamenco-like composition, further enhanced by the lamentation of John McKay's organ playing. The band were more than mindful, even fearful, of the prospect of pleasantries in the form of meetings, playing corporate games and being manipulated and exploited, everything The Banshees were resolute they wanted no part of.

Therein lies the band's perpetual dilemma: exposure and commercial success versus remaining on the periphery as outsiders, calling all the shots, being completely in control, but with little wealth or recognition. The occasional £10 handout from manager Nils Stevenson would certainly have proved both less than desirable and sustainable in the long run.

Lyrically, 'Overground' chronicles a time of impasse and indecision, as Steve Severin remarks: 'You can either go along with the way things are or... It's very personal to the band on one level. The whole thing about the uncompromising Banshees. It's saying that we can change to go overground but at the same time we know we'd be worse than ourselves.'[187] 'Overground' is another mini psychodrama, a conversation or inner monologue about the loss of identity and relinquishing all of one's ideals for fame.

'Carcass'

"'My mother had her son for tea"… when you think about it, every day can be really cruel yet so laughable.'[188] Siouxsie Sioux.

One of the few songs written during the short spell with Pete Fenton on guitar, lyrically, 'Carcass' is an aberrant, societally transgressive tale about, according to Sioux, 'a butcher's assistant who can't get girls and so he falls in love with a lump of meat on the slab and so that he can be like the object of his affection, he cuts off his own arms and legs.'[189]

Sioux and Severin's appetite for macabre, clandestine stories was also tinged with often acerbic gallows humour, whether found in the pages of a pages of a tabloid newspaper or one of the books etched on the psyche of those of a certain generation, such as 'Struwwelpeter' by Heinrich Hoffmann, a book of ten illustrated children's cautionary stories describing the gruesome results of misbehaving, including 'Geschichte vom Daumenlutscher' (The Story Little Suck A Thumb), where a mother warns her son Konrad not to suck his thumbs. However, when she leaves the house, Konrad resumes his thumb-sucking and the nomadic tailor his mother warned him about appears and cuts off his thumbs with giant scissors.

'One day, Mamma said, "Conrad dear,
I must go out and leave you here.
But mind now, Conrad, what I say,
Don't suck your thumb while I'm away.
The great tall tailor always comes
To little boys that suck their thumbs.

And 'ere they dream what he's about
He takes his great sharp scissors
And cuts their thumbs clean off, — and then
You know, they never grow again".'[190]

There is also The Velvet Underground's 'The Gift', with its lyrical narrative centring around a lovelorn Waldo Jeffers, who has engaged in a rather non-reciprocal, long-distance relationship with his college girlfriend Marsha Bronson. Waldo's separation anxiety-ridden paranoia about Marsha's possible sexual infidelity, despite her promises to the contrary, reaches a peak when Waldo decides to mail himself inside a cardboard box from his hometown of Locust, Pennsylvania, to Marsha's residence in Wisconsin.

The delivery takes several days to ship, from Friday to the following Monday. Waldo anticipates the sheer delight Marsha will feel when she opens the box to find her beau ensconced within. In Wisconsin, just before the mysterious delivery arrives, Marsha is in conversation with her roommate Sheila Klein about Bill, a man whom Marsha slept with the previous night, extolling the virtues of his sexual prowess.

When the package appears at the door, Marsha and Sheila wrestle with the box, trying to open it by various means, while Waldo waits excitedly inside. Unable to open the box, cross and frustrated, Marsha retrieves a sheet metal cutter belonging to her father from her basement and gives it to Sheila, who stabs straight through the box and right through the centre of Waldo's head 'which split slightly and caused little rhythmic arcs of red to pulsate gently in the morning sun.'[191] John Cale delivers Lou Reed's lyrics with perfectly deadpan irreverence.

Steve Lillywhite remarks that 'Carcass' is rather at odds with the rest of the album: a 'two- dimensional song, it doesn't have mystery; it doesn't build the picture of what I'm talking about. Those first three songs set the world that makes me want to be in it.'[192]

I am not entirely in agreement with Lillywhite with regard to the song, partly due to the enveloping, sweltering seduction of John McKay's guitar playing (perhaps McKay's genius was such that he could make the runts of the litter into show-winning pigs) and the lower register rumbling of Steve Severin's bass playing.

The song needs, I feel, to be contextualised in terms of the band's predilection for the flippant and frivolous, as Sioux reflects: 'People always miss out on the humorous aspect of what we do, or rather the facetious aspect...'[193]

True, 'Carcass' may not have the depth and complexity of other songs on The Scream and is perhaps more redolent of an oeuvre more recognisable in the songs of Sham 69 or The Cockney Rejects, hybridised with the stomp of The Dave Clarke Five's 'Bits and Pieces', replete with handclaps. Running at three minutes and 49 seconds, 'Carcass' does rather run out of steam after two and a half minutes, so, perhaps Lillywhite does have a point.

'Helter Skelter'

Already an established staple of Siouxsie and The Banshees' live set list, 'Helter Skelter', originally recorded by The Beatles in 1968 for 'The Beatles' album, colloquially known as the 'White Album', (a favourite of Sioux's) is a barnstorming cover, overflowing with breakneck energy as it builds, beginning with several, preternaturally punctuated resonant bass guitar notes appearing from a dark void of silence and joined by the embryonically haphazard, abstract, metallurgic, feedback-infused strumming of John McKay's guitar. Sioux follows with a biliously expectorated vocal and then the belabour of Kenny Morris's drums. The song has all the histrionic hallmarks of the German Expressionist cinematography so beloved of Steve Severin.

Sioux was acutely aware of cult leader and murderer Charles Manson's interpretation of 'Helter Skelter'; Paul McCartney claimed that Manson had 'interpreted that 'Helter Skelter' was something to do with the four horsemen of the Apocalypse'[194] and 'I still don't know what all that stuff is; it's from the Bible, 'Revelations' — I haven't read it so I wouldn't know. But he interpreted the whole thing... and arrived at having to go out and kill everyone... It was frightening, because you don't write songs for those reasons.'[195] The Manson association would not have been lost on Sioux or Severin, given their predilection for the salacious, macabre and voyeuristic, all of which would manifest themselves in subsequent songs.

It might seem incongruous to include a cover song on the band's debut album, considering the band's admirable, dogged insistence on avoiding any semblance of being part of a musical canon or genre, yet somehow the song in its rightful place on an album that explores aspects of nihilism and whose title was influenced by the Eleanor and Frank Perry-directed 'The Swimmer', released in 1968. Starring Burt Lancaster, the film explores the psychological unravelling of its protagonist Ned Merrill as he swims his way home through the pools of his neighbours, each one providing a cumulative unveiling of Ned's chequered, misdemeanour-laden past.

It wasn't as though the band had a deficit of songs to include on 'The Scream' as is evident on the subsequent 2005 reissue. A regular feature of the Banshees' live set since its first airing at The Oaks in Manchester on 17 May 1977, 'Helter Skelter' is its own entity and captures the skittish energy of a band in the throes of embracing, albeit ambivalently, a headlong flight into what would become mainstream commercial success. The song also encompasses the abandoned thrash and Catherine-wheel twisting cajolery of the original.

'Mirage'

'Mirage' has been resolutely transformed in the studio into a rich, multi-layered, almost symphonically swirling two minutes and 49 seconds of beautiful, cascading sound where one can discern the multi-tracking of voice, guitar, bass and drums, all to stunning effect.

'Mirage' signposts much of the ensuing studio experimentation the band would utilise so effectively on subsequent albums. It is no surprise that guitarists such as The Edge, who 'wouldn't be The Edge without John McKay'[196] according to Steve Lillywhite, Robert Smith, Steve Albini, Johnny Marr, Jamie Reid and Kevin Shields set so much store by John McKay's guitar playing, the angularity and inklings of discord that are juxtaposed by an enveloping warmth, which can be discerned on 'Mirage' by acoustic as well as electric guitar. Retrospectively, one can also see the shape of things to come for Lillywhite, pretty much unarguably the inventor and pioneer of the 'big sound' that prevails on U2's debut 1980 album 'Boy', as well as offerings by The Killers, Big Country, The Psychedelic Furs and Simple Minds.

Lillywhite's modus operandi of collaborative facilitation, melded with innate understanding of the importance of creating space in the music, as well as the democratisation of every instrument, creates a panoramic vista of a band's music and, to illustrate this, Lillywhite remarks of The Scream: 'It has its harsh edges, but they're not harsh edges that hurt. It's a pleasurable listen, and without saying it sounds like Simply Red or something like that, you can have all the angst, but it has to make you want to be in that world. It's really important to build this world that you feel the artist is comfortable in. I was aware of the fact that I always make an artist's album. One of my least favourite things is when I'm chatting to a producer, and they say, "Oh, you know, I had to fire my drummer." Who are you, when you have to fire the drummer? Maybe the drummer's job is not just the drumming; normally it isn't. Normally the drummer's job is to say to the singer as well, "I hate your lyrics on that song; write better lyrics." You don't know; your job as a producer is that you produce the band'![197]

'Metal Postcard (Mittageisen)'

The bilious venom of 'Metal Postcard' on the 1977 Peel Session is no less smartingly visceral on 'The Scream', but this time it is delivered at a slower tempo, rendering the song even more menacing; a hybrid of death march and apocalyptic vision, in keeping with the John Heartfield 'Hurrah, die Butter ist Alle'! 1935 montage.

The meticulous orchestration of every fragment of the postcard-size Heartfield image is mirrored in the Banshees' song, which permeates every fibre of one's being with metronomic intensity. We can almost taste the metal of the family's inversely sumptuous repast and Metal Postcard propounds the cautionary and catastrophic pitfalls inherent in' propaganda. Again, Lillywhite's empathetic production works with the song to ensure that both artistry and tenor are realised to full effect.

'Nicotine Stain'

'Nicotine Stain' 'Started off when I had both my hands full and I had a cigarette. I had to hold on to it and I could feel the fumes all around my face. I had to look in the mirror to see that my face hadn't gone brown. I just got to thinking how nicotine could soak up all your body.'[198] Siouxsie Sioux.

From the macro to the micro with regard to lyrical concerns after the polemical sting of 'Metal Postcard', 'Nicotine Stain' focuses on perhaps more mundane, 'kitchen sink'[199] matters; a composition comprising two minutes and 57 seconds' of existential catastrophising about the problems of unseemly addiction.

The narrative of the song pertains to the realisation that we are predisposed to making decisions that are clearly detrimental yet incurably seductive, potentially interminable, and 'that habits are very disgusting, and you realise how addicted you are to them. You try to find the usefulness of your habits, you try to justify them.'[200]

'Nicotine Stain' is one of a few songs on 'The Scream' where guitar, drums and bass begin at the same time. 'The Scream' is a reflection of a band experimenting with a plethora of arrangements and sounds, pointing to the future direction of the band. It is another song driven by the melodious, nuanced inflections of John McKay's guitar playing, with a couple of transcendental instances where it is almost a guitar solo two minutes and 23 seconds into the song, fitting the ebb and flow.

Through nuanced light and shade, McKay bevels the hard edges, placing a metaphorical flower down a gun barrel. Voice, guitar, bass and drums all collude to create another mini-drama redolent of 'The Scream's' oscillating, nervous energy encompasses the neuroses of living in one's own head; the escalation of the seemingly anodyne and domestically humdrum into a scenario approaching an atomic catastrophe. Sioux's vocal is beautifully expressive, building from the matter of fact to a Patti Smith-like faltering, yet perfectly executed, yelp.

'Suburban Relapse'

'The Scream' recording of 'Suburban Relapse' is replete with multi-layered, almost symphonic orchestration and melodrama, as the slowly building sonic tension, so reflective of the tenor of the album, is affected by the poking and stabbing of instrumentation, especially with Kenny Morris's epic drumming, following the manic Sioux vocal.

Morris aligns his precision to maximum effect when Sioux utters 'snaps'; the most brutal and fatal of stab wounds. Morris's expressive playing on 'Suburban Relapse' gives the song its menace, every fill and pattern an expression of total immersion and empathy for the downtrodden, subjugated protagonist of the song. The band plays aggressively, as though they are painting the grisliest scene imaginable; a soundtrack to all the tensions and dysfunction being played out behind a myriad net curtains.

It is panoramically filmic in its scope, akin to the tense voyeurism of Hitchcock's 'Psycho' and 'Rear Window'; from the simmering to the boiling over and then the scalding; the passive perpetrator at the end of their passive and subservient tether. John McKay adds a further layer of visceral complexity through the addition of a searing saxophone, which is reminiscent of the saxophone playing on David Bowie's instrumental 'Newkoln', which appears on the 'Heroes' album released in 1977.

'Suburban Relapse' ends with that most universally recognisable of suburban sounds, the ding-dong of a doorbell. One can sense that what awaits inside might not be conducive to polite conversation.

'Switch'

'This is the way the world ends
This is the way the world ends

This is the way the world ends
Not with a bang but a whimper'[201]

'The Hollow Men' T S Eliot

'The Scream' reaches its end with an introspective, existential denouement; a narrative about authoritarian, hierarchical subservience, whether one's certainties lie in religious, scientific or political dogma. 'It all comes down to the same thing: the hypocrisy of it all.'[202] 'Switch', consciously or otherwise, is a paean to libertarianism.

'Switch' bookends 'The Scream'; an aural finale equivalent to the previously mentioned film 'The Swimmer', which sees the psychological degeneration of Ned Merrill, as every aquatic encounter crescendos until Merrill limps dejectedly through dank, overgrown foliage to reach his final destination, the family home. He shakes the wrought-iron gates open to encounter the forlorn, untended tennis court covered in Autumn leaves, and painfully approaches his dilapidated, abandoned house. Merrill frantically turns the door handle to try and enter but the door is locked. We, the viewers, can enter through one of the broken windows to view the few remaining family effects in front of the fireplace — a broken tennis racket and several cardboard boxes — on the other side of the door through which Merrill is so desperately trying to enter. We are privy to the inner recesses of Merrill's psychological malaise, exemplified by the miserable interior of his former home. Merrill finally realises the magnitude of his own abandonment and aloneness, and breaks down, withering and foetus like in the doorway, in the torrential rain.

The song begins with a melodious and melancholic guitar refrain and is joined initially by soft, reflective drumming and bass guitar. Sioux joins to complete the ensemble, along with the wistful saxophone playing of John McKay. Sioux envisaged that 'the song... was going to be very fragmented with three different sections.'[203]

'Switch' is reflective of the band's increasingly experimental disposition and willingness to stretch out. It is by far the most adventurous track on 'The Scream', exemplifying the band's innate understanding of the importance of light, shade and space, juxtaposing the barbed with the melodious. At six minutes and 53 seconds, 'Switch' is the longest song on 'The Scream', incidentally 26 seconds longer than Radiohead's 'Paranoid Android', also composed of several parts. Akin to the tolling of a bell, no sooner has Sioux uttered 'humanities' than McKay's guitar chimes the single-chord fanfare for Sioux's lyrics to take flight, singing of GPs trying medication out on patients with 'drastic side-effects.' Lyrically, 'Switch' ostensibly alludes to the addiction of religion, drugs and any manifestation of dependence, resulting in a downward volution of addiction or inculcation.

'The Scream's' release in November 1978 and its ensuing success attracted a cavalcade of journalists lining up to interview the band, including Paul Morley from the NME, and Jon Savage and Pete Silverton from Sounds.

Morley's interview comes across as the most forensically studied, alluding to J G Ballard, Bertolt Brecht and Arnold Schoenberg, painstakingly dissecting both musicality and meaning, and striving to elucidate the brilliance of both band and debut album.

In the interview, Morley maintains that the band aren't as dour and difficult as the reputation that had started to gain momentum in the press. Instead, Morley encountered an erudite and articulate ensemble, willing to engage on the premise that the tenor of the interview was intelligent and allowed the band to maintain more than a modicum of mystique, especially where questions attempted to both probe and deconstruct aspects of their dark craft: 'From the listener's point of view, you don't want to rob them of using their imagination, and if you're saying, "This song is about a boy next door", then the listener doesn't have to ponder.'[204]

In the interview, the inference is that the band used any negative press to their advantage, almost feeding off pejorative reviews to strengthen their collective resolve. Sioux maintained that 'If someone said something genuinely constructive but heavily critical, and on reasonable grounds, it would sink in a lot more. I wouldn't just think they were being stupid for no reason at all. I'd probably question it with myself. But whether I'd change is a different thing...'[205]

Morley infers that there is no further latitude for poking the band with a stick to dredge up further thoughts about journalistic, bilious miasmic vernacular so the topic is laid to rest.

The band is willing, however, to discuss the debacle leading up to their eventual signing with the Polydor label, at one point more than toying with signing with the BBC so they could legitimately release the February 1978 John Peel Session as an EP.

It was clear that the band were in seemingly interminable limbo because no one with any semblance of clout was going to any of the band's live gigs. The eventual signing to a major label wasn't without its travails, as John McKay suggests: 'At first Polydor thought that we were a bit of a joke, like always asking for things. They didn't really think we were serious, that it was just our "gimmick." But they soon realised that it's something that we're going to carry all the way through. Keep hassling them for little bits and details.'[206]

Contextually, in terms of the usual 'terms and conditions' governing the relationship between band and label, it was rare for any band to have carte blanche with regard to artistic freedom and licence, and certainly not with a major label. Siouxsie and The Banshees put paid to this, although, as Kenny Morris stated, this was not as utopian and plain sailing as it sounded back in 1978: 'As far as control goes, we can ask them to do things and pressurise them to do things, but it's like constantly swimming against the tide. Because they just hold you back all the time. We have to be at Polydor a lot of the time, pushing them and repeatedly telling them to do things.'[207]

In Morley's interview, he also alludes to the impact the single 'Hong Kong Garden' had in the wake of them signing to Polydor, with its 'mystery and enigma... coupled with the similarly seductive reputation of the group itself... its flickering eroticism, its simple beauty pushed it deep into the charts. People really did care! The Banshees really were that subtle! That observant! That good!'[208]

The hiatus of a month between recording the single and its release meant that the band had near enough forgotten about it until the ensuing frenzy on its release on 18 August 1978. The band were ensconced in writing 'The Scream' at the time and were clearly more than a little blindsided by the response to it, although John McKay's insouciance implies that the success of the single, replete with silver disc status, was more of an eye-rolling drag than cause for celebration, stating 'The silver disc was like one of those little gold stars — you get a pat on the head and a little gold star like at primary school. It was a bit ridiculous. They were going to present it, but we refused any presentation.'[209]

Steve Severin's take was that 'It's funny thinking that 250,000 people have got 'Hong Kong Garden' in their homes. It just meant to us that a lot more people were going to buy the album.'[210] Severin and McKay's views on the success of 'Hong

Kong Garden' are perhaps speculative, predictive soundbites; the cumulative effect of which would lead to the band's almost calamitous dissolution in 1979.

Morley's appetite for 'The Scream' is more than apparent, describing the album as 'unlike anything in rock. It is not, as some would say, chaotic; it is controlled.'[211] He also clearly appreciates every band member's contribution to the work, stating 'Each instrument operates within its own space, its own time, as if mocking the lines of the other instruments. Known rock is inverted, leaving just traces of mimicry of rock's cliches; satire that often bursts with glorious justification into shaking celebration (as on 'Helter Skelter').'[212]

Morley praises the album for avoiding the pitfalls of rock cliches, innovating to create its own individual oeuvre born out of The Velvet Underground, David Bowie and Marc Bolan. Morley describes Sioux's voice as 'Staggering... dropped, clipped, snapped prominently above this audacious musical drama, emphasising the dark colours and empty, naked moods.'[213]

Morley's empathy, journalistic skill and clear excitement about the band's modus operandi elicits further candour about their individual and collective ambitions. Severin acknowledges that, within the ensemble, there are 'four very powerful egos... so I'm certainly not going to sit back and just play a rhythm, like Eno's theory of the anchor bass and drums.'[214]

What is clear in the interview, and is writ rather large on 'Overground', is the perpetual wrangling, bordering on existential crises in maintaining the balance between artistic integrity and the inevitable weight of expectation that comes with success, as Kenny Morris so succinctly explained: 'You have to maintain that line between the traditional and the unconventional all the time. But I can't see us slipping and producing something traditional.'[215]

Lyrically, Morley compares Sioux's lyrics to the syntax of the novels of J G Ballard, creating landscapes which 'Are those of the living room and of the mind; the same thing: confinement. The music reflects this private, clinical landscape, the tensions and euphorias of day-to-day living. There is a twisted passion, but no compassion, and that really is unnerving; the record's fragments seem almost a calm before the storm, which can be seen as being the album's final track 'Switch', where even a mental breakdown is dispassionately detailed, Siouxsie's voice grossly, offensively parodying mental collapse.'[216]

Morley is acutely aware that the band understands the emotive power of the nihilistic motif as it appears in most of 'The Scream'; finding the ideal, yet temporary, panacea or anaesthetic for the perversity of the boring, futile and mundane 'that can erupt into violence, aggression, suicide, breakdown, perversion. This is what the Banshees depict, slanted from the way they themselves were brought up, mundanely 'comfortable' and middle class. Their use of 'Helter Skelter' in this is crucial: *"When I get to the bottom I go back to the top of the slide."* Roll the boulder up, roll the boulder down...'[217]

The interview catalyses the Banshees' dichotomy: the limbo of being caught between thought and expression; the endless repetition of journalists' generic questioning and probing in interviews that came with the band's newly acquired fame as pop stars, and the refusal to proselytise, 'not ramming... things down people's throats, because there would be no point in doing that'[218] even though the ensemble's collective antennae was markedly attuned to responding with more candid polemic than alacrity.

John McKay exemplifies both dilemma and collective antithesis to the normative rock cliché: 'A little bit more of the population are willing not to go out and have a good time and hide all the rest of their personalities in the back of their brains, so they don't have to think about anything.'[219] The band pre-empts the inevitable quizzing about 'Hong Kong Garden' and how this has created a division between new converts and established 'purist' Banshees' fans who 'said they don't like the new audience because they've only come for the single, but we love that. And we love playing the single every night. Although I can understand people do get precious.'[220]

Morley's crediting the band with erudition elicits from the band a philosophy that is part manifesto, part forward-thinking game plan, with Sioux and Severin the indubitable, pragmatic authors, standing front of house. Kenny Morris chimes in with his own take on the band's ambitious proclamation, stating that Siouxsie and The Banshees had 'never been dictated to by modes of music or modes of the times or the press, and that's something we strove for from the beginning, and we've got a strong hold on that.[221]

The Morley interview provides insight into how the band want to present themselves, whether on Top of the Pops or the Old Grey Whistle Test. They possessed a meticulous understanding of camera angles and the inherent juxtapositions of miming with performing live. As independent film aficionados, both Sioux and Severin understood and could navigate the complexities of the confines of choreographed camera angles, ensuring memorable performances that were the antithesis of the visceral, unpredictable and untethered nature of performing live.

By the same token, the band had travelled in a short space of time from sweatbox venues like The Nashville to the Hammersmith Odeon, notable not only due to the audience capacity differential but also because the Hammersmith Odeon was a seated venue, not the band's natural habitat by any stretch of imagination. However, the band's increasing popularity ensured that their music would reach a larger audience and would attest to a band that had earned their spurs through playing venues that could be classified as the rougher end of the gigging spectrum; it was also increasingly unlikely that the band, putting as many artistic miles as they could between them and punk, were less likely to be spat on.

Sioux remarked 'We've had some really good reactions at seated gigs. It is very alienating for a group like Siouxsie and The Banshees to play a place like Hammersmith Odeon, and we like that.'[222]

Performing live on the Old Grey Whistle Test came with its own challenges, as Severin comments: 'On the Old Grey Whistle Test we knew we were dealing with 24-inch and we knew what two songs we wanted to do, and we put a lot of thought into it, how we were going to move. It's totally different from a gig, where your eyes can go everywhere.'[223]

In the Mark Paytress biography, Sioux remembers spending a lot of time 'screaming at the cameramen to shoot close-ups of fingers over guitar frets and take away the red and green lights. We had a very precise idea of what we wanted.'[224]

Morley's acute understanding of the machinations of pop music and the ebb and flow of contemporary musical trajectory caused him to remark that Siouxsie and The Banshees were 'another new rock group caught in the distorting and destructive glare of publicity and post-punk hypocrisy, vulnerable to cynicism and disrespect from people who by their own broadcast ideals should be on their side.'[225]

'Aesthetics is to artists as ornithology is to birds' Barnet Newman

Not all articles and reviews when 'The Scream' was released were so thoughtful. Pete Silverton's review of the album in Sounds on 14 October 1978 acknowledges 'Hong Kong Garden's' causation of expectation, citing the single as 'neither predicted nor predictable',[226] although the review of the album itself rarely focuses on the tenor and brevity of the music, preferring to regurgitate more hotchpotch of retrospective and current soundbites and titbits, dating back to the band's early live forays in 1976, commenting 'While Siouxsie has grabbed the front pages with her often just this side of tacky Bromley chic and the occasional flash of tit (no, that's not sexism, far from it, she knew just what she was doing when she strutted her stuff back in 76 — first create the frame and only then follow it with substance).'[227]

There is almost a sense of the begrudging; the band had chanced their way into the Polydor portals, although 'well aware that they were working on an important album — even if it was only the magnitude of their own fractious egos which convinced them.'[228]

This is an article that pays little attention to the multi-layered nuances of the album, its filmic narrative influences and the certitude that one of the roles of art is to take the temperature of the time in which it is being made, whether socially, economically, politically or, especially for the Banshees, musically.

Guitarist John McKay is singled out for his contribution to the album, working 'his way round the frets like a master who's just discovered the reaches of his own talent and is stretching himself to the very limits of his technique and abilities — he even makes fairly standard chordal thrashes and lurches sound fresh, probably because they sound that way to him.'[229]

Steve Morris's playing is described as a 'hump beat laced with suburban artiness,'[230] a hybrid of the Glitterband stomp and Mo Tucker, while Silverton describes Severin's bass playing as 'barely discernible'[231] and buried in the mix.

The review does mention several of the album's songs,

where Silverton writes 'there is a definite width of material (from the languorous obliqueness of the seven minute 'Switch' through the maybe tongue in cheek black humour of 'Helter Skelter' and 'Carcass' to the simplicity of 'Nicotine Stain')'[232] although Silverton is keen to labour his point that none of the songs on the album are as good as 'Hong Kong Garden'.

Silverton's lukewarm review, rather than being any form of cultivated critique, volunteers the album as a 'set of demo tapes'[233] and 'the Banshees' stage show with a couple of new songs, which far from being the clearing out of dead wood it could have been, is a fascinating documentary of a band at an early stage of development, when they're still learning about each other, when their drive to leave a testament for posterity overwhelms their desire to come up with the perfect record.'[234]

Diametrically and refreshingly in opposition to Pete Silverton's review, Kris Needs' article in ZigZag magazine, a publication better attuned to the sensibilities of more esoteric and underground musical genres, started in April 1969 by English music journalist and rock music historian Pete Frame, provides a much more contextualised and insightful narrative in which he frames the album, beginning his appraisal of 'The Scream' akin to the William Blake aphorism that, 'Without unceasing Practice nothing can be done: Practice is Art. If you leave off you are lost,'[235] citing 'Countless gigs and the John Peel sessions'[236] as indicators that the album was well worth the wait.

Needs both acknowledges and praises the cerebral attributes of the band, noting that 'the Banshees... already succeeded on a couple of counts because they want people to think and question.'[237] Needs recognises the tenacity of a band 'Unbothered by their relatively little studio experience'[238] in making a record 'so uncompromising, powerful and disturbing, yet so captivating and ENJOYABLE.'[239]

Needs recognises the dramatic timbre of the music, observing that 'The Scream' is 'like a film that does you in (The Devils, Performance, The Exorcist — my examples).'[240] Needs' pinnacle of praise is the list of albums he puts it on a 'classic album' par with, including 'Diamond Dogs, Roxy's first, Berlin, and Nico's last three.'[241]

Describing the album as an 'aural monster'[242] aided and abetted by producer Steve Lillywhite, Needs provides an insightful track listing narrative, as well as acknowledging the significant contribution of every band member. 'When the needle first hits vinyl it's the primeval swamp wailings of 'Pure', an eerie fanfare, which seep out before the dam breaks and out bursts the unstoppable grand power of 'Jigsaw Feeling', a song of disorientation and bewilderment. The sound is huge, sometimes awe-inspiring. John McKay's guitar is a one-man maelstrom of nightmare riffs and counter-melodies sparking from a sheet of jagged repetition. Steven Severin pumps in the full-stops and commas with heart-beat bass punctuation.'[243]

Needs, as with Silverton's Sounds review, acknowledges Kenny Morris's 'Glitter Band stomp'[244] and within the band's 'bed of deep sound Siouxsie intones, soars and becomes another instrument.'[245]

The themes of suburban drudgery are also realised, especially in the dysfunctional, barbed 'Suburban Relapse'. Needs describes the lyric as 'the central heating advert housewife succumbs and breaks under the pressures of monotony — "I'm sorry that I hit you but my string snapped." The track is a nerve-shattering rampage of thunderous frenzy, careering to the breakdown and the end, when the doorbell rings. (What grisly sight greeted the eyes of the Avon lady?)'[246]

Rather than eschewing relatively older and more established Banshees' staples 'Carcass' and 'Helter Skelter',

Needs embraces the songs, describing them as 'meaty (sorry), beaty and witty, being the already-much-written-about tale for a love-struck butcher, while the Fab Four ditty rises from it's clashing, jarring birth into a frenetic mutilation.'[247]

'Switch' is characterised by Needs as the 'most adventurous thing the Banshees have done'[248] and 'Sioux's best vocal performance.'[249] Acknowledging the complexity of the song, Needs extolls Sioux's unique approach to singing such 'complicated lyrics and sections with mournful, moving control and shades of Nico in the chilling long notes. Panic and passion creep in as the band rise and fall, and you realise that Siouxsie has become one of our most mesmerising and individual singers, if you hadn't already.'[250]

Describing 'The Scream' 'as one of the most remarkable debuts ever,'[251] Needs also acknowledges the uncompromising nature of the band: 'Siouxsie and The Banshees have stuck to their pure route. Without fuss they've emerged the other side with a scream of triumph.'[252]

And the band played on...

> 'Fame is a fickle food
> Upon a shifting plate
> Whose table once a
> Guest but not
> The second time is set
> Whose crumbs the crows inspect
> And with ironic caw
> Flap past it to the
> Farmer's corn
> Men eat of it and die'[253]

> Emily Dickinson

Dovetailing with the release of 'The Scream', Siouxsie and The Banshees continued their 58-date tour with a gig at the Hemel Hempstead Pavilion on 11 October 1978. Things are beginning to change for the band. Their punk following, post-Polydor signing, has diminished, with early fans discerning something of the Judas about the band. How could they forsake their punk principles by signing to a major label?

A notion Steve Severin found utterly risible, recollecting that 'Shortly into the (1978) tour, we turned up at Glasgow Apollo in a stretched black Mercedes. This obviously incensed the "real" punks because, when we came out after sound-checking, they'd dumped a rubbish bin on the hood of the car and scratched "Capitalist…" down the side. We found it hilarious, and it became a catchphrase for years to come. Our security men weren't taking any chances, though, so when we finished the gig we ran straight out through the back door in to an inconspicuous van with towels over our heads. I remember saying, "We've arrived. I feel like David Cassidy."

This was an important tour for the band that saw them playing larger-capacity venues replete with support acts including Nico, whose stint with the band was to prove short-lived due to the pop sensibilities of the audience and also because the performance comprised solely of Nico playing harmonium. Severin remembers Nico being present for 'about half a dozen dates before she got sick of being booed offstage and quit.'[254]

The audience's antipathy towards Nico was a bit of a body blow to a band that cited The Velvet Underground as a major influence, although there were other contributing factors that meant that Nico might have been slightly musically compromised, including the fact she was in the throes of heroin addiction, about which Severin remarked 'She was pretty out of it on smack at the time and, I have to admit, a rather sad, shuffling figure.'

The 1978 tour proved more fruitful for other support acts The Human League, Spizz Oil and Cabaret Voltaire. Phil Oakey (Human League lead singer) had a Siouxsie and The Banshees' epiphany three or four dates into the tour when he realised what set The Banshees' apart from other bands around at the time, recounting 'standing at the side of the stage, I suddenly got it. To me, punk sounded like skiffle or protest music. The Clash and The Damned played really simple rock 'n' roll, Buddy Holly-era stuff with tougher lyrical themes. The Banshees were different, unique. The four of them made something that's not been before or since. They were all born to be in that band.'[255]

Behind the scenes, the personal relationship between Sioux and Severin had come to an end halfway through the 1978 tour. Nils Stevenson, The Banshees' manager, who by all accounts had something of a crush on Sioux, encouraged Severin to end the relationship in order to 'maintain the balance'[256] within the band. Severin felt that his relationship with Sioux had no bearing on the band's functionality and internal dynamic, proposing that it was 'Quite the reverse. In terms of coming up with the concepts and bringing them to fruition, it was absolutely vital to the identity of the band.'[257]

'John eats flowers and talks to dogs when he's drunk.'[258] Kris Needs.

ZigZag journalist Kris Needs followed the band on tour for two days in late November when the band were bookending their 1978 tour. Needs writes of the unadulterated fun that he and the band had offstage, in contrast to the way the ensemble were painted as po-faced harbingers of doom by much of the music press, witnessing the band 'get pissed, mess about... but always remain true to that hour on stage.'[259]

It is during the tour that the band aired two new songs

'Premature Burial' and 'Playground Twist', the latter of which was initially recorded as a demo at Pathway Studios in North London in June 1978, before recording 'Hong Kong Garden', and subsequently at Air Studios on 24 November 1978 between the penultimate and final gigs of the 1978 tour.

The two gigs that Needs attended are the Winter Gardens in Malvern on 15 November and the Locarno Club in Portsmouth. Needs describes the calm before the blizzard-like storm during the period after The Human League and Spizz Oil have finished their sets, when Siouxsie and The Banshees take to the Winter Gardens' stage in front of a 1200-strong crowd, writing that 'the echoey hall adds to the weight and density of the churning Banshees sound... Like as a rhythm machine for feet and guts Kenny Morris' drumming is unorthodox, primitive (in a tribal sense) and far removed from the clicking hi-hats of the fly-strength paradiddle merchants. Steve's bass aims likewise, being again individual, vital to the surge and without homage to any of the instrument's conventions.

John McKay slashes riffs, but steeped in a piranhic panorama of flurries and counterattack strange chords.'[260] Needs characterises 'Sioux's voice as a vital part of the sound... It often carries the melody and the mood. Just listen to the devastating 'Switch', the way she veers from almost wistful observation to chilling warning. It's just a great voice, handled with ever-increasing control for effect... what she's singing, which are lyrics of dramatic, incisive insight and... emotion. I mean, you can't get much more emotionally affected than through the nightmare un-coordination of 'Jigsaw Feeling' or the turbulence of the housewife's snapping mind on 'Suburban Relapse'.[261]

Needs comments that the setlist comprises 'all the (Scream) album, minus 'Carcass' but plus the 'Prayer' (my ultimate favourite) and 'Staircase'. The latter will be the next single. Don't hold it next to 'Hong Kong', it's just another facet, a metallic waltz. More disorientation and confusion. I can't wait to hear how it's gonna sprout in the studio.'[262]

The band signed post-gig autographs and Needs joined them for some refreshment at the hotel bar where John McKay made considerable inroads into a bottle of gin, ate a yellow flower bloom and attempted to strike up a conversation with an elderly golden retriever. Sioux, aware the effect a night on the tiles will have on her vocal cords, decides to have an early night.

Needs was again impressed by the band's live performance, with a set 'swamped in the magnificent power roaring from the stage. 'Helter Skelter', 'Staircase', 'Mirage', 'Metal Postcard', 'Jigsaw Feeling', 'Switch', 'Hong Kong Garden', 'Nicotine Stain', 'Suburban Relapse', 'Overground', 'Pure', 'Lord's Prayer' are the songs played. Siouxsie is on top form which means blitzing through numbers with a simmering passion which spikes her usual menace and grace. Her eyes blaze as she motivates round the stage, arms swinging, legs kicking like a deranged Bluebell girl. She stalks the group, who don't move much as they concentrate wholly on venting that sound.'[263]

Needs' 'favourite moment of '78 came when the group segued from the tortured soul of 'Pure' into the all-out cleansing ferocity of 'Prayer'. Rapid bass, pummelling drums and terrifying fractured guitar take the course the gig dictates and tonight it's mesmerising as Sioux whoops, sings and intones her gamut of rages.'

Needs teases a plethora of responses from the band about where they were, where they are currently and where they want to be regarding touring, making records and band dynamic. Sioux describes the strains of hotel hopping and of one audience melding into another, commenting 'It's like we've been staying in hotels day in day out and you can't remember what the last hotel was like or where you were or what the town was and sometimes that was the same with the audience. They were reacting the same, and it was so that we were doing bigger places or something like that, probably the fact of us attracting people because of the single, and they were becoming quite samey.'[264]

The band was acutely aware that many of the audience have come along simply to get near to a band that is successful; the phenomenon of fame, 'to be near somebody who's had a hit single, to get to the front, and the other people, the hard core following, aren't that bothered about that sort of thing so they're probably on the edge and watching. That's disturbing in a way, but it's inevitable.'[265]

The band was excited about the soon-to-be-released single, although Needs points out that it doesn't have the ear-worm pop-like catchiness of 'Hong Kong Garden'. However, Sioux 'never banked a lot on 'Hong Kong' being successful. We knew it would have an element of success, but whether it got in the charts as high as it did or not... to us and the way we work, it would not determine what the next single would be or anything.'[266]

In Need's interview, the band alludes to the push and pull between artistic integrity and Polydor's predilection for packaging, with Sioux stating, 'They can influence what we put out. They can try — they can't in the contract. They can try and put us on a compilation album...'[267] which is what Polydor tried to do, when they announced their New Wave Sampler, with opening track 'Hong Kong Garden'. The band were quick to kibosh this, telling the record label that it was for the good of their relationship with the label to do this.

Needs provides a timely snapshot of a band incontrovertibly serious about their craft. Siouxsie and The Banshees appeared to have the world at their feet: hit first single; hit first album; sold out tour; momentum and column inches aplenty.

That difficult second album and other travails

There is an inevitability, bordering on the cliche, about the outcome when four headstrong band members have individual visions for a band's direction. In the instance of Siouxsie and The Banshees, it was perhaps more a case of the increasing marginalisation of Kenny Morris and John McKay, both of whom saw the band as more of an experimental aural art form, with a 'visual' stage performance, including a slide show of the kind that support band The Human League had used on the 1978 tour, using powerful, evocative imagery in tandem with the emotive, swirling Banshees' dark soundscapes. Kenny Morris was becoming particularly impassioned about the direction of the band, commenting 'The Banshees were so important to me. I could play the fucking drums the way I wanted to and all that, but I wanted much more.'[268]

'The Staircase (Mystery)'

'The first cracks began to appear around the time of 'The Staircase (Mystery)'. Everything was hunky-dory until then. We were on a mission. Yes, Siouxsie and I had started the band, so it was our band, but we tried to make sure that everyone's opinion was listened to. But Kenny tended to run around in circles, never saying very much. He'd say, "We need visuals." Siouxsie and I and Nils would say "We've got no money, so let's concentrate on the next gig. All that can happen in time".'[269]

Recorded at Air Studios on 24 November 1978 and released on 23 March 1979, 'The Staircase (Mystery)' was the band's second top 40 chart single, peaking at number 24 in the UK singles chart. In essence, 'The Staircase (Mystery)' exemplifies Siouxsie and The Banshees' modus operandi, their way of taking control and endeavouring to have complete artistic autonomy. 'The Staircase (Mystery)' is their 'Kid A': the wish to confound expectation and not follow formula.

If there is any obvious DNA strand beginning to appear then it is the band's love of creating a dramatic narrative, reflecting Siouxsie's admiration for the work of Alfred Hitchcock. The video for the single was in part inspired by the staircase murder of private detective Milton Arbogast in the film 'Psycho'. No sooner has Arbogast stealthily climbed the staircase in the Bates Motel when he is ambushed, driven through with a kitchen knife and falls down the stairs where he is stabbed multiple times. Siouxsie commented 'There's something about a staircase. It's so unpredictable and exciting at the same time. That feeling of displacement, vertigo when you're at the top looking down or at the bottom looking up.' Siouxsie Sioux.[270]

If 'Hong Kong Garden' is light and poppy, despite its lyrical narrative based on the racial discrimination Sioux witnessed at a local Chinese takeaway, 'The Staircase (Mystery)' takes the listener into a place of gloaming, descending into a dark spiral. Sioux maintained that the lyrics of the song possess an observational granularity, an entity one might observe and use every day without giving it much thought.

Sioux mused 'The words are getting more complicated… It's a waltz and is about an unsolved mystery,'[271] reflecting her increasing depth and maturity as a songwriter and lyricist. There is also a deepening and perhaps darkening of Sioux's gallows humour, as she reflected 'it's very much a memory of them (staircases). Especially in my house, people were always falling down the stairs in it.'[272]

Produced by manager Nils Stevenson, the song begins with guitar and bass working in parallel, creating the dramatic tension associated with the work of Bernard Hermann or 1960s Hammer Horror soundtracks. Again, John McKay's guitar howls and the minor chord refrain can be heard in stereo, like a melancholic conversational exchange once Kenny Morris's drums join, following the pulsating bass line, and when Sioux's vocal comes into play, the evocatively filmic song is in full flow; everything working in perfect gothic harmony.

This is clearly not standard chart fodder or music that can be readily commodified. However, it is worth noting that a glance at the UK charts reveals an eclectic list of songs including Art Garfunkel's 'Bright Eyes', 'Wow' by Kate Bush, 'Tragedy' by the Bee Gees, 'Everybody's Happy Nowadays' by Buzzcocks and Blondie's 'Heart of Glass'. 'The Staircase (Mystery)' is a rollercoaster of an emotive song packed into three minutes and 15 seconds, with a dreamlike, quiet and understated bridge segueing into perfectly choreographed handclaps as the song reaches its climax, culminating in Sioux's Siren-like vocal and the clankingly discordant piano that ends with a single-note homage to The Beatles' 'A Day In The Life'.[273] The band sound more locked in than ever and Siouxsie and The Banshees are becoming fully conversant, grabbing the attention of the listener to generate thrills and spills and, most of all, to entertain.

The video for the song aired on Top of the Pops 24 April 1979. Directed again by Clive Richardson, the video starts with a shot of a music box cloche with a ballroom-dancing couple atop a white grand piano, and melds into Siouxsie and The Banshees performing the song, with Sioux dancing with abandon, dressed impeccably in Nehru-type shirt and white trousers, Severin and Morris in black, and John McKay ever so slightly incongruous in what could be described as a lumberjack shirt.

The band looks stylish and moody, and even though

complicit in the cosmetically superficial act of miming, Richardson's direction creates a mesmerising performance, including a cutaway to a slow-motion black and white film of a middle-aged man with raincoat and briefcase climbing a metal staircase against backdrop of what looks like an urban or industrial hinterland, until he suddenly falls backwards, tumbling down the stairs; a nod to the fate of 'Psycho's detective Aborgast. The video is compositionally perfect and both attuned and empathetic to the tenor of the song, which concludes with Sioux at the grand piano, mimicking the automaton movements of the dancers trapped in the cloche as her hand crashes down on the keys.

The B-side of the single, a cover of T. Rex's '20th Century Boy', originally released on 2 March 1973 and a staple of Siouxsie and The Banshees' live performances, is an antidote to the enigma of 'Staircase'. Coming in at two minutes exactly, it is a riotous, fast-paced, joyous stomp, with no little semblance of Rockabilly[274] or Psychobilly[275] such is its velocity. Beginning with guitar feedback and a Sioux yelp, the song keeps up a magnificent pace with Morris and Severin providing the pulsating, stomping rhythm which is the glue that holds the song together.

Chapter 5

'Join Hands' (or not) 1979

'When we were making the 'Join Hands' album, it was outrageous — we weren't even speaking to each other in the band. It was really, really fucking hard; it was ridiculous. But we couldn't understand — you don't go and lose the likes of Steve Lillywhite, you don't do that. Like I said, there was no democracy at that time. We were barely speaking to each other, it was a joke.'[276] Kenny Morris.

'Join Hands' was such a shock to the system,' admits Steven Severin, the band's bassist and, with Sioux, a Banshee from the beginning. 'We'd been working to our own pace right up until June 1978 when we got signed. Now, just after Christmas 1978, we were asked to write a second album while at the same time having to fit in promotional visits to the continent. We were all having to work twice as hard as before.'[277]

The Banshees were going through the process of recording an album of intense breadth and depth yet, behind the scenes, creative tensions were beginning to simmer and eventually boil over. Recorded at AIR Studios between May and June 1979, Join Hands was released on 7 September of the same

'The Bromley Contingent', Linda's Place, October 1976.

100 Club Festival, 20 September 1976.

Steve, Kenny, Siouxsie and PT Fenton.

1976 rehearsal.

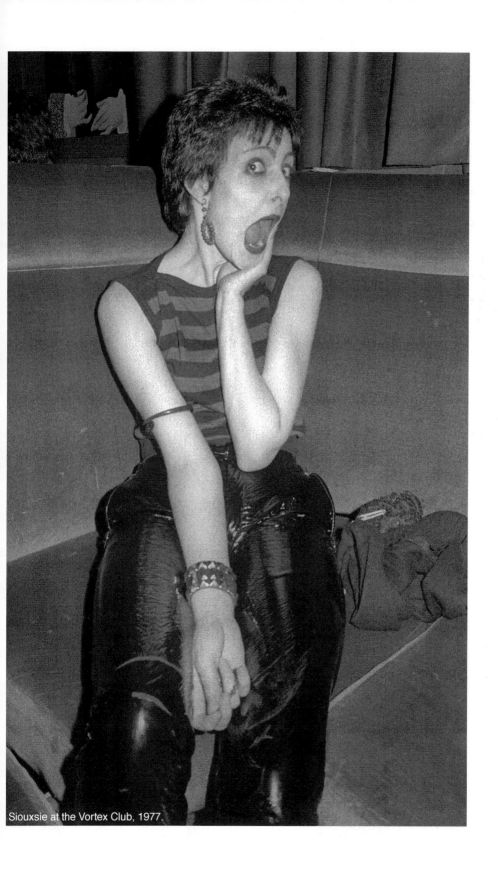

Siouxsie at the Vortex Club, 1977.

Vortex Club, 1977.

1977.

Vortex Club 1977.

1978.

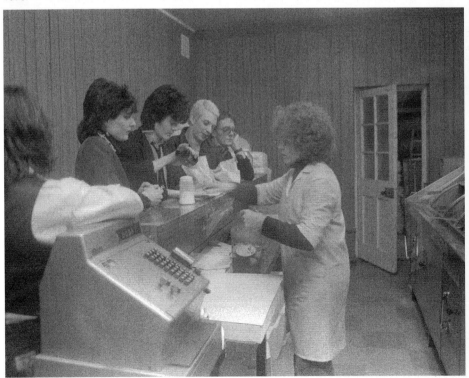

At the chippie, 1978.

Nashville Rooms, 7 January 1978.

Siouxsie, Kenny, John and Steve 1978.

Siouxsie and Steve Severin.

Siouxsie and Steve Severin, 1978.

Kenny Morris, Notre Dame Hall, London, 1979.

Rebecca's, Birmingham.

Rainbow Theatre, London, 1979.

Madrid, 1979.

With Robert Smith, October 1979.

Recording Kaleidoscope, 1980.
Inset opposite page: Budgie during the video shoot for Happy House, 1980.

Video shoot for Happy House, 1980.

John McGeoch.

year. The band were on a mission to write and release original music that set out to be consciously diametrically opposed to every rock 'n' roll cliche. Siouxsie and The Banshees were fully, and conceivably painfully, aware that they had set a bar for themselves that, if not beyond reach, could barely be touched.

For context, the maelstrom and revolution of punk was ostensibly over, and the band found themselves part of a new era of breakthrough bands such as The Cure and Joy Division, both of whom would plough their own important furrows.

What price success? The band may well have had been able to rule with regard to artistic output, but no sooner had 'The Scream' been released that the call came through from Polydor requesting the second album. If 'The Scream' was an album reflecting Steve Lillywhite's abilities to ensure cohesion and work with the band both as an ensemble and as individual members to ensure the best possible unified and successful outcome, the doubling up of production duties, with both manager Nils Stevenson and Mike Stavrou at the helm for 'Join Hands', proved slightly trickier.

Nils Stevenson was certainly 'tight' with the band, especially Sioux and Severin, whom he had known from the outset. Vocally effusive about the band's 100 Club debut in 1976, he had offered his services as their manager, having previously been the Sex Pistols' road manager and an instrumental part of the Johnny Thunders and The Heartbreakers story, especially in assisting the relocation of guitarist Thunders and drummer Jerry Nolan to the UK after leaving US band The New York Dolls.

Scrutinise Stevenson's 1979 CV and there is no mention of his credentials as a producer. American producer Mike Stavrou had come from a high school and college radio background, with duties including production engineer, DJ and director of programmes, production and promotion.

He worked as both in-house producer and chief engineer at Eastern Recording Studios in Virginia from 1972-1974 before joining AIR Studios in London as a sound balance engineer.

Part of Stavrou's attraction for the band was his work with Marc Bolan on his final album 'Dandy In The Underworld':[278] Bolan was idolised by Sioux. Stavrou proved a divisive presence for Kenny Morris and John McKay, who called him 'A little shit'[279] and 'a joker.'[280] There was talk initially of employing either John Cale or Tony Visconti as producer, but both were tied up with other projects so couldn't commit.

Stevenson felt that Stavrou, a fledgling producer, would listen to the band's ideas. This is where the dynamic of the band became particularly askew, with Sioux and Severin in favour of Stavrou's way of working; exacerbated by 'making decisions without consulting John and Kenny in anything like the depth... done before.'[281]

However, drafting in Mike Stavrou was presented by Stevenson as a fait accompli to all band members. Things were moving apace for the band; decisions needed to be made quickly and this included the artwork for the album, which was put together by the triumvirate of Polydor in-house designer Rob O'Connor, filmmaker John Maybury and Nils Stevenson. Maybury had initially been drafted in as the album's art director.

The artwork for the font cover was a black and white image from a Holy Communion card, showing children joining hands. The image had been photocopied several times, so it had become grainy, pixilated and distorted, and a little like a still from the 1960 British horror film 'The Village Of The Damned'.[282] However, this was to prove problematic because Polydor, when presented with the image by Nils Stevenson, gave a flat 'no', citing copyright reasons and the religious nature of the content.

Rob O'Connor, in-house Polydor designer, was asked
to draft an alternative cover and recalls the design process:
'The 'Join Hands' sleeve that eventually made it to the shops
featured four of the soldier statues cut-out from a press shot
of the band, I believe taken by Adrian Boot for the NME or
some other paper. The real battle for us was to convince the
company to use textured board and make it a gatefold. The
lack of colour helped to win the day. The wreath of poppies
was devised to help add colour and create a graphic device
for use on merchandising. I've seen the odd T-shirt with the
soldiers on even recently. I've always liked the illustration of
the band on the inner spread — it was the only part of the
original design that survived.'[283]

The result was a last-minute, rushed compromise of sorts:
a gatefold sleeve with the effective but austere front cover of
four soldiers, originally designed as an embossed image but
judged to be non-cost effective and time consuming, set against
a sea of white; John Maybury's inner-sleeve charcoal drawing
of all four band members with the track listing underneath
in capitalised Times New Roman font; and plain black back
cover. As Rob O'Connor explains, the only colour to break
up the otherwise monochromatic front cover is the red of the
poppy wreath, between band name and album title, echoed as
an image on the record label B-side.

Sioux recalls that 'John and Kenny hated the artwork.
As far as Severin and I were concerned, the image we used
of soldiers on the sleeve was perfect as an alternative to the
original idea, which we all liked. There was conflict in Iran and
bombings in London and it all seemed to fit. It wasn't any pro-
miliary message; we just wanted to capture the spirit of what
things were like at the time. Severin had written 'Regal Zone',
which summed all that up and, along with 'Poppy Day', made
the cover much more relevant. John (Maybury) did some nice

line drawings of the band which we used inside the album.'[284]

The 2006 digital remaster includes the original track listing of 'Poppy Day', 'Regal Zone', 'Placebo Effect', 'Icon', 'Premature Burial', 'Playground Twist', 'Mother/Oh Mein Papa' and 'The Lord's Prayer', plus bonus tracks 'Love In A Void' (7" AA Side) and 'Icons'. The remaster also has extensive liner notes by Siouxsie and The Banshees' official biographer Mark Paytress. To coincide with Record Store Day 2015, the band released the album on vinyl with the original artwork as they had intended in 1979. The Maybury front cover had been fully reinstated, with charcoal drawings adorning the inner gatefold and lyrics printed on the sleeve containing the vinyl. The track listing was also as originally conceived with 'Infantry 'ending side two, rather than 'The Lord's Prayer'.

Sioux was effusive about the 2015 release, commenting: 'I've always loved the artwork John Maybury presented for 'Join Hands' and it's wonderful to see it again after all this time... Along with the inclusion of 'Infantry', here it is finally to have and behold in all its full glory.'[285]

Severin was similarly delighted, commenting 'Not only does the album now look how it was intended but now boasts the original track listing. I can't really remember why 'Infantry' was left off originally. Maybe we felt we hadn't the time to develop it a bit further, maybe because it wouldn't have fitted into the live set. Either way, it's here now for posterity.'[286]

The band had been touring since 5 January 1979, the first eight gigs of which included the Empire Theatre in Paris, the Markthalle in Hamburg, the Kantino Club in Berlin, the Teatro Barcelo in Madrid and the Paradiso in Amsterdam; returning to the UK for a series of dates on 29 August, just over a week before the release of 'Join Hands', recorded during the interim gigging hiatus of May and June 1979.

The band aired new songs 'Premature Burial', 'Playground

Twist' and 'Placebo Effect', as well as 'Icons', all of which seemed to fit in well alongside material from 'The Scream'. However, the band realised that they had a distinct deficit of material when they halted their gigging schedule to begin work on 'Join Hands' and it was clear that, unlike their debut, the range of songs and ideas just wasn't there. This wasn't helped by the increasing tensions in the band; conflicts exacerbated by expectations, exemplified by Severin commenting that (John) 'McKay couldn't churn out the riffs like he'd been doing before. He was probably working at the same pace, but it just wasn't quick enough.'[287]

Set against a backdrop of increasing in-fighting and differences of opinion, the quartet entered Air Studios in early May 1979, finishing 'Join Hands' around four weeks later. The actual duration of the album including ideas for songs and writing had taken nearer to six months. Steve Lillywhite had lifted a curtain on the band's distinctive sound for 'The Scream', 'Join Hands' saw The Banshees opting for a far denser, almost overpowering and oppressive production. Mike Stavrou was simply enabling this aural compactness, which itself mirrored the tenor and subject matter of the album.

'Poppy Day'

The album opens to the chiming reverberation of church bells; not celebratory but ominous, it is here that the austerity of the 'Join Hands' album cover starts to mirror the content of the music and vice versa. Enter the searing guitar of John McKay, the harmonious pulse of Severin's bass and Kenny Morris's austere snare drum, accompanied by a disembodied handclap, all paving the way for Sioux's haunting vocal refrain, sounding like it has been recorded backwards through a phaser. The lyrics owe more than a little debt to 'In Flanders fields' by the Canadian poet, physician and Lieutenant-Colonel John

117

McCrae, having been selectively lifted verbatim from the original poem.

'In Flanders fields the poppies blow
Between the crosses, row on row,
 That mark our place; and in the sky
 The larks, still bravely singing, fly
Scarce heard amid the guns below.

We are the Dead. Short days ago
We lived, felt dawn, saw sunset glow,
 Loved and were loved, and now we lie
  In Flanders fields.

Take up our quarrel with the foe:
To you from failing hands we throw
 The torch; be yours to hold it high.
 If ye break faith with us who die
We shall not sleep, though poppies grow
  In Flanders fields'[288]

In Flanders Fields by John McCrae

Probably the most quoted and recited poem from World War One, McCrae was moved to write the work on 3 May 1915, after the funeral of fellow soldier Lieutenant Alexis Helmer, who died in the Second Battle of Ypres. The poem almost didn't see the light of day due to McCrae's dissatisfaction with it. It was first published on 8 December 1915 in Punch magazine.

'Poppy Day' was initially recorded as part of a John Peel session at the BBC's Maida Vale Studios on 9 April 1979 and aired on 16 April 1979. The session also included 'Placebo

Effect', 'Playground Twist' and 'Regal Zone'. It is easy to discern the influence of McKay's playing on Killing Joke's Geordie Walker, who, on being asked about his influences, cited 'The guy in the original Banshees on 'The Scream'. Apparently, that guy had just learnt to play, and he came out with these chord structures that I found very refreshing. The guy's been ripped off so much, he started that flanged chord thing.'[289]

It is worth noting that Severin's bass-guitar playing is becoming much more sophisticated and more discernible in the mix, taking more of a lead role. Of 'Poppy Day', Severin commented that "'Last November 11, I was watching the TV when they had the two minutes' silence in memory of the war dead and I thought, wouldn't it be nice if there were music for it." A leaping notion... silence set to music.'[290]

After the introspection of 'Poppy Day', 'Regal Zone' starts like an aural battering ram, with the triple assault of guitar, bass and drums. McKay's saxophone lends a louche, sleazy and unexpectedly discordant layer to the song, a sort of inverse Roxy Music, which melds into the realms of a heralding march; a proclamation of sorts, which is entirely in keeping with the tenor of the song's title.

Morris's drumming creates the menacing tension in the song, with the metronomic use of crash cymbal, like a cat 'o' nine tails whip, as the song alternates between the tension and release of verse and chorus. Its sensibilities lie in the realms of the spectacle of theatre and Victorian freakshow, and one can readily envisage Sioux as a sort of demented ringmaster: "Roll up, roll up." This is no longer the intimate, domestic melodrama of the suburbs. The chintz curtains are not twitching anymore. Instead, they have been wrenched down to reveal the spectacle within. Sioux's lyrics more than hint at the futility of war and its hierarchy, For king/queen and country, Sioux equivocates with 'For the good of the land, / For the love of the man',[291] akin to Isaiah 1:19, 'If ye be willing and obedient, ye shall eat the good of the land.'[292]

'Regal Zone'

The song is, according to both Sioux and Severin, an observation on the unfolding political situation in Iran, culminating in uprising and revolution. On 16 January 1979, Shah Mohammad Reza Pahlavi fled Iran and went into exile. Pahlavi was the last Persian monarch and he assigned all his duties to a regency council and Shapour Bakhtiar, who was an opposition-based prime minister.

Ayatollah Khomeini, who had spent the previous 15 years in exile due to his opposition to the previous Shah, was invited back to Iran by the government, returning to Tehran to be greeted by several thousand Iranians. The Shah's royal reign collapsed shortly after Khomeini's return, on 11 February, when both guerrilla fighters and rebel forces overpowered troops loyal to the Shah in armed street fighting, bringing Khomeini formally to power.

Subsequently, Iranian people voted in a national referendum to become an Islamic republic on 1 April 1979, orchestrating and approving an established theocratic-republican constitution whereby Khomeini became supreme leader of the country in December 1979. It is estimated that between 1980 and 1985, following the revolution, between 15,000 and 40,000 Iranians in opposition to the Ayatollah's regime were executed.

Remarking on the events of 1979 and how these had a direct impact on his lyrics for 'Regal Zone', Severin commented: 'It is absurd to say that your emotions when watching, say, a TV news item on Iran (the starting point of 'Regal Zone') are unreal just because you aren't out on the streets of Teheran yourself.'[293]

'Placebo Effect'

'It was all very well to say, "Drink me," but the wise little Alice was not going to do that in a hurry. "No, I'll look first," she said, "and see whether it's marked 'poison' or not.'[294]

Like an inverted pop song, 'Placebo Effect' is imbued with menace and gloriously industrial-sounding guitar, redolent of World War One mechanisation — the first war in which modern weaponry, including quick-firing artillery, was used — accompanied by Severin's bass. Cymbal and bass drum, courtesy of Kenny Morris, whose snare drum has a weighty echo, add to the effectiveness of the rhythmic reliance of the song.

Sioux's spoken vocal, melding into transcendent expression, sees her savouring every single intoned word. The song moves, ponderous and snake-like; every bilious, lyrical utterance followed assiduously by guitar, bass and drums. All four members of the ensemble are locked in and work synergistically in tandem to create a mesmerising song that is rich with imagery, seemingly decrying the faith put in faux science, amulets, totems and faith healing, looking for a panacea or cure all for every conceivable ill in mind or body. Believing. Superstition. Looking for answers and meaning.

Apparently, the impetus for the song 'came from hearing a programme on Capital Radio, when one of the station's resident Kildares was discussing the kind and colour of medicaments that different nations most favour. Apparently, the UK goes for pills while the French like suppositories and the Italians injections.'[295] The sentiment of the song corresponds entirely with Sioux's vehement opposition to any form of organised fanaticism.

'Icon'

'Icon' begins with the ponderous riffing of John McKay's guitar and what sounds like flanged, muffled explosions in the background, joined tentatively by Kenny Morris's bass drum. After the opening introspective lyrical refrain 'My eyes went up to heaven',[296] the song suddenly leaps into a cornucopia of galloping and embellished optimism after the third verse: an extraordinary volte face after the sobriety of 'Poppy Day', 'Regal Zone' and 'Placebo Effect'. Lyrically, it is no less visceral than the previous three songs, yet it is musically more upbeat, almost as though the band is in perverse mode — think you know who we are? Think again.

What is certain is that Sioux is stretching her vocal range to the limit and there is no shortage of fireworks or gymnastics. According to Severin, the idea for the song was 'inspired by Dervishes getting themselves into such a state that they could put needles through their heads. Our interest in that state is a theme that runs through our work.'[297]

The state that Severin alludes to could also be reflective of the 'ramping up' in intensity that the band were experiencing; the non-stop 'Dervish-like' treadmill of album–tour–album that is not unfamiliar for bands in the throes of both increasing popularity and success.

Sioux echoed the sentiment when, interviewed in 1986, she remarked, 'There's amazing religions in the East where they go into states of… Dervishes and they put skewers through their skin, I don't know what that's called, they go into mad Dervishes, chanting and mantras and that. I'm just fascinated in the power of the mind over the body I suppose, and what's outside, not just the mind, what other elements are involved in it; you can endure an incredible amount of pain without faltering, again, when the adrenalin and drive is pushed.'[298]

It might also have been the case that the song was in part a paean to simpler, more optimistic and less fraught times for the band, a touch of wallowing in nostalgia. Sioux often sought refuge in the escapism of film and television as a child, and would have no doubt been no stranger to the solace provided by children's programme 'The Flashing Blade',[299] the theme tune of which canters at the same rate, although it doesn't share the same biting lyrical content: 'Those words hang like vicious spittle / Dribbling from that tongue / Close your eyes to your lies / Force feed more pious meat.'[300]

However, 'The Flashing Blade' was a programme made about war and was based on historical events during the War of the Mantuan Succession (1628–31) between France and Spain and its allies. Sioux commented that 'Musically, 'Join Hands' was an uncompromising album and it still sounds modern today. We were lonely and isolated and that comes across in the music. It's an extreme record but a very brave one and that's why I still have a soft spot for it.'[301]

Contextually, 'Icon' can be placed in the same canon of 1981's 'Juju', especially songs such as 'Spellbound' and 'Voodoo Dolly', both of which have the same rush-of-adrenaline timbre. 'Icon' is a song that is new and unchartered musical territory for the band and, as a result, the song sounds a little like it doesn't quite know when it has ended, almost, but not quite, descending into chaos. One can imagine Kenny Morris kicking his drumkit over and John McKay leaving his guitar against the amp to create a wall of screeching feedback moments after 'Icon' has finished.

Jon Savage, reviewing 'Join Hands' for Melody Maker in 1979, thought 'Placebo Effect' and 'Icon' were the best songs on the album, commenting 'Placebo Effect' has a stunning flanged guitar intro, chasing clinical lyrics covering some insertion or operation: whether this is sex or some other medicine is unclear. It winds down, spaciously, into the apocalyptic (again!) 'Icon' that 'Siouxsie begins slowly, and a little awkwardly. The band then slip into one of the oldest tricks in the book — the Bo Diddley rhythm — and make it their own: the brilliantly reverbed guitar is a perfect foil for Siouxsie's soaring and, for once, emotional vocal.'[302]

'Premature Burial'

'She presented all the ordinary appearances of death. The face assumed the usual pinched and sunken outline. The lips were of the usual marble pallor. The eyes were lustreless.'[303] Edgar Allan Poe 1844.

'I just tried to embellish and make bigger anything that they did. The musical ideas are all the bands.' I had no real input on that at all. The vocals were double tracked to give them some light and shade. I can't remember whether I use backwards reverb on 'Premature Burial' but I was really enjoying playing around with backwards reverb and adding sounds like you're in London, and there's this big mist, and then out of the mist, the sound or the character coalesces into this solid form. I thought it suited the song. I was basically just using various mixing techniques to try and embellish the sound. It was easy to hear where the band were going with the song; I was the catalyst that tried to help them make it more obvious.'[304] Mike Stavrou.

Every song on 'Join Hands' is an event: a deliciously embellished story or vignette. If 'The Scream' is a microscopic examination of the lunacy of the humdrum, 'Join Hands' turns its sonic gaze outward towards a fickle and mercurial world where nothing is certain and there is an increasing proliferation of information to navigate. There is darkness but also black humour, which the band embraced but meant they were often tarred with a misguided and misinformed 'humourless' brush.

Both Sioux and Severin shared much of the same jocular aesthetic about the ridiculousness of situations, whether real or imagined. One of their literary influences was the American writer Edgar Allan Poe 1809–49, known and revered for works incorporating the macabre, as well as mystery and science fiction.

'Steve (Severin) claimed Edgar Allan Poe (on whose short story the song is based) was a sort of Gothic comedian and Siouxsie said the single line 'Oh what a bloody shame' was there to make the doominess of it all feel silly... and yet they came back to discussing the song in terms of the weighty theme of social claustrophobia (the 'burial' image equals limiting factors like race or youth fashion cults).'[305]

Poe was one of the first proponents of the short story, one of which, 'The Premature Burial', cites several instances where people have been buried alive, which, Poe writes 'Is, beyond question, the most terrific of... extremes which has ever fallen to the lot of mere mortality. That it has frequently, very frequently, so fallen will scarcely be denied by those who think. The boundaries which divide Life from Death are at best shadowy and vague. Who shall say where the one ends, and where the other begins? We know that there are diseases in which occur total cessations of all the apparent functions of vitality, and yet in which these cessations are merely suspensions, properly so called.'[306]

Most of the precipitously subterraneously interred are tended back to full health, excepting the woman that died of an unaccountable illness and had assumed all of the peculiarities associated with being dead: 'The eyes were lustreless. There was no warmth. Pulsation had ceased. For three days the body was preserved unburied, during which it had acquired a stony rigidity.'[307]

Three years later, after being posited in the family vault, her husband opened the iron door of the tomb and 'how fearful a shock awaited the husband, who, personally, threw open the door! As its portals swung outwardly back, some white-apparelled object fell rattling within his arms. It was the skeleton of his wife in her yet unmoulded shroud.'[308]

The premise for the story is Poe's own cataleptic condition, which leads him to become paranoid that this will lead to his own premature burial. Poe describes his catalepsy in detail: 'Sometimes, without any apparent cause, I sank, little by little, into a condition of hemi-syncope, or half swoon; and, in this condition, without pain, without ability to stir, or, strictly speaking, to think, but with a dull lethargic consciousness of life and of the presence of those who surrounded my bed, I remained, until the crisis of the disease restored me, suddenly, to perfect sensation. At other times I was quickly and impetuously smitten. I grew sick, and numb, and chilly, and dizzy, and so fell prostrate at once. Then, for weeks, all was void, and black, and silent, and Nothing became the universe.'[309]

The author writes of one particularly vivid, cataleptic trance-induced vision where he is led by the hand by an unseen figure who beckons Poe to witness all those who have been buried alive, which by far outnumber those who are actually dead, writing 'the unseen figure, which still grasped me by the wrist, had caused to be thrown open the graves of all mankind, and from each issued the faint phosphoric radiance of decay, so that I could see into the innermost recesses, and there view the shrouded bodies in their sad and solemn slumbers with the worm. But alas! the real sleepers were fewer, by many millions, than those who slumbered not at all; and there was a feeble struggling; and there was a general sad unrest; and from out the depths of the countless pits there came a melancholy rustling from the garments of the buried.'[310]

Poe makes elaborate, intricate plans to ensure that, should his catalepsy be mistaken for death, he can mitigate his fate 'Among other things, I had the family vault so remodelled as to admit of being readily opened from within. The slightest pressure upon a long lever that extended far into the tomb would cause the iron portal to fly back. There were arrangements also for the free admission of air and light, and convenient receptacles for food and water, within immediate reach of the coffin intended for my reception.'[311]

The story's final denouement involves Poe believing he has been buried alive, surrounded by a wooden casket, with the smell of damp soil permeating his nostrils. This is not the comfortable, lined and cushioned receptacle he instructed, nor is there any discernible device to free him from this precipitous incarceration. It transpired that Poe had not, in fact, been buried alive; instead, he was accompanying an expedition by the James River in Richmond, Virginia, when a storm curtailed the day's activities and Poe and his friends sought refuge in a sloop whose cargo consisted of garden waste. 'I slept in one of the only two berths in the vessel — and the berths of a sloop of sixty or twenty tons need scarcely be described. That which I occupied had no bedding of any kind. Its extreme width was eighteen inches. The distance of its bottom from the deck overhead was precisely the same. I found it a matter of exceeding difficulty to squeeze myself in. Nevertheless, I slept soundly, and the whole of my vision — for it was no dream, and no nightmare — arose naturally from the circumstances of my position — from my ordinary bias of thought -- and from the difficulty, to which I have alluded, of collecting my senses, and especially of regaining my memory, for a long time after awaking from slumber.'[312]

The song starts with the fading in and out of John McKay's

guitar, resembling the reverence and quietude of a church organ at a funeral service. However, it doesn't take long for rumble of bass guitar and drums to come to the fore, Sioux uttering 'This catacomb compels me', akin to one of the many scenes in the words from the William Friedkin directed 'The Exorcist',[313] which sees a levitating Regan MacNeil (Linda Blair) being read the Catholic Rite of Exorcism, repeated multiple times, by Father Merrin (Max Von Sydow) and Father Damien (Jason Miller) as they try to exorcise the demon that possesses her.

The mood of Poe's story is captured with the weighty portentousness of the music, creating a sense of calamitous foreboding as the grains of damp soil hit the unfortunate occupant's coffin lid. It also describes the state of helplessness associated with the imprisonment of catalepsy, perhaps not only as a literal condition but also a metaphorical one; the inescapable truism that we are all trapped within our minds, as well as our skin.

The notion of premature burial was, Poe asserts, not an uncommon worry, in the nineteenth century. It is an inescapably grotesque notion but not without, as Sioux's lyrics suggest, its own gallows humour — 'This blissful suffocation, It is driving me to pain, Oh what a bloody shame' — perhaps indicating some understated resignation to this unfortunate fate. The song bears many of the trademarks one associates with gothic narrative, including transmogrification in the form of 'zombierama', and evocative, monastic litany-like chanting 'We're all sisters and brothers', the result, apparently, of 'choir effects; just lots of tracks of them.'[314] Sioux's background vocal 'swoons' evoke Poe's catalectic paralysis as he descends into his unsolicited altered state. 'Premature Burial' broke new ground for Siouxsie and The Banshees and is, perhaps, the closest they had come to date in realising such an all-encompassing cinematic vision.

'Playground Twist'

'Siouxsie's fascination for the macabre finds an expression that suits it in a swirl of child-like disorientation and terror. Controlled, clipped and powerful, a great song.'[315] Jon Savage.

Released as the band's third single, on 29 June 1979, 'Playground Twist' has the ominous menace one associates with many Hitchcock films, especially the crows in the playground scene in 'The Birds',[316] where socialite Melanie Daniels (Tippi Hedren) smokes a cigarette as flocks of crows quietly gather on the school playground behind her. We observe Daniels, immaculately dressed in a green tailored suit and coiffured hair, lighting her cigarette as children from the Bodega Bay School house sing a rendition of 'Risseldy Rosseldy',[317] based on a traditional Scottish folk song 'Wee Cooper O'Fife',[318] first referred to in print in texts from the late 1880s. 'Wee Cooper O'Fife' describes a cooper (a person trained to make wooden casks, barrels, vats, buckets, tubs and troughs from timber staves that were usually heated or steamed to make them pliable) who beats his wife, after he has draped her in sheepskin, for refusing to cook, sew, clean and carry out other domestic drudgery.

> 'The Cooper has gane to his woo' pack,
> Nickety, Nackety, noo, noo, noo,
> And he's laid a sheep's skin on his wife's ba'ck,
> Hey Willy Wallacky, hoo John Dougal,
> A lane, quo'Rushity, roue, roue, roue.
>
> It's I'll no thrash ye for your gentle kin,
> Nickety, Nackety, noo, noo, noo,

But I will thrash my ain sheep's skin,
Hey Willy Wallacky, hoo John Dougal,
A lane, quo'Rushity, roue, roue, roue.'

From 'Wee Cooper O'Fife'

'Risseldy Rosseldy' is far more anodyne, eliciting no overt spousal punishment, but the message of the potential violent repercussions of indolence still looms large.

'She swept the floor
But once a year,
Risseldy, rosseldy,
Mow, mow, mow,
She swore her broom
Was much to dear,
Risseldy, Rosseldy,
Hey bambassity,
Nickety, nackety,
Retrical quality,
Willowby, wallowby,
Mow, mow, mow.'

The scene from 'The Birds' has three intertwined elements that, all combined, add to the all-encompassing imminent threat. Hitchcock has orchestrated the scene so the song being sung by the schoolchildren and the gathering of the crows, which eventually cover the school playground climbing frame entirely, are synchronised with Daniels lighting-up and smoking her cigarette, until, discerning a solitary low-flying crow in her peripheral vision, her gaze turns to the sea of birds, causing her to warn of the avian danger and seek refuge in the schoolhouse.

'Playground Twist' is another Siouxsie and The Banshees song of epic proportions, drama and ambition. Producer Mike Stavrou recalls, 'I thought this could be a single. The tubular bells that I hired in could have been straight out of Mike Oldfield's collection; these were literally giant, orchestral tubular bells that are taller than I am! I really wanted them. The bass riff was great, but I wanted it to ring in your ear so the tubular bells would double the bass part. I thought, okay, well, the bells are a percussion instrument, I'll get the drummer to play them, because he's a percussionist. Well, he couldn't quite play them, get the phrasing or quite get the timing so it would really match the bass. So, then I asked the bass player, maybe he might want to play the bells, because he knew the timing. As it transpired, Severin either didn't want to do it, or he did it and it wasn't right either. So, I'm in the studio tape operators' hitting record, and I am also playing the tubular bells because I know it's supposed to go down, down, down, down, really simple. And the band were not too impressed because it sounded like a hit now. Sorry, guys. But I think that's why I'm here.'[319]

A song, Sioux reflects, about 'the cruelty of children and that whole aspect of being thrown out into the playground in the winter in howling gales and left to fend for your-selves. It's not the sort of thing you're supposed to write pop songs about,'[320] 'Playground Twist' would have chimed with any 1970s' schoolchild dreading the thought of the hierarchy and potential brutality of the playground, as it encapsulates perfectly the sense of dread and fending for oneself that Sioux mentions.

Every pastime, whether Follow the Leader or Pass the Parcel, has an element of pecking order, leading or following, winning or losing. The psychological wounds and eventual scarification of name-calling proliferate in the 'wild west'

131

hinterland of the playground, which, in the context of the song is something of a contradiction.

The swirling sonic vortex is created by multi-layered instrumentation, including John Mckay's phased guitar and the multi-tracking of Sioux's voice, a technique on which producer Mike Stavrou was very keen. Unusually for a Banshees' song, the bass guitar introduces the song, but it isn't long before the operatic nature of the song is in full effect with guitar, bass and drums joined by tubular bells.

Sioux's initial vocal refrain 'Hanging, Hanging, Hanging' is appropriately onomatopoeic as she drains every possible elucidation from the phrasing. The imagery conjured by the song is that of the playground as battlefield — 'Running from your enemies' — the sense of being left to fend for oneself; as well as implying capture by the enemy, 'Falling on your knees' and 'Get down on your knees' not only represent the rough and tumble of the playground but also conceivably reference the enforced ritual common in many primary schools of pupils having to recite the Lord's Prayer.[321]

Sioux's phrasing of the word 'knees' is echoed by the crash of Kenny Morris's cymbals, which adds to the metaphorical playground 'storm.' 'Get down on your knees' could also be referring to one of the many playground games that were played by children in the 1960s and 1970s, such as 'Stuck in the mud', a variety of tag that sees the person who has been 'tagged' having to stand still (seen as being stuck in the mud) until they are set free by another, who has crawled under their legs. An elementally potent game that saw children running all over the playground, trying to avoid being tagged, while those stuck screamed for someone to get on their hands and knees and under their legs.

A game like British Bulldog was more combative, giving children the chance literally to overpower their playground enemy, using less than honest and fair tactics, and dole out some physical punishment. The beginning of the game started with one 'bulldog' trying to capture other children attempting to run from one end of the playground to the other without being captured. Subsequently, every child captured would become a bulldog counterpart until, eventually, there would be as many bulldogs as there were runners and inevitable annihilation would ensue as personal grudges were enacted, all under the aegis of 'play.'

'Playground Twist' exudes the omnipresence of danger, either real or a product of a child's febrile imagination. Every part of the playground ritual has a sinister side. The allusion to the nursery rhyme 'Three Blind Mice',[322] first published in 'Deuteromelia' or 'The Seconde part of Musicks melodie'[323] (1609) adds to the song's overtones of cruelty; it has been suggested that 'Three Blind Mice' has its origins dating back to Mary I's blinding and execution of three Protestant bishops when the parliament of 1553 repealed most of the Protestant legislation.

However, the original makes no overt allusion to the act of 'blinding' the mice themselves and historical records attest that Bishops Hugh Latimer, Thomas Cranmer and Nicholas Ridley, who became known as the 'Oxford Martyrs'[324] were burnt at the stake. The song's reference to 'farmer's wife' could conceivably refer to the massive estates owned by Mary and her husband King Philip II of Spain. The allusion to 'Dame Iulian' is curiously anomalous as Dame Iulian refers to Dame Julian, also known as Julian of Norwich, who lived from 1342 to 1416. She is best known for her book 'Revelations of Divine Love' (or Showings). She lived in times of turmoil and rejected the prevailing notion that suffering was a punishment from God. Instead, she believed that God loved people and wanted to save everyone.[325]

'... shee scrapte her tripe licke thou the knife' probably refers to the act of scraping the entrails from the bellies of the mice, 'tripe' being the name for stomach lining, more readily associated with the edible delicacy from cattle or sheep.

'Three Blinde Mice,
Three Blinde Mice,
Dame Iulian,
Dame Iulian,
the Miller and his merry olde Wife,
shee scrapte her tripe licke thou the knife'

The equally cruel contemporary adaptation is more readily accessible than the original, although it is clear that Sioux had looked into the origins of the song; never one to shy away or stray from the truth, she uses the 'entrails' of the 1609 version.

'Three blind mice. Three blind mice.
See how they run. See how they run.
They all ran after the farmer's wife,
Who cut off their tails with a carving knife,
Did you ever see such a sight in your life,
As three blind mice?'[326]

The video for 'Playground Twist', again employing the talents of the band's director of choice Clive Richardson, has the band playing their instruments on a chequerboard stage surrounded by stainless steel scaffolding, which also serves the purpose of a climbing frame. Sioux is literally 'hanging' from the climbing frame as the song begins.

Throughout the mimed performance, the band look animated yet composed, immersed in their instruments, naturalistic, putting heart and soul into the performance, even though they are surrounded by children who are swinging and climbing on the multi-levelled frame, jumping off it, and running and walking across the stage. Dressed in black and white, with Sioux looking particularly striking in a Breton shirt, the band coheres with the chequerboard stage, in contrast to the colour of the children's clothing. Like Hitchcock's crows, cameras swoop and focus on every band member and on the children from myriad different angles, creating a fluid dynamism as well as a sense of disorientation.

Sioux rules this imaginary playground as she dances around the stage until, right at the end of the song on the cue of the repetition of 'Drown', the children set upon her, and she is drowned by a sea of bodies as the song fades. The single's sleeve design, accredited to Delga Press,[327] is a curious felt-tip drawing with a proliferation of green dominating the image; a cross between a child's visual description of a recreation ground with elements of Edvard Munch's 'The Scream'.[328]

'Mother/ Oh Mein Papa'

'I remember having fun with the music box and Mother. The band brought in their own music box. They said, "We're going to record this." I wasn't quite sure what was going to happen next, but I thought a music box can be kind of boring. So that's when I mentioned the idea of putting the music box on a turntable and running it at 33 RPM, because that's the speed of the record. I put a microphone behind the music box that went into reverb; a microphone to the left of the of the turntable that only went to the left channel, dry, a microphone on the right that only went to the right channel, and a microphone in the front that went to the centre. So, as the object spins, it's not only just moving, it's actually three dimensional. If you listen to it on a nice pair of speakers, you'll hear that. I also put the music box inside another box, so the sound was very directional... I wanted it to be like the spinning beam of a lighthouse; when it's facing back it's little literally away from you and when it's really close it's right there in front. Anyway, that was just a fun little thing the band liked.'[329] Mike Stavrou.

Hauntingly beautiful, 'Mother' is an expression of familial complexity, with Sioux remarking 'It's very close to home. It's personal but I'm not hung up about it. I've deeply loved my mother. I've gone out and got pissed with her. Called her by her first name. But at times she's been this disapproving figure and I've hated her I think.'[330]

The music box alluded to by Mike Stavrou has the soporific lulling effect of a child's mobile suspended above a cot, so it seems appropriate that the sound should have been recorded on a turntable. It's conceivable that the band, and Stavrou, were experimenting with an early incarnation of a Fairlight synthesizer,[331] which, using microprocessor technology, could create sounds evocative of acoustic instruments through digital sampling and was a more user friendly and less cumbersome alternative to the established Moog.[332] However, Stavrou recalls that all the additional sounds were simply recorded and edited 'old school.'[333]

Fairlight or not, 'Mother' certainly provides the listener with a foretaste of combined psychedelic and polyphonic adventure of 'Kaleidoscope', which took full advantage of this revolutionary digital technology.

There is also a sinister, elemental dimension to 'Mother'; it as though one can discern the whirring of an inverse music box in the background, evoking the proximity of 'Hitchcockian' menace. The song is reminiscent of hiding-behind-the-sofa psychological horror films or 'Neil Gaiman's 'Coraline',[334] in which the young protagonist discovers an identical apartment to her own through a locked door, having been warned by mice not to enter, where she finds her 'other mother' and' other father', identical to her own parents, except that both have buttons sewn onto their faces instead of eyes.

In 'Mother', some hidden spectral commination awaits beyond a forbidden locked door. This unnerving sonic rumble, present at the beginning of 'Mother', comes to a crescendo with the song's final refrain: 'The love you won't forget (The thing you grow to hate).' The lyric is strewn with barbed contradictions, as echoed in the music box and its polarised mechanical dirge. Each line of the song's lyrics has its counterpart; a call and response or sotto voce form of polychoral antiphony.

'Mother' segues into 'Oh Mein Papa', with the ethereal lyrical refrain:

'Oh my papa
To me you're so beautiful
Always the same'[335]

The words run in parallel with the slowing down and eventual stopping of the music box, as the mechanism of metal prongs shudders to a halt. The multi-layered sound puts one in mind of track six of 'Ninth Wave (the)' on side two of Kate Bush's 1985 album 'Hounds of Love',[336] a suite of seven songs based on a film called 'The Ninth Wave' and born from 'The idea of this person being in the water, how they've got there, we don't know.

But the idea is that they've been on a ship and they've been washed over the side so they're alone in this water… horrific imagery, the thought of being completely alone in all this water. And they've got a lifejacket with a little light so that if anyone should be travelling at night they'll see the light and know they're there. And they're absolutely terrified, and they're completely alone at the mercy of their imagination… such a terrifying thing, the power of one's own imagination being let loose on something like that. And the idea that they've got it in their head that they mustn't fall asleep, because if you fall asleep when you're in the water, I've heard that you roll over and so you drown…'[337]

'Oh Mein Papa' is replete with what could be construed as Siren[338] calls as Sioux's voice slips from the consciousness of 'Mother' into the semi-conscious hallucinations of 'Oh Mein Papa', harking back to the younger Siouxsie in her sickbed.

'Oh Mein Papa' is based on a German song 'O Mein Papa', written by Swiss composer Paul Burkhard[339] in 1939 for the musical 'Der schwarze Hecht'[340] and subsequently reproduced in 1950 as 'Das Feuerwerk'[341] to a libretto by Erik Charell,[342] Jürg Amstein[343] and Robert Gilbert.[344]

Nostalgic and wistful, it was originally sung by a young German woman remembering her beloved, once-famous clown father. It has also been recorded by Lyss Assia[345] and Björk,[346] as well as a version by Lancashire trumpeter Eddie Calvert.[347]

Unlike the conflicted and barbed 'Mother', if it is autobiographical in any shape or form, 'Oh Mein Papa' is a beautiful, poetic eulogy to Sioux's late father, whom she clearly had a great attachment to, and empathy with, accepting, even embracing, his every flaw. It is almost Haiku-like in its simplicity: an evocative lament. The original song, adapted into English by lyricist John Turner[348] under the title 'Oh! My Pa-Pa', the song is a serene, heartfelt air; free of cynicism and imbued with innocent feeling.

'The Lord's Prayer'

'It's really important to have 'The Lord's Prayer' on this album.

We probably won't do it on the next tour, only on occasions when we feel like it.'[349] John McKay.

'She could hear a voice above her, chanting. Such a lovely sound. What was he singing? Impossible to understand. Now louder. Not too loud, please. Uncle Ben, it's too loud. You're hurting my ears. Oh stop! Stop! Softer now. Much better. More understandable. What were the words? They sounded familiar. Evil from us deliver... Not us lead... This us give... The Lord's Prayer! That was it. But he was saying it backwards. How strange and fascinating. She would be late back and the warden would be angry. But that didn't matter. What a story she would have to tell her friends. By her head, his insane eyes gleaming, Russel began to moan. Purity. Chastity. Virgin. Sacrifice. No one like this. Frenzy. Beauty. Milk-white skin. Running red. Red over white. Church. Hate. Rome. Hate. Rome. Rome. Excommunicate. Prison. Never again. Too clever. Revenge. Teach them. Teach them all. Peggy. Teach her. Outcast. Hate. Hate. Janet. Save her. Pure soul. Purify. Glorify. Sanctify. No more. No more. Live. Rise. Revenge.'[350] 'The Benefactor' Walter Winward.

'I think it was really important for us to put 'The Lord's Prayer' on (Join Hands) because so many people were pretending it didn't exist, pretending we were this "singles band." There were all these other sides to us and I'm really glad it got on there.'[351] Steve Severin.

'That's a gleeful mockery of religion or any other fanaticism — for the Beatles or whatever. We're just spanners in the works of uniform progression.'[352] Siouxsie Sioux.

Conceivably Siouxsie and The Banshees' most ambitious

song to date, in part inspired by 'The Benefactor', a short and rather transgressive horror story by Walter Winward about the grooming and subsequent ritualistic murder of an orphan girl by a rich benefactor, and harking back to the seminal 1976 100 Club gig, committing 'The Lord's Prayer' to vinyl may have been the exorcism or sonic catharsis needed to sooth the less than fully functional and increasingly strained dynamic within the band: two against two, the result of which was the band's temporary dissolution.

At 14 minutes and eight seconds, 'The Lord's Prayer' is extraordinarily epic; its length more akin to something from prog rock. Although it bears no resemblance, in any shape or form, to anything from 'Tales From Topographic Oceans'[353] by Yes, the entirety of which clocks in at 81 minutes and 14 seconds, with the longest track, 'Ritual (Nous Sommes du Soleil)',[354] running at 21 minutes and 35 seconds, it nonetheless shares some parallels with the underground strains of Space Rock[355] pioneers Gong[356] and Hawkwind,[357] both of which would incorporate elements of improvisation through the synergistic melding of rock and jazz elements.

The song is introduced by Severin's bass strumming, followed by Kenny Morris's 'Ready? (I'm ready!)' and Sioux's clarion call of 'O! I'm gonna get you in the end!' What ensues is tantamount to the most resolutely defiant, spleen-laden outpouring stream of consciousness, akin to a disjointed dream state redolent of the final passage of Winward's short story, providing a lyrical smorgasbord with words from W.C. Fields,[358] Mohammad Ali,[359] Batman,[360] The Beatles, Dillinger[361] and Bob Dylan.[362] John McKay's guitar refrain is not a million miles away from David Bowie's 'The Gene Genie',[363] echoing the band's idolising of the mercurially brilliant singer-songwriter.

'By the time we did 'Icon', my hand was really damaged;

then I had to play 'The Lord's Prayer'. So, Sue (Siouxsie) and I went for a cup of coffee. John McKay had left the studio to go somewhere else; he came back in time. However, we said "alright, we're gonna do this." So we went back into the studio, did 'The Lord's Prayer', and if you listen about halfway through, I kind of stopped — it's just because I was exhausted. Then all of a sudden I come back with a really, really long drumroll. I suddenly got my energy back... And you can hear Siouxsie say "Carry on, carry on, carry on!" What they left out was her saying "Carry on, Kenny, carry on!." Then we finished it... after we recorded it in that studio, apparently they never played it again.'[364]

The recording retains all the raw energy and spontaneity of the original 'Sister Ray' improvised and extemporised template and, for context, it has to be remembered that 'The Lord's Prayer' was an early live staple of the band, which, ironically, proved to be their saviour when Robert Smith, on tour with The Cure as Siouxsie and The Banshees' support act, suggested to a beleaguered Sioux and Severin that they join The Cure on stage and play an extended version of 'The Lord's Prayer' as a three-song encore at Aberdeen's Capitol Theatre the day that Kenny Morris and John McKay fled the 1979 tour, at least to placate The Banshees' audience who had waited patiently to see the band.

Smith's intervention was not entirely altruistic, as he realised that the sudden disarray of The Banshees could lead to a less-than-happy experience and memory of the gig for The Cure fans at a time when the band were beginning to break through on the back of their first album 'Three Imaginary Boys', which was released on 11 May 1979.

Mike Stavrou was unambiguously enthusiastic when asked about 'The Lord's Prayer', 43 years after its release, praising its untethered ambition. Stavrou maintains that the band knew exactly what they wanted and witnessed the extraordinary transformation of a band that were introspective, quiet, thoughtful and studious, commenting, 'When the red light comes on, it's kind of play time, in a very uninhibited, non-stressful kind of way. And it's fascinating to watch ... The sound balance engineer is really just a backroom boy, who just needs to keep up with everything and stay out of the way.'[365]

One cannot deny the sheer chutzpah of 'The Lord's Prayer', which closed side two of 'Join Hands' on its original release in 1979. Unwittingly or otherwise, it put a marker down to distance Siouxsie and The Banshees from their punk and post-punk peers. The band witnessed, and were an instrumental part of, the 1976 revolution and would continue to confound expectation through sheer bloody-mindedness, inventiveness, creativity and imagination, never bowing to formula, commercialism or the tyranny of record company diktats.

'Join Hands' peaked at number 13 in the UK charts, where it stayed for one week in mid-September 1979. Reviews of the album ranged from effusiveness to empathy but also elements of incredulity and a soupçon of disappointment.

Writing in Melody Maker, Jon Savage's review on 1 September 1979 described the album as uneven, seeing 'Join Hands' as little more than a curiosity and folly, commenting 'A year ago, the Banshees had a hit, a Top 10 single ('Hong Kong Garden'), the crossover pop audience and the punk audience. Credibility, critical acclaim, and pop prowess. Whatever you thought about them (and, as ever, the non-debate reverberated through the music press), they were an integral part of the matrix. Finally, they wore their clothes nicely — perfect. Blink... and it's gone!'[366]

Having seen the band on tour in 1979, Savage opines that the band were below par, citing a gig which took place at Friars in Aylesbury on 30 August, a week before the official release of 'Join Hands', and suggesting that this is indicative of 'the problems this sudden success entailed: the group was not only struggling to maintain the constant command over instrument and atmosphere needed for the new league they'd entered, but the renowned cold, insulting facade that they, in particular Siouxsie, had erected made it difficult for them to cope with the fact that they weren't underdogs anymore.'[367]

Perhaps Savage sensed the increasing discontent pervading the Banshees' camp and could see this affecting the band's live dynamic. Essentially, this must have been an exhausting time for Sioux and, indeed, the rest of the band, all of whom were in their early twenties and trying to live up to their own expectations and, even if perversely and somewhat begrudgingly satiate the appetite of both hardcore fans and those fans they had picked up through the stellar success ear-worm of Hong Kong Garden, not to mention the treadmill of seemingly endless interviews.

Savage isn't entirely averse to the album, commenting on the cohesion of side one as the songs segue into one another, 'The first, 'Poppy Day', is a short, powerful evocation of the Great War graveyards in Flanders. McKay's phased guitar scythes out a barrage of sound while the bass carries the tune. 'Regal Zone' opens with an urgent flurry, muted slightly by McKay's sax: it shifts into an urgent, insistent claustrophobia, with lyrics of snapshot atrocity images.'[368]

Savage also praises 'Placebo Effect' and 'Icon', citing 'the brilliantly reverbed guitar… a perfect foil for Siouxsie's soaring and, for once, emotional vocal.'[369] When critiquing side two of the album, Savage mentions the recent single 'Playground Twist' as 'underrated'[370] and cites 'Sioux's fascination for the macabre[371] as finding 'an expression that suits it in a swirl of child-like disorientation and terror. Controlled, clipped and

143

powerful.'[372]

One can discern that Savage pays little attention to most of side two, describing 'Mother' as 'mawkish rather than evocative',[373] perhaps a rather off-the-cuff comment that does little to penetrate the complexities of familial relationships.

Savage finds 'The Lord's Prayer' an unsatisfactory limboed mezzanine that is neither art nor music, and that 'Siouxsie methodically pulls the wings off the Lord's Prayer over a Banshees boogie which, when it shifts, provides the only moments of interest. It's not art, not proper noise... The 100 Club one liner (and myth), taken out of context, is made absurd. Lost in space, the Banshees frequently sabotage improved and impressive technique and ideas with ponderous, humourless pretension. At its worst, Join Hands is unforgivably necrophiliac; at its best, it captures the power of which the Banshees are capable. Translated practically, all this means: listen before you buy.'[374]

It was always inevitable that 'Join Hands' would divide both audiences and critics. However, some reviews of the album proved more favourable and responsive to Siouxsie and The Banshees' sonic, occasionally oblique, odyssey, among them the Sounds journalist Pete Silverton.

Silverton had more compassion for the 'plight' of the band, at the time 'in the unenviable position of becoming everybody's favourite whipping boys and girls.'[375] Silverton contextualises his review through the lens of expectation concomitant with being signed to a major record label with acts as diverse as the Bee Gees and Jimmy Pursey, and the inevitable 'metric of success' comparisons post 'Hong Kong Garden' and 'The Scream', commenting 'I can't think of anybody outside the band and their manager who thought the Banshees would become Top Of The Pops regulars with their first single.'[376]

'The Staircase (Mystery)' peaked at number 24 in the UK charts, with the semi-acoustic introspective and experimental B-side 'Pulled To Bits, lyrically not dissimilar to 'Playground Twist', peaking at 28. Subsequently, 'Mittageisen', appearing on 1978's 'The Scream' and re-released as a single in September 1979 with the lyric sung in German, with the B-side 'Love In A Void', peaked at number 47.

There was also the emergence of new bands such as Joy Division and The Cure who were bringing their own brand of dystopian introspection, fanning the flames that Siouxsie and The Banshees had very much already ignited. The band's malady reflected the capriciousness and range of musical tastes, which included the Mod revival, Ska, New Wave, New Wave of Heavy Metal, Disco, Soul and Soft Rock.

Where and what was Siouxsie and The Banshees' market share? Silverton suggests that 'The Banshees had simply become boring. There was little left to say once they'd established their own domain and carved out their own little patch of the rock'n'roll universe (which quite likely includes hating being referred to as rock'n'roll).'[377]

Silverton comments: 'Why think of the Banshees when you can thrill to the exciting world of Joy Division or, at the other extreme, the whole new mod movement? Much as they hate the idea, the Banshees are now established, in much the same position as, say, Whitesnake. There's no longer anything particularly exciting or original about them — if you've heard the first album and the singles, you'll know, with only maybe one exception, what this album will sound like without even listening to it.'

Warming to his theme, Silverton also points to second-album-itis, comparing the stunning debut of 'The Scream' with The Clash's eponymous 1977 album 'Give 'Em Enough Rope', released in 1978, commenting 'Almost inevitably, the album bears the same relation to The Scream as Give 'Em Enough Rope did to The Clash. Where the first album represented the collected efforts of a year's writing, the second had to be written almost to order and what it loses from not being kicked around the brain cells for a year, it gains in thematic cohesion.'[378]

The travails of producing a seamless follow-up with comparable fanfares and clarion calls was always going to prove challenging, with an inevitable perfect storm of often sneering, destructive and lazy critical appraisals and the hunger for the next big thing. On measure, Silverton is sympathetic to the band and the review of the album itself is considered and, for the most part, pithily praiseworthy.

He writes, 'Ringing in the new album with a peal of bells, 'Poppy Day' sets the tone for the whole 46 minutes — about as cheerful as Chesterfield. But, like all the Banshees' stuff, it doesn't somehow make you feel like cutting your wrists any more than watching Dirty Harry makes you feel like shooting people.'[379]

Silverton spotlights John McKay's guitar as a dominant force, 'prowling around like caged lions',[380] as well as Severin's increasing mastery of the bass guitar, which no longer thuds 'around the bottom of the sound, giving you the impression that it was distorted when it wasn't.'[381] Sioux's vocals have a 'clarity... like it was a thing of treasure.'[382] 'Regal Zone' is deemed a 'more aggressive, more neurotic, more dynamic and even more demonic offering. If songs were ever mini-epics, this would be it — it both frightens and reassures.'[383]

'Placebo Effect', 'Premature Burial' and 'Playground Twist' all receive brief praise, and Silverton comments on 'Mother' that 'Sue sings soft and quiet backed by a music box. Placed as it is between 'Playground Twist' and the storming inferno of 'The Lord's Prayer', it's very delicacy displays a

146

touching confusion.'[384]

There is a more extended discourse reserved for arguably Siouxsie and The Banshees' most divisive recording, 'The Lord's Prayer', which, Silverton pronounces will 'no doubt raise a few hackles — Dylan certainly won't cover a Banshees song on his next album and I doubt if Cliff Richard will put it in his star choice. It's fourteen minutes of rage and twisted bitterness which includes Sue "quoting" from the likes of 'Twist and Shout' and the 'Yodeley-ee' song in The Sound of Music. Both frightening and absorbing, it'll probably get them in the News of the World. It deserves better.'[385]

Silverton prognosticates that 'Join Hands' will not necessarily procure Siouxsie and The Banshees a whole swathe of new fans, advising one to 'buy it if you liked the last album and run as fast as you can in the opposite direction if you didn't. It's probably best you don't ask yourself why you like the Banshees. I'm sure in my case it's an aberration.'[386]

Writing in New Musical Express on 1 September 1979, journalist Paul Morley reviewed both The Slits 'Cut', released on Island Records, and 'Join Hands'. Sensing the winds of change with regard to what Morley posits might conceivably be a period of reflective consolidation for Siouxsie and The Banshees, he suggests the band 'have finished their personal exploration and are hovering.'

The balances and marks of 'Join Hands' differ little from the devastating levels exploited on 'The Scream'. They're scuffling in a corner; increasing the melodrama, heightening the tension, smoothing away the scratches, leaning towards a saturated, exaggerated punk MOR.'[387]

A 'self-confessed Siouxsie and The Banshees sycophant',[388] Morley is nonetheless critical of what he perceives as the album's shortcomings; an unevenness that, at its centre, is a cohesive 'addictive'[389] side one and 'infuriating'[390] side two, citing what could be 'second LP confusion…'[391]

In opposition to Banshees' detractors, who consider the band 'ponderous and presumptuous,'[392] Morley waxes lyrical about the five songs on side one of 'Join Hands': 'Poppy Day', 'Regal Zone', 'Placebo Effect', 'Icon', and 'Premature Burial' are all addictive Banshee mini-dramas with strange, deliberately incomplete structures. It's not a new Banshee trait, but it remains … irresistible.'[393]

Morley's critique of the second side of the album is less positive: 'Side two is a mess; at best Sioux endearing, at worst infuriating.'[394] 'Playground Twist', however, has Morley's unconditional approbation, naming it one of his 'favourite singles of the year.'[395]

The schismatic 'Lord's Prayer' is, albeit conflictingly, deemed by Morley as 'simply a superfluous exercise in banal improvisation with defective chanting and ranting. I probably love it, but I'm not allowed to say that.'[396]

The tail end of Morley's review implies that 'Join Hands' is a rather in-between state of affairs, somewhere in twilight limbo between the gutter and the stars, 'hovering',[397] with the expectation that what ensues musically will see the band 'fly off somewhere more fulfilling and radical.'[398]

Chapter 6
Aftermath

'We left at the most perfect time. The next thing you knew, we had the New Romantics and everything to follow. Everybody knows that the original line-up of Siouxsie and the Banshees was the best.'[399] Kenny Morris.

Between late August and the first week in September 1979, cumulative hairline cracks that formed during the fractious making of 'Join Hands' were beginning to take on the appearance of a discernible fault line. The whirlwind of breaking ten days into a short European tour at the end of April 1979 to record 'Join Hands', and then reconvening to tour the UK with a further 23 dates, was to prove the tipping point beyond which there was no return.

The 'Join Hands' tour started on 29 August 1979 with a warm-up gig at Bournemouth's Stateside Centre. The setlist for the gig is 'Playground Twist', 'The Staircase (Mystery)', 'Metal Postcard', 'Premature Burial', 'Placebo Effect', 'Icon', 'Regal Zone' and 'Hong Kong Garden'.

There is an apparent darker, brooding edge to the band's performance, befitting the newer material, with John McKay's guitar leading the menacing charge, phased to the nth degree on 'Playground Twist' and replicating the smorgasbord of expressive sounds so exquisitely prevalent on both 'The Scream' and 'Join Hands'.

The complexities of 'Premature Burial' are executed with absolute mastery by the band, replete with all of the thrashing melodrama redolent of the studio version. Kenny Morris's drums keep a tight, metronomic beat that has a ramped-up intensification on 'Placebo Effect' and 'Icon', the latter of which sees Severin's bass being utilised as more of a lead instrument. This does not sound like a band on the cusp of imploding.

The recording from the gig might be lacking, exacerbated by the apparently poor sound quality at the gig itself, but one can glean enough to discern that Siouxsie and The Banshees are a tight, rehearsed, creative and imaginative ensemble, capable of moments of inspired, sublime and transcendent brilliance. 'Hong Kong Garden' ends the set with adrenaline-fuelled alacrity. Not bad for a 'warm-up' gig.

'After the warm-up show, we got the ferry to Ireland, where we discovered that none of the gear had turned up. The guy who was meant to bring everything over had fallen asleep at the border and wasn't going to be able to make it in time.'[400] Steve Severin.

The first 'proper' date of the tour was a less than auspicious omen, with the Royal Ulster Constabulary diktat in force that no more than 12 people could gather at one time, lest constituting a 'riot', so many of the fans who had turned up to see the band couldn't queue and were instead being moved on, walking around Ulster Hall for hours or, as Siouxsie and The Banshees discovered, seeking refuge in the local hotel bar, where the band had to explain what exactly had happened to their gear.

It transpired that The Banshees, as well as support band The Cure, would borrow equipment from local band The Outcasts, much to the chagrin of John McKay, as much of the set for him required a host of effects pedals. The ensuing set was one of 'rudimentary'[401] make do and mend improvisation, with an apparent desperate reconfiguration of the setlist.

An expeditious decision was also made that The Cure headline the gig, with one disappointed Banshees' acolyte commenting 'For a Siouxsie fan, who adored and played to death 'The Scream', this gig ought to have been a classic but turned out far from it.'[402]

The band's lengthening fissure was reflected in an observation by journalist Kris Needs, who was accompanying the band on the Join Hands tour, that 'It was quite noticeable that Kenny and John's preference for each other's company within the band had grown into a practical self-isolation.'[403] Kenny Morris also remarked 'We'd be on the tour bus sitting separately. Steven would have his own seat, Nils and Siouxsie would be sitting together. Me and John would be sat at the back.'[404]

The schism of Sioux, Stevenson and Severin in one camp and McKay and Morris in another was being played out with disagreements within the band and tense, tour bus quietness.

The eventual severance and dissolution of the Sioux, Severin, McKay and Morris belies Morris's memory of the band when they were in full flight, evoking their synergistic alchemy: 'Everyone's playing the lead line at the same time, and it's very difficult to do — but there it was being done instinctively. Whoever brings the song into the space, everybody puts their parts into it, and it becomes the sum of its parts. There isn't one song where you're just keeping time in the background: your style creates atmospherics, power, and it's painting with sound.'[405]

This is a far cry from the monochromatic misery recalled by Severin during the final vestiges of the current incarnation: 'The very last photo session we did together was down at Camber Sands and you can tell from the pictures that they're not enjoying it, because both of them look stoned and pissed off.'[406]

Severin readily admits that both Morris and McKay were being kept out of the band's decision-making, reflected in the lack of an invitation to be a part of the Camber Sands photoshoot: 'They hadn't been party to the decision to do the shoot and had been told to come along. That probably made them feel even more excluded, but it wasn't like we'd consciously decided to annoy them.'[407]

The Vanishing

'It was a Saturday morning, and we had an in-store signing scheduled at the local record shop. Yet again, no one told John (McKay) we were doing it, so he was in a strop by the time he got there. This was about lunchtime, and we were supposed to be going down to the soundcheck immediately afterwards, but the signing was a fiasco right from the off.'[408] Steve Severin.

The 'fiasco' to which Severin alludes gathered momentum the day the band were due to play a gig at Aberdeen's Capitol Theatre, preceded by signing of 'Join Hands' at Other Records during the afternoon, aspects of which were Spinal Tap-like, except that Other Records was teeming with excited, expectant fans waiting for their copy of 'Join Hands' to be signed by the band.

The only, rather significant, issue was that Polydor hadn't sent anywhere near enough albums to be sold or signed, so The Banshees were having to sign copies of 'The Scream' and singles instead. No sooner over the threshold of the shop, John McKay apparently uttered, 'I hate this fucking record'[409], having no compunction about walking straight up to the turntable where 'Join Hands' was playing and gleefully putting on The Slits' 'Cut', which had been released the same week.

McKay was also considerably exercised about not being told about the signing, fanning the flames of disaffection further. McKay and Morris went into Situationist mode, deciding to start giving away copies of 'Join Hands' stamped with 'Promotion Only — Not For Resale', prompting Sioux to push McKay and call him an 'idiot or something. Nothing too nasty.'[410]

This was the apparent catalyst that led to McKay and Morris walking out of the record store, 'It seemed like they'd been waiting for the signal and that shove from Siouxsie was it.'[411]

'...there seemed to be a strange undercurrent when we arrived at the Capitol Theatre for the soundcheck. Where were Kenny Morris and John McKay? They didn't seem to be in the building, as Siouxsie and Severin did the soundcheck on their own.'[412] Lol Tolhurst.

Sioux and Severin, the two founder members, initially thought that the walkout was nothing unusual and nothing more than 'another day, another strop'[413] and 'didn't seem too out of the ordinary'[414] and it was unequivocal that the four band members would meet at the soundcheck. It turned out that this was not to be. After leaving Other Records, Morris recalls walking 'down the street in tears'[415] disconsolately returning to the band's hotel to plan a hasty retreat.

With £200 between them, McKay and Morris gathered themselves and their belongings and made their getaway by taxi to Aberdeen airport where they boarded a small charter plane to Manchester, where McKay's uncle lived. Sioux describes a scene straight from the 1979 film 'Escape From Alcatraz'[416] when she and Severin discovered that Morris and McKay had 'stuck their pillows under the blankets with their tour passes on them and just run off.'[417]

Apparently, the only comment uttered by Morris and

McKay was to 'Banshees' manager Nils Stevenson as he caught them speeding off in a cab outside their Aberdeen hotel: "We can't take the pressure".[418]

The sudden departure of Morris and McKay a mere two days into the band's biggest tour to date elicited more than a little bile from Sioux and Severin, after the initial 'devastation and... sadness.'[419]

Sioux comments: 'They were just pathetic. The band were growing apart. John and Kenny were going off into ga-ga land, totally abstract nonsense.'[420] Warming to the theme. Sioux elaborates 'They seemed to become more immature. I always had hopes for John, until he got tight in with Kenny. The more he got involved with Kenny the more Kenny fucked him up.'[421]

Sioux believed that any differences the band may have had could be resolved while on tour, and 'it would obviously get better if the band were forced together. But they never made the effort.'[422] Ray Stevenson comments, 'Morris and McKay leaving was such a stupid thing to do. Their complaints were justified but the way they dealt with it was not.'[423]

In an interview with Nick Kent, published in New Musical Express on 22 September 1979, two weeks after the tumult of Aberdeen, Sioux and Severin are still coming to terms with their unceremonious jilting. Severin commented: 'IT'S THE LAST thing we imagined happening, particularly in the totally underhand manner it did. We knew they were unhappy to a certain extent...'[424] yet he maintained that both former members were committed to the Join Hands tour, always replying "Yes, we want to do it"[425] when asked about their commitment. A more conspiratorial viewpoint conjectures that, during live gigs, both McKay and Morris would try to put Sioux off her stride with the interjection of a guitar intro during Sioux's between-song-audience badinage and

'Occasional percussive slice-ups.'[426]

There are comments about tensions within the band that could be traced back to the recording of 'The Scream', agitation that was a basic ingredient of the band's modus operandi: 'In a way it was an integral part of what we did. There's always been that kind of tension there simply because both Kenny and John literally walked into Siouxsie and The Banshees and they could never quite get over that — especially John, because he'd seen the band onstage.'[427]

Severin maintains that McKay was never fully at ease with his poacher turned gamekeeper role but maintains that he and Sioux 'were constantly trying to make him feel a part of the group while letting him express himself musically as he desired.'[428]

Further examination also reveals a dissimilitude of disappointment for the way 'The Scream' turned out which, considering the open wound caused by the departure of Morris and McKay, is perhaps unsurprising; Siouxsie thought 'Me, Nils and Steve were totally aware that 'The Scream' as it finally came out was not what we wanted, but John and Kenny either weren't aware of its failings or wouldn't admit it.'[429]

Severin takes a more introspective view, opining that 'recording 'The Scream' was the first really traumatic time for the band, simply because it was our first record.'[430]

The interview discloses the frustration of trying to find a producer suited to the band's sound and the fact that 'Join Hands' was recorded in a fragmented fashion.'[431] If there was tension and arguing during the recording of 'The Scream', there was also transparency because the band were recording in the studio together and would face each other to address any issues immediately 'But with 'Join Hands' the process was almost completely different because it would be us going in first and recording backing tracks and then Siouxsie would go in and record her vocals. So on one level there'd be none of that out-and-out bickering, but on the other hand the animosity would take the form of behind-the-back bitchiness.'[432]

Sioux maintains that both McKay and Morris showed a distinct lack of interest in the 'Join Hands' project 'that manifested itself in everything from refusal to participate in interviews through to non-appearances at 'Join Hands' mixing sessions.'[433]

This perceived deficit of interest and apathy meant Morris and McKay were not wholly involved in the final mixing of the songs, which Sioux cites as, 'Partly as a matter of policy, but more because they'd lost confidence in themselves as far as matters of judgement were concerned.'[434]

Sioux's vehemence about Morris and McKay during the interview with Nick Kent extends to her thoughts on the guitarist and drummer's relationship with each other, insisting, 'I think that it is of paramount importance that you get across that they'd worked up a nice little marriage with each other and that they'd travel up their own arseholes with each other and console each other! That's when the trouble really started, when they became really, really fucked up!'[435]

Financially, there was also the not insignificant matter of bankruptcy if all remaining tour dates were cancelled, with Severin quoting a figure of £50,000 invested. This was raised partly by promoter Dave Woods but, more importantly, the majority of the money was put in by the band themselves, investing all their earnings from 'The Scream' and 'Hong Kong Garden' to subsidise the Join Hands tour. The band had to take a hit to their finances to the tune of £5,000 in deposits on halls for five cancelled gigs.

To try and redress the balance a little during the interview, Kent suggests that perhaps Morris and McKay were doing their level best to hold their own to equal the powerhouse of

Sioux and Severin, eliciting the rapid response from Severin that 'Sioux and I are no way a unit unto ourselves. It was the whole operation and John and Kenny went off on their own. They'd antagonise Nils and Dave Woods on a business and touring situation, just everyone was alienated.'[436]

The interview concludes with a wariness about continuing as a band with a permanent line-up, with Severin suggesting that he and Sioux would be the indissoluble nucleus and work with a series of different musicians, qualifying the acerbity of his observations with 'The feeling I have now, possibly due to having been jilted by two people we've worked with solidly for two years and who I really thought I knew. But the more I think about it the more I see it as being the one sure way of staying fresh, of destroying the idea of a group as a marriage.'[437]

And The Band Played On...

'Do you think you guys could go back out and play some more songs? I don't think the Banshees are going to be able to play tonight.'[438] Dave Woods.

No strangers to improvisation after the equipment debacle in Belfast two days before, Sioux and Severin would again enlist the services of Robert Smith in anticipation that the dematerialised Morris and McKay would turn up. Sioux and Severin faced the crowd and, verbatim, let them know exactly what had happened; their guitarist and drummer had absconded and those attending the gig could have their money back if they so wished.

It is a measure of Sioux and Severin's tenacity that they would not bow out that night without making a pertinent gesture and not let the fans down entirely. Smith suggested 'The Lord's Prayer' and Sioux and Severin joined The Cure on stage to round off what has become the most dysfunctional, yet ultimately defining, evening of The Banshees' history.

Onstage, Sioux was in no mood for gestures of contrition towards the two escapees, as recounted to journalist Mark Paytress: 'I seem to remember telling the audience that if they saw John and Kenny they had my permission and blessing to kick the shit out of them. We masked the devastation and the sadness with a "fuck you" celebration. After the gig, me, Severin and Robert Smith, Lol Tolhurst and Mike Dempsey from The Cure sat at the hotel and drank as much alcohol as we could get inside us.'[439]

Plan B

'My first memories of drums was 'Zulu'[440] with Michael Caine... the Zulu warriors had a spear and a shield and were rapping the spear against the shield; a hundred spears hitting a hundred shields... that was the sound. I thought, that's what drums should be like.[441] Budgie.

Peter Edward 'Clarke' Clarke, born 21 August 1957, grew up in St Helen's, one of the less salubrious parts of Liverpool. The son of a joiner turned publican, Clarke's musical education was an eclectic mix of rhythm and blues, courtesy of teenagers playing Beatles' covers on the local bandstand, and his brother and sister's record collections, which included PJ Proby, The Kinks, The Troggs and The Pretty Things.

Clarke's mother died when he was 12 years old, a similar experience to Sioux's, especially with regard to the ensuing trauma and sadness endured; for Clarke this meant a period of recuperation with an aunt in Southport. Clarke joined the school choir and experienced a gravitational pull towards the more creative side of the school curriculum, including art, poetry and woodwork. With limited career prospects, except a job at one of the local glass factories, Pilkington or Ravenhead,

Clarke's initial aspirations gravitated towards architecture, although, in retrospect, he felt this was too lofty a yearning.

Picking up a snare drum at a local secondhand shop and joining forces with his friends David Jones and Alex Peachey not soon after the death of his mother in 1972, Budgie reflects: 'I didn't become a wild kid. But with the blessing of my dad I joined up with some of the guys who knocked on my door and said, "You can play drums." I ended up playing the cabaret circuit.'[442]

The knock on the door for Budgie proved a seminal and defining moment, and the 'Leather Dog, Furry Boots' experiment was born, culminating in a recording on a C30 cassette tape, replete with bespoke artwork, which 'sounded rubbish.'[443]

In common with Sioux and Severin, Clarke gravitated to the more esoterically underground spectrum of musical genres, citing German bands Faust and Amon Duul II as being surprisingly popular where he grew up, perhaps in no small part due to Clarke and his peers searching for the most atypical music they could find to outdo each other in discovering sonic weirdness.

After the 'Leather Dog, Furry Boots' experiment, Clarke met Chuck Richardson, an Opportunity Knocks wannabe who 'fancied himself as a cross between Elvis Presley and Cliff Richard.'[444] After being invited to join Richardson's band, Clarke found himself wearing a crushed-velvet jacket and bow tie and auditioning for working men's clubs in Runcorn and Warrington, playing Elvis Presley standards 'Teddy Bear', 'Hound Dog' and 'Don't be cruel'. Deemed a little too old fashioned as a bequiffed frontman, Chuck Richardson was sacked by the rest of the band.

Clarke's evolving musical tastes conceivably reflected a quest for his own identity, an advancement that included his love of T. Rex and Roxy Music as well as Led Zeppelin and Emerson, Lake and Palmer. The heavier the music, the more Clarke could get lost in it, accompanied by a bottle or two of Newcastle Brown Ale at the Geraldo Club in Lord Street, St Helen's.

Having undertaken an art foundation course at St Helen's College, where Clarke was immersed in an array of experimentation in painting, drawing, photography and sculpture, he found the subsequent Fine Art degree course at Liverpool Polytechnic too constraining, and was far from enamoured with his tutors' 1960s conceptual aesthetic, although as a first-year undergraduate, wishing to take control of his own, he recounts with no little fondness how liberating it was to take control of his own hirsute aesthetic, cutting his hair and dyeing it black, wanting to 'be a cross between Francis Bacon and Bryan Ferry.'[445]

One year into the course, it was becoming apparent that Clarke's possible career leanings were towards music, due in no small part to seeing bands at The Revolution Club in Mathew Street, latterly Eric's, where it moved after a brief incarnation in the basement of the Fruit Exchange in Victoria Street.

Clarke saw the Sex Pistols, their only Liverpool gig, on 15 October 1976, as well as The Clash and The Ramones. The experience of being 'pinned... to the back wall'[446] by the depth of sound created by The Clash's drummer Topper Headon and The Ramones' Joey Ramone was to prove a seminal moment.

One night at Eric's, Clarke met two old friends who were in a band called The Spitfire Boys and was invited to join. The full band line-up was Paul Rutherford (aka 'Maggot') on vocals, Peter Griffiths (aka 'Zero') on bass, Dave Littler (aka Jones) on guitar and Pete Clarke (aka Blister) on drums.

The line-up recorded one single in October 1977 on Robert Kingston Production Ltd records (RKO), with 'British Refugee' on the A-side and 'Mein Kampf' on the B-side. It was around this time that Clarke was christened with his nom de plume 'Budgie', after coming to the rescue of a budgerigar brought to his bedsit by Paul Rutherford and Holly Johnson, latterly of Frankie Goes To Hollywood. Ironically, Clarke had also made some gainful forays into budgerigar breeding before going to art school, the revenue from which enabled him to buy his first drumkit.

The Spitfire Boys' 'British Refugee' is in prototypical Ramones mode, with a semblance of The Clash's attitude, coalescing with the melodic proclivities of Television for good measure. The band is tight, and Budgie keeps a solid beat with several restrained drumrolls. The overall sound has a rhythm and blues/skiffle orientation, with the guitar playing redolent of Dave Edmunds, a reminder that, for many young bands starting out in the mid to late 1970s, the tendrils of rock 'n' roll were never far away.

The vocal delivery and lyrics are derivative, unimaginative and strained: straight from the book of 'how to sing punk', compelling Budgie to comment 'The singer was completely crap… He wore safety pins and stuff,'[447] and belies aspects of musicality that are at the core of the song.

The rather more incendiary sounding title of the B-side 'Mein Kampf' is more of a thousand-miles-an-hour affair; one minute and 22 seconds of hardcore thrash, again owing its structure and speed to The Ramones. One can clearly hear the influence of Joey Ramone on Budgie's fledgling drumming.

With no deficit of musical heritage emerging from the 1960s, from its most famous sons The Beatles, as well as Gerry and the Pacemakers, Cilla Black, The Searchers, Billy J Kramer and The Hollies, the late 1970s saw a renaissance and resurgence of musical movers and shakers that would dominate the charts in the early 1980s, ploughing their own distinct musical furrow, due in no small part to the punk and post-punk effect with bands the Sex Pistols, The Clash, The Damned, The Ramones and Siouxsie and The Banshees taking to the stage at Eric's.

One such band, Big In Japan, reads like a future who's who of Liverpool musical royalty and was to prove fruitful for Budgie as The Spitfire Boys had ground to a halt after the release of their one and only single. The transience of hopping from band to band as they formed and, more often than not, imploded shortly afterwards, was de rigueur.

Put together by the mercurial and entrepreneurial Bill Drummond, whose initial career was as a theatre scene painter and carpenter, when, while working on a staging of 'The Illuminatus Trilogy'[448] at the Roundhouse in London, he told the crew he was popping out to buy some glue and never returned, Big In Japan's members included, among others during the period 1977 to 1979, Drummond (latterly of The KLF and K Foundation) Jayne Casey (latterly artistic director and member of Pink Military and Pink Industry), Ian Brody (latterly of Lightening Seeds), David Balfe (latterly of The Teardrop Explodes, Echo And The Bunnymen and the subject of Blur's 'Country House'), Holly Johnson (Frankie Goes To Hollywood), Budgie and Clive Langer (latterly record producer, working with Alan Winstanley).

Independent label Zoo Records was formed by Drummond and Balfe to enable the release of records by Big In Japan. 'Brutality, Religion and a Dance Beat' was released on the Eric's[449] label in 1977 as a seven-inch split single, with 'Big In Japan' the A-side and 'Do The Chud' by The Chuddie Nuddies the B-side.

The song 'Big In Japan' is not without parallel to The

Yardbirds' version of 'Train Kept A Rollin' released in 1965; a joyous, anthemic stomp with some East Asian seemingly nonsensical interpolation towards the end of the song. An EP 'From Y to Z and Never Again' was released on Zoo Records in 1978 and included 'Nothing Special', a louche, introspective song, with a vocal not dissimilar to Lena Lovich; 'Cindy and the Barbi Dolls' comes across akin to a novelty song, with a rather helium-effected vocal from Jayne Casey, balanced by the more sombre tones of Ian Brody.

'Suicide a Go' has elements of Tom Verlaine and complex, overlayed guitar playing by Drummond, Brodie and Langer. 'Taxi' emanates its own evocative menace, reminiscent of late-night bars and seedy after-hours clubs, driven by Budgie's echoing drums and Ambrose Reynolds' evocative bass. The band recorded one Peel Session, recorded 12 February 1979 and broadcast on 6 March 1979. The three songs recorded were 'Suicide High Life', 'Don't Bomb China Now' and 'Goodbye'.

Playing in Big In Japan was to prove an affirming musical experience for Budgie, with minor celebrity status and an unofficial residency at Eric's. Budgie's sense that, musically, Liverpool's star was on the ascendent proved prescient with the rise of Elvis Costello, The Teardrop Explodes, Echo And The Bunnymen, Frankie Goes To Hollywood, The Las, Nightmares On Wax, Dead Or Alive and The Mighty Wah. However, it wasn't long before Budgie had set his sights on moving to London, piling his 'rucksack, a cheese plant and… racing bike into the back of a van…'[450]

Budgie played both drums and bass guitar on Clive Langer and the Boxes' EP 'I Want the Whole World', including the tracks 'The Whole World', 'Lovely Evening', 'I Know I', 'Those Days' and 'Simple Life'. All songs on the EP are not readily categorised in terms of genre, but there is the discernible thread of light-touch pop sensibility running through all the songs, almost prog in some places with smatterings of reggae and the added richness of sonic texture through Ben Barson's keyboard playing.

Budgie was gaining experience of working in a bone fide studio and Langer put him in touch with Glen Matlock, as Matlock recalls: 'I met Budgie through Clive Langer. Budgie… turned up in London trying to find something more happening, and there was a guy called Steve Lindsey who ran the studio and was the bass player in Deaf School. The Burning Sounds record that Creation put out, some of the stuff on there comes from the Warner Chappell studio. People were in and out doing different things on other people's stuff. I remember Mick Ronson came down one day and said, "I'm not playing guitar, I'll play drums".'[451]

Rather serendipitously, through Langer's manager, Budgie joined The Slits when original drummer and founder member Palmolive left the band on the cusp of recording their debut album. He recalls, 'My first band was called Spitfire Boys and Paul Rutherford, the singer, would later become the other singer in Frankie Goes To Hollywood with Holly Johnson, who was in my other band, Big In Japan… Paul was a big fan of The Slits, Ariana especially (Ari Up) and we eventually got to do a support slot, opening for The Slits. So, we got to know them; we'd stayed round at Ari's mum's place just off the King's Road… I'd moved down to London, after The Spitfire Boys and I'd hooked up with a manager, Frank Silver was his name. Frank was, unusually, managing a drummer… all he had to manage was me, and my dog. Frank, suddenly, quite unexpectedly, got the job of looking after The Slits. That's how I got the gig.'[452]

Budgie felt he brought some order to the band's more natural habitat of chaotic spontaneity and, Viv Albertine recounts, had 'The right attitude, just because of the company he keeps... He's inventive, has a light touch, is rock-steady and, most important of all, has no problem whatsoever with Ari (Up) giving him extremely detailed instructions about the rhythms, the hi-hat patterns and no cymbal bashing. He's respectful and confident.'[453]

Budgie's playing on 'Cut' is playful, colourful, characterful and solid, complementing the angularity of Viv Albertine's guitar playing and effortlessly in tandem with Tessa Pollitt's driving bass. It is the sound of a band having an absolute blast in the Ridge Hill Farm Studio in Rusper.

Budgie's tenure with The Slits lasted for two years, during which time the band recorded their much-lauded album 'Cut', released on 7 September 1979 on Island Records. Produced by reggae guitarist and bass player Dennis Bovell, who was moonlighting, producing 'Cut' during the day from 1 April 23 April 1979 and travelling into London at night to co-produce Lynton Kwesi Johnson's 'Forces of Victory',[454] considered one of the most important reggae records ever made.

'Cut' is a melding of a plethora of reggae influences and is clearly distant from the punk flock regarding any well-ploughed furrow courtesy of The Clash and The Damned, although The Clash drummer Topper Headon's playing was to prove oracle-like for Budgie, who reflected that 'The Slits were opening for The Clash on the 'Sort It Out' tour. I was side stage every night, watching Topper. Amazing.'[455] Budgie also recounts his early experiences of reggae, 'hearing a lot of Reggae in Britain because of the Jamaican population... so I grew up with Reggae chartbusters with The Upsetters and The Cimarons...'[456]

One can discern Budgie's rhythmic contributions to 'Cut'. He follows the music instinctively and empathetically, adding to its colour and vibrancy and lending it polyrhythmic personality. The absolute joy of the first track on side A, 'Instant Hi', sucks one into a world of the band's tipping-point chaos with its innate feel for the music, rather than technical musical precision.

There is palpable punk sensibility on 'Shoplifting', which has borrowed something of The Clash's DNA; Budgie's studied appreciation of drummer Terry Chimes and, especially, Topper Headon coming to the fore. There is dramatic tension on 'Typical Girls', a foretaste of Budgie's work on 1980's 'Kaleidoscope', adding panoramic, cinemascopic gravitas, and servicing each song so its story can be told.

Ironically, considering Budgie's changes of band allegiance, Paul Morley reviewed 'Cut' at the same time as' Join Hands' on the release of both albums, summarising his thoughts of 'Cut': 'Cut isn't laid back. It's mangled and savage, petty and contradictory: cultured depravity and nursery rhyme gothic pop.'[457]

'Cut' reached number 30 in the UK album charts and the single 'Typical Girls' with the B-side a cover of Marvin Gaye's 'I heard it through the grapevine' peaked at number 60 in the UK singles chart. 'Cut' has received many retrospective plaudits for its originality and influence, with Kurt Cobain listing the song 'Typical' Girls in his top 50 favourite recordings of all time.

In 2004, 'Cut' was voted 58th in The Observer's 100 Greatest British Albums list and it was also included in the book '1001 Albums You Must Hear Before You Die'.[458]

Live footage, filmed by Don Letts,[459] of The Slits playing 'Man Next Door' as part of a festival line-up at Alexandra Palace that included The Pop Group, The Raincoats, Au Pairs and John Cooper Clarke on 15 June 1980 demonstrates Budgie's indomitable immersion in the music; he anchors a joyous performance that is only a hair's breadth away from pandemonium.

Encountering Siouxsie...

While still residing in Liverpool, Julian Cope played Budgie the B-side to 'Hong Kong Garden', 'Voices', in preference to the A-side with, as Cope perceived it, its more commercially attractive elements. What struck Budgie most was the austerity of Kenny Morris's playing; the absence of any drumming pyrotechnics à la Ginger Baker or Keith Moon, although Budgie's playing may lie somewhere between the two, just straightforward, imaginative drumming without the augmentation of a high hat.

After seeing Siouxsie and The Banshees play in Liverpool, Budgie was so enamoured and intrigued by their sound, he fashioned 'a little sculpture of Siouxsie out of modelling wax and wire.'[460]

He reveals that 'The first Spitfire Boys gig was going to be opening for Siouxsie and The Banshees at Eric's. But in those days, you had to get there early and fight your way onto the stage, and we lost.'[461] Siouxsie and The Banshees had lit a small but perhaps not insignificant conflagration for Budgie regarding the synergy of music and high art.

With The Slits' 'Cut' released, rather ironically, on the same day as 'Join Hands', coinciding with the Morris and McKay unceremonious getaway, and thinking that The Slit's gig was over as Budgie had never envisaged drumming with the band as a long-term prospect but identifying that it was his 'first real opportunity to anchor something, to use... drumming to hold all the chaos together.'[462]

Budgie, rather to his incredulity and surprise, after an alleged tip off from the Sex Pistols' Paul Cook, got a phone call from Nils Stevenson, somewhere between the Banshees' tour hinterland hiatus of 7 September and 17 September 1979, asking him to audition for the band he was managing.

Budgie's immediate thought was that Stevenson was

looking after several bands and wanted him to audition for one of them. There was absolutely no way this could be Siouxsie and The Banshees, could it? Surely it was another, lesser band Stevenson had in mind, although the news had broken about the Banshees' having a tour to fulfil. But no, it was an audition for a band he admired, his diminutive modelling wax and wire sculpture of the singer perhaps a serendipitous amulet of sorts?

Budgie's approach to the audition, which took place close to Camden's Music Machine, assumed that the band wouldn't be looking for anything approximating anything else, and he endeavoured to purge himself of everything he had assimilated: 'I tried to forget everything I'd learned and go in as untutored as I could. It was all about having a blank canvas in front of me, musically, and seeing where I could go with it... I used Kenny's old drum kit, which meant it had the Banshees' sound to it.'[463]

Both Sioux and Severin took to Budgie's playing instantly, Sioux recounting, 'We knew he was good straight away.'[464] Finding a guitarist was a different matter entirely, with Sioux's patience on a knife edge and with no attempt to hide her disdain or consternation 'at how many completely crap guitarists there were and how they genuinely thought they were perfect for the band.'[465]

After leaving The Models and in the middle of rehearsals for the short-lived Rema Rema, Marco Pirroni was asked by Nils Stevenson if he wanted to audition for the Banshees. With more than a feeling of 1976 100 Club deja vu, only this time with two albums' worth of songs to learn, Pirroni tried out with Budgie present. A subsequent phone call later the same day from Sioux elicited a thanks but no thanks from both parties.

Budgie 'played through two days of auditioning guitarists,

who mostly seemed to think the Banshees were an offshoot of the Steve Gibbons Band, before they'd conceded to the inevitable and asked Robert Smith of The Cure, already tour support, to stand in with them for the duration.'[466]

Drafting in Smith, despite his admiration for Siouxsie and The Banshees and his offer to do a stint with the band so they could finish the tour, wasn't reservation free, with Sioux recounting, 'At first we thought "He's great but we can't." Then we checked and rechecked with everyone concerned with his band and now we're sure there's not going to be any resentment or worries that we're trying to steal Robert.'[467]

Budgie wasn't entirely sure he had passed the audition as there was no overt acknowledgement but, instead, an 'unspoken assumption.'[468]

With five cancelled gigs after Aberdeen, yet the insubordinate mind set, wilfulness and determination to carry on, Sioux and Severin had found both guitarist and drummer so they could salvage the remainder of the Join Hands tour.

'The pain and the panic of the previous week just melts away.'[469]

The first live outing with new Banshees Budgie and Smith was on 18 September 1979 at the De Montfort Hall in Leicester with the following setlist:

'Poppy Day'
'Playground Twist'
'Regal Zone'
'The Staircase (Mystery)'
'Metal Postcard' (Mittageisen)
'Premature Burial'
'Switch'
'Overground'

'Icon'
'Jigsaw Feeling'
'Mirage'
Hong Kong Garden'
'Suburban Relapse'

Sioux began the gig, 'Swathed in an old mac and pink scarves,'[470] by announcing 'This feels like the first gig we have ever done and that's a good feeling.'[471]

The set comprised 13 songs from the first two albums, with the addition of singles 'The Staircase (Mystery)' and 'Hong Kong Garden'. Considering the lack of time spent putting the new line-up of Siouxsie and The Banshees together, a total of three days in fact, this performance is nothing short of remarkable. Not seamless or faultless by any means, faltering in places, it nonetheless propounds a defiantly strong, creative and resilient band, capable of confounding expectation, especially in tackling some of the newer (even for Sioux and Severin) live airings of complex songs such as the epic 'Premature Burial', which they handled with great flair. 'Jigsaw Feeling' is played with a renewed urgent zeal and, ten songs in, galvanises the band.

NME journalist Kris Needs, reviving his 'Banshees' journalist in residence' role, reviewed the gig and was overwhelmed as 'a full De Montfort Hall accept them with open arms, and in return they are given over an hour of power and passion.'[472]

Describing the gig as 'an Event,'[473] Needs praises the 'same fire and invention with which he (Budgie) saved The Slits on The Clash 'Sort It Out' tour: He's got down Kenny Morris's basic drum patterns, and the parts he considered "boring" have been spiced up with deadly new rolls and accents.'[474]

Needs is equally effusive about the deftness with which

Smith alternates between guitars and the requisite mood of each song, careful to replicate John McKay's phased, flanged and atmospheric guitar tone. There is more attack in Severin's bass playing. The most affirming acclamation is received for 'Siouxsie, still the most compelling of them all… everywhere, skipping, marching, jumping, pumping every morsel of passion into every onstage second — despite a soaking from some pathetic water-tossing bonehead.'[475]

A Perfect Storm Turned Sublime…

After the brief but significant interruption to the band's tour, Sioux felt both vindicated and elated about not suspending the Banshees' activities but, instead, carrying on, for both the sake of the band as well as the loyal fans. De Montfort Hall proved a defining 'phoenix from the ashes' moment for both Sioux and Severin as the tour continued despite almost insuperable odds.

This performance, and the remaining 18 days of the Join Hands tour, represented a newfound cohesion and camaraderie that had been absent when disagreements fragmented the band during the recording of 'Join Hands'. What had appeared to be an inevitable dissipation now had more potential than ever.

For Robert Smith, playing with Siouxsie and The Banshees, especially that first night, proved an empowering experience and led to a complete volte face in his perspective on what kind of music he wanted to make: 'Being a Banshee for the rest of the tour really changed my attitude to what I was doing.'[476]

At a time when he was dealing with the pressure of being the frontman of The Cure, with its emerging mini soap opera culminating in the departure of bass guitarist Michael Dempsey after the final night of the Join Hands tour at the

Hammersmith Odeon, Smith could at least, albeit temporarily, meld into a band and just play the music.

Budgie, perhaps partly due to the 'revolving door' modus operandi he had both witnessed and been a part of in Liverpool, having been in The Spitfire Boys, Big In Japan and The Slits, all within a period of three years, wasn't making any assumptions that his stint with Siouxsie and The Banshees would last any longer than the remainder of the Join Hands tour.

As for Sioux, a culmination of exhaustion, heavy drinking and the de rigueur perversity of being spat at during gigs, had resulted in her contracting hepatitis. By the end of the Join Hands tour, Sioux took a month off to recuperate and begin working on new material, including the songs 'Tenant', 'Drop Dead' and 'Happy House', remarking, 'Despite the illness, I was feeling very inspired, probably because the first time in ages the pressure was off.'[477]

Sioux also reflects, 'I went onstage bright yellow at the end. I didn't know I had it until I went yellow. I thought it was just a cramp. I was supposed to go into hospital, but I didn't. I can't bear hospitals. I was in there for just over a day and I hated it. Some of the people knew who I was... I didn't want them looking into my bedpan. And there was always some vampire lurking, wanting to take samples of your blood.'[478]

John Alexander McGeoch

Born 25 August 1955, Greenock, Inverclyde, there are distinct parallels between the creative trajectories of Budgie and John McGeoch regarding attending art school. In fact, if only for accuracy, by the time John McGeoch joined Siouxsie and The Banshees in 1980, four of the bands' six members had studied Fine Art, including Kenny Morris and John McKay.

It is perhaps no coincidence that the Banshees' third album,

'Kaleidoscope', possesses a cornucopia of multi-layered, rich, aural textures that, as the title suggests, evokes, both through the music and lyrics, an immersive and fascinating wealth of unearthly visual delights.

McGeoch's first electric guitar was bought for £25: a Commodore that he used to play with his first band, the 2d Sparklers, latterly Slugband. McGeoch was the youngest member of the band, playing his first gig when he was 14. Known as Ian by his family and friends, the Scottish Gaelic for John, he and his family moved from Greenock, with its rich industrial heritage including waterpower being used to process imported goods and shipbuilding, to Goodmayes, near Romford in Essex, where the McGeoch family managed an electrical goods store called Trident, residing in the flat above the shop.

McGeoch's early loves were martial arts, reading, creating artworks in an array of media and imbibing the music of bands such as Led Zeppelin and Deep Purple, as well as Rory Gallagher. McGeoch made friends easily and was adept in adapting to new surroundings and situations.

At 16, he enrolled at Redbridge Technical College and started Saturday-morning guitar lessons at Loughton College with Mark Knopfler, who was also an English lecturer there on weekdays. McGeoch undertook a one-year art foundation course at Thurrock College, taking a year out to work as an untrained psychiatric nurse at Goodmayes Psychiatric Hospital before becoming a Fine Art undergraduate student at Manchester Polytechnic in 1975.

The move to Manchester was to prove fruitful for McGeoch in myriad ways. Manchester was on the cusp of becoming a cultural hub; a northern university town engendering a spirit of pioneering experimentation that was to manifest itself over the coming years. The Who, Fleetwood Mac, The Rolling

Stones and David Bowie adorned the stage of Manchester's Free Trade Hall with regularity and punk was about to break in 1976.

McGeoch's experience of art school in the 1970s was not untypical, especially in terms of Fine Art. One would be given a studio space, pointed in the direction of the library and, basically ordered to 'go forth and make art', often with the scantest of directives or project briefs, attested to by Liddy Papageorgiou, a fellow Fine Art student and friend of McGeoch: 'The first day we were all put into this big studio to draw whatever we saw, and most people were drawing a view outside the window or something. Standing right in front of me was John, so I decided to draw him from the back.'[479]

McGeoch struck up a friendship with Malcolm Garrett, a graphic design student who had also started at Manchester Polytechnic in 1975. Garrett went on to design record sleeves for, among others, Duran, Buzzcocks and Simple Minds. Garrett played McGeoch Buzzcocks' 'Spiral Scratch', which elicited from him an initial... "It's fuckin' rubbish"[480] to a more subsequently receptive "Actually it's quite good,"[481] realising that this wasn't about the studied, technical virtuosity heard in the work of Ritchie Blackmore or Carlos Santana, but was more instinctive or attitude laden, something McGeoch understood through his fine art forays, 'He'd just get his paints and dive in and paint, experiment with shapes, materials and marks that he made in the most genius way.'[482]

McGeoch was approaching music the same way he was approaching making art, with the same spirit of experimentation: a tape loop here, an all-day improvisational jam session there, with his friend Ciaran Harte, by all accounts an accomplished and rather brilliant guitarist, who recalls that, 'I was in Manchester from October '75 to June '76 and that was when we would do our jamming. I was into tape recorders at that point, so I would set up my Sony TC-377, we'd rig that through his hi-fi system in his flat, get drunk and just leave in on echo as we played.'[483] However, McGeoch was resolute in wishing to focus on his Fine Art degree so his other talents would remain latent, at least for the time being.

On 4 June 1976, The Sex Pistols played at Manchester's Lesser Free Trade Hall, a gig set up by Buzzcocks Howard Devoto and Pete Shelley. It is a date that has gone down in history as it lit the touch paper for a plethora of Mancunian post-punk and new wave bands, among them Joy Division, The Smiths and The Druitti Column.

By 1976, McGeoch was endeavouring to see as many bands as possible, developing a voracious appetite for whatever bands he could see playing the various Manchester pubs and clubs. The city was becoming an exciting, vibrant melting pot of musical genres, which also facilitated the growth and flourishing of cultural diversity, bringing 'white punks together with their black counterparts, largely first or second-generation sons and daughters of immigrants from the West Indies.'[484]

As was the case in other major cities such as Birmingham and London, reggae and dub were becoming massive, both in terms of live performance and also in illicit clubs, many of which operated beyond midnight until 5am or so, that were springing up all over Manchester, replete with sound systems.

Originally established in Kingston, Jamaica in the 1950s, these were souped-up, customized, amplified mobile systems with low, rumbling, immersive bass. McGeoch loved the experience of being in these clubs: the beat, the rhythm and the feeling that, wherever he went, friendship could be found.

McGeoch saw The Clash, The Jam, The Ramones and Buzzcocks play The Electric Circus in the Collyhurst area of Manchester, all of which would have played a role of the development of his musical psyche, but perhaps there is one gig, which took place on 13 April 1978, unbeknownst to McGeoch at the time, that would prove to be the most significant, as friend Dave Atherton recalls in Rory Sullivan Burke's biography of McGeoch: 'John and I saw Siouxsie and The Banshees at Rafters and I remember him talking to Siouxsie after the show.'[485]

'The guy I share a house with can play all the guitar parts to Marquee Moon.'[486] Malcolm Garrett.

Through stealth and no little guile, so John McGeoch could meet Howard Devoto who was toying with the idea of putting a band together, housemate Malcolm Garrett invited Devoto to a party at their flat in March 1977. Devoto knew that he didn't want anything resembling punk, instead being after something more nuanced, 'as indicated by the advert I placed for musicians "to play fast and slow music".'[487]

This ad was placed in the window of the Virgin record store and garnered interest very quickly, so much so that it was snatched, conceivably as a piece of Devoto memorabilia. If this was Garrett's game plan, it worked; McGeoch and Devoto hit it off and, soon after, Magazine was inaugurated. One of the advert responses was from Stockport Art College graphic design student and novice bass guitarist Barry Adamason, who had acquired a bass guitar that he had yet to equip with a full set of strings.

Devoto's advert provided the necessary spur and impetus for him to do so. Local drummer Martin Jackson, who had been in a band called The Freshies with Chris Sievey, latterly Frank Sidebottom, and Billy Duffy, latterly of 'The Cult', also replied, and by August 1977, armed with songs 'The Light Pours Out Of Me' and 'Shot By Both Sides', the full band, with the addition of keyboard player Bob Dickinson who had worked with 'Cabaret Voltaire', went into full rehearsal mode.

Having sent demos to several record companies, the band were signed to Virgin Records, courtesy of Simon Draper, managing director and head of A&R, due in part to the growing reputation of Buzzcocks and an awareness of the songwriting talents of Howard Devoto and Pete Shelley. Draper was also drawn to what he perceived as a band that were more thoughtful and cerebral, and most certainly easier to deal with than Sex Pistols.

Magazine's first gig was at the Electric Circus, a two-day swan song for the venue on 1 October and 2 October 1977, as it was on the cusp of closure. Other bands on the bill were Buzzcocks, The Fall, Warsaw (later Joy Division), John Cooper Clarke, The Worst, The Negatives, Steel Pulse and The Drones.

Sounds journalist Jon Savage described Magazine thus: 'Immediately, they're more musical than the other bands so far, capable of different textures — the sound isn't as clear or as confident as on the demo tapes, but this is understandable, and more than complemented by the visual presence of the band. Still the centre of attention is Devoto: on stage he's a curious, compelling performer, awkward yet graceful, commanding yet ambiguous.'[488] The band's second gig was at Rafters on 28 October.

The band's first release on 20 January 1978 was the single 'Shot By Both Sides', written by Pete Shelley and Howard Devoto. The B-side, 'My Mind Ain't So Open', was written by McGeoch and Devoto. 'Shot By Both Sides' reached number 41 in the UK singles charts and the band made their Top Of The Pops debut on Thursday 16 February 1978, an appearance noticeable for the song being lopped in half, robbing the viewers and listeners of John McGeoch's majestic guitar solo, which was an undeniable high point of the song.

'Shot By Both Sides' showcases McGeoch's versatility and

range as a guitarist, adept in playing both rhythm and lead. The song itself is nothing short of a masterpiece and was lauded by guitarist Johnny Marr as one of his favourite songs of all time. It clearly has some Buzzcocks DNA and a smattering of Television, plus the pop sensibilities of Blondie, although it is essentially powered by originality, partly attributable to McGeoch's virtuosity, whose searing guitar parts drive the song's four minutes and four seconds of melodrama.

'That's why it's called 'Real Life'. There's not many albums that deal with the same concerns... Lou Reed's 'Berlin' does. It deals with things that no-one else does.'[489] Howard Devoto.

Magazine's debut album 'Real Life', produced by John Leckie (Be Bop Deluxe and XTC), was recorded between March and April 1978. McGeoch was endeavouring to balance his musical commitments and his Fine Art degree, so stints at Ridge Farm Studio in Surrey were intermittent, with McGeoch calling in to record the guitar parts and travelling back to Manchester to complete paintings for his final show.

The album's 'seminal' credentials are due in no small part to how unlike punk it sounds, as though fashioned from an entirely different, otherworldly aesthetic, aided and abetted by Dave Formula's keyboards (Formula replaced Bob Dickinson before the album was recorded) adding mood, atmosphere and texture to the album, evocative of parts of David Bowie's 'Low' or 'Heroes', and kickstarted by the first track, 'Definitive Gaze'.

Devoto's fast and slow music request bore the fruit he desired; the blistering tempo of 'Recoil' dutifully fulfilling the latter, with McGeoch releasing his inner guitar hero. Fuelled by an incendiary drumbeat and Formula's ARP Odyssey oscillating synthesizer, this is less than three minutes of gonzoid, dextrous experimentation; imagine the bastard son of Motörhead and Emerson, Lake and Palmer with an added smattering of Tom Verlaine's vocals and one has an idea of the unabashed nature of the song.

'The Light Pours Out Of Me' is epic in its sonic vision; another Magazine song driven by Martin Jackson's solid drumbeat and John McGeoch's Glitter Band riff. The album's finale, 'Parade', is a gorgeous Jaques Brel-like, understated lament, with a layer of wanton smouldering added by the brief but beautiful saxophone solo provided by McGeoch. Devoto's lyrics and vocal delivery, the latter a cross between Scott Walker and Jaques Brel, denote both the erudite and articulate, informed and enriched by an array of literary sources, while also embracing aspects of twilight Soho sleaze.

There is a sense that 'Real Life' confounded critics, especially after the kerfuffle caused by 'Spiral Scratch'. Sceptics felt that this was less a cohesive band and more a vehicle for Devoto's vision and ideas. However, there was no doubting the musicality and ambition of the album, as described by Jon Savage's review of 'Real Life', which appeared in Sounds on 3 June 1978, where he finds the album more than a little JG Ballard-like and Orwellian with 'its subtle air of irony, menace and paranoia. Quietly disorientating — things are not as they seem.'[490]

It is conceivable that the title of the album alludes to the great escape and solace to be found in art, creating one's own reality, while also holding up a mirror to a world in a state of unnerving flux, the embodiment of which is the record sleeve, a striking monotype of four disembodied, floating, angular faces emerging from the textural blackness, evocative of aspects of German Expressionism and the mask-like faces in Picasso's 'Les demoiselles d'Avignon'.[491]

The album cover was designed by the artist Linder Sterling who had studied graphic design at Manchester Polytechnic from 1974 to 1977. Linder had also designed the photomontage cover for Buzzcocks' 'Orgasm Addict' single, released on 4 November 1977. Much of Sterling's early work was influenced by Hannah Hoch (1889–1978), a pioneer of politically oriented montage and photomontage.

For Savage, 'Real Life' reflects a sort of dystopian inverse universe, with its inhabitants having anything but fun. 'Parade' begins with cocktail piano by Dave Formula, played nonchalantly to an empty lounge, with Devoto leaning on the piano, very weary: 'They will show me what I want to see...' Winston Smith after Room 101.'[492] 'Motorcade' also conjures visceral playbacks of Abraham Zapruder's[493] silent 8mm colour film capturing the assassination of John F Kennedy on 8 November 1963 prophesying, exposing and amplifying the perpetually unfurling series of unpalatable international news events being played out in living room televisions on a daily basis.

In 1978, among other events: 'The former Italian prime minister Aldo Moro was kidnapped and murdered by the Red Brigades; Pope John Paul I, head of the Roman Catholic church for just over a month, died, and Carl Bridgewater, a 13-year-old paper boy, was shot dead after disturbing a burglary in Staffordshire. Georgi Markov, a Bulgarian dissident, was murdered in London with an umbrella that carried a poison pellet. In Jonestown, Guyana, 918 people died in a mass suicide.'[494]

This was the same year that 'The musical world said goodbye to Keith Moon, Jacques Brel, and — most notoriously of all — Nancy Spungen, who was stabbed to death in the Chelsea hotel in New York by Sid Vicious of the Sex Pistols.'[495]

Savage also discerns the eye of the artist in Devoto's observational lyrics; always playing the role of the outsider looking in, enabling him to 'perceive the strangeness and 'otherworldliness' in everyday life, to see things and people in a different way through isolation…'[496]

Regarding the musicianship, Savage comments: 'Any doubts about the band's playing are resolved convincingly. Devoto's singing is less forced, less scratchy than it's been known to be, and more relaxed (especially on the superb 'My Tulpa' overdubs). The bass and keyboards (Barry Adamson and Dave Formula) are near faultless throughout, the former providing the essential humanising ingredient of flexibility and spunk, the latter creating whatever sound pictures are necessary to complement Devoto's lyrics. Martin Jackson's drumming is rock solid (the opening to 'Recoil') but sometimes follows the beat rather than drives it, making the lavishness of the music dangerously top heavy. And occasionally John McGeoch's guitar solos tread near heavy metal clichés, although his choice of tone is impeccable throughout, especially on the otherwise undistinguished 'Burst'…'[497]

'Real Life' peaked at number 29 in the UK album charts. It featured in Robert Dimery's book '1001 Albums To Hear Before You Die'[498] and was ranked 37 in Uncut's '100 Greatest Debut Albums'[499] in August 2006.

There were two non-album singles released in 1978: 'Touch And Go', released on 14 April 1978, the B-side of which was a rendition of 'Goldfinger' (not for the first time named in this book), composed by John Barry, Leslie Bricusse and Anthony Newley. 'Give Me Everything' with Captain Beefheart's 'I Love You Big Dummy' was released 17 November 1978.

Magazine played a total of 46 dates in 1978, 32 of which were between July and December, after the June release of 'Real Life', including gigs in Paris, Amsterdam, Belgium (supporting Patti Smith) and Vienna. Much of the coverage of the UK gigs seems to centre around Devoto, whether alluding to his hairline, self-consciousness as a performer or proficiency as a vocalist. Pete Silverton's 100 Club gig review is a case in point: '… he (Devoto) seemed all too conscious that great things were expected of him, that the eyes of a small, elite world were beaming hard on him. So he tried too hard and ended up looking like a subdued but equally self-obsessed Stiv Bators.'[500]

Little or nothing is written about the rest of the band's musicianship or the songs themselves. Ian Penman's NME Lyceum London review is similarly Devoto focused: '… Devoto is the first performer to effectively mirror my ever-present sense of doubt apropos rock music in the live arena (emphasis on viewing), rock musicians in the PR stocks (exchange of versions), and rock criticism…'[501] portraying Devoto as a sort of anti-vocalist's vocalist; a meta version of himself. Again, the band, including McGeoch, scarcely get a look in.

No sooner had the 1978 tour ended than the band started recording what was to become 'Secondhand Daylight', in January 1979. Produced by Colin Thurston, who had co-engineered David Bowie's 'Heroes' in 1977 and Iggy Pop's 'Lust For Life', also released in 1977, 'Secondhand Daylight' signals further movement away from punk. The album has more overt keyboard presence, a foretaste, perhaps, of the ensuing renaissance of the synthesizer, which would have greater prominence in many 1980s' bands, crossing the bridge between New Wave and New Romanticism.

There is a distinctive introspection to the album, not least the Malcolm Garrett-designed album cover denoting an apocalyptic hinterland, the centrepiece of which is a decapitated head on a wooden stake. The title itself suggests a world retreating into itself; a life lived through the diffusion of nicotine-stained net curtains and the desensitisation of the cathode ray, evidenced from the beginning of the first track on side A 'Feed The Enemy', with a soundalike smattering of the Beach Boys' bittersweet 'God Only Knows' from the celebrated 'Pet Sounds'[502] album, bringing the listener into a world of introspection with Devoto's opening lyric 'It's always raining, over the border.'[503]

Sonically, it does have parallels with 'Low'-era David Bowie regarding the use of swirling synthesizer and the deployment of McGeoch's saxophone. 'The Thin Air' could have come straight from Hansa Tonstudio.[504]

Ostensibly, this is an album of maturity and musicality; not a million miles away from the 1970s German bands Neu and Can beloved of Bowie and, indeed, Siouxsie and The Banshees' Steve Severin. The album peaked at 38 on the UK album charts, below par and the band's expectation when compared with 'Real Life'.

There was a sense that previous devotees, including journalists, expectant of something in closer to Buzzcocks territory, may have felt they were being given short shrift, as the band's musical arc moved tangentially further away from the ten minutes and ten seconds' aural dynamite of 'Spiral Scratch'; instead, it is more of an unashamed and unembarrassed experimental coalition, the result of which defies compartmentalisation or categorisation.

Writing in Uncut in November 2000, Paul Morley reflects that: 'Their second album, 'Secondhand Daylight', came extravagantly wrapped in a non-punk, non-new wave, non-minimal, over glossy gatefold sleeve, and that combined with an instrumental track and keyboard-heavy production led to a suspicious response.'[505]

McGeoch's guitar parts are discernible but take more of a back seat compared to 'Real Life', except for the final track on side B, 'Permafrost', where McGeoch's guitar drives the song with menace, first in the background with all the attack of Steve Jones playing on 'Nevermind The Bollocks' and subsequently the flanged, phased wail as the song progresses, matching the dark tenor of Devoto's sinister lyrical refrain 'I will drug you and fuck you, On the permafrost.'[506]

Nick Kent critiqued 'Secondhand Daylight' favourably as a coming of age for Magazine, proffering, '... where previously there was half-realised potential, there is now an austere sense of authority to the music. This becomes clear from the first bars of 'Feed The Enemy'. These are very Low-period Bowiesque, right down to the stray saxophone bleats and lulling synthesiser chords, both of which are sublimated into the dank neo-Gothic sound to which Magazine seem so partial (the same ingredients precede the first moments of the second side as well).'[507]

Despite what 'Secondhand Daylight' lacked in terms of commercial sales, and McGeoch's dissatisfaction with the album, the band embarked on a 40-date international tour of the UK, Europe and North America, beginning at Malvern Winter Gardens on 16 April and ending at the Commodore Ballroom in Vancouver. The band also played venues in Austin in Texas, Los Angeles, San Fransisco, Seattle, Washington and New York. There were also gigs in Brussels and Paris.

John McGeoch's last hurrah with Magazine was playing on the band's third album 'The Correct Use Of Soap', released in May 1980, which was to prove something of a volte face for McGeoch, with '... a collective push to give John more space to express himself than on Secondhand Daylight ...'[508] and 'There was a definite feeling that we needed more guitar, it needed to be featured more. So, we went into it with that idea.'[509]

Despite the reinvigorated and distinctly upbeat strains of 'The Correct Use Of Soap', there were tensions emerging within the band, with McGeoch feeling that he was giving his all and that his desire to press ahead with taking the band to what he felt were stratospheric creative heights was not reflected by Devoto, whose concerns were becoming focused on the band's financial constraints. This ultimately '… would signify the beginning of the end, the end of a viable working relationship and also, eventually, the end of Magazine.'[510]

The album was produced by Martin Hannett who had worked on Joy Division's 'Unknown Pleasures'[511] a year previously, as well as producing The Druitti Column and John Cooper Clarke. Whether or not McGeoch's contributions are more to the fore on 'The Correct Use Of Soap' or otherwise is immaterial. His aim was never to showboat, but to be an integral part of a great band.

The attention Devoto was garnering was becoming a distraction from the band as a collective, especially as Devoto was not the easiest of interviewees, often challenging journalists whose response to this tended to be less than favourable, as if to say 'You're the musicians, play the music, and who the fuck does Howard think he is with all the Dostoyevsky quotes? That's our job.'[512]

'The Correct Use Of Soap' was McGeoch's favourite Magazine album, as it was, it transpires, for the majority of the band. Johnny Marr reflected that: 'I understand that not all members of Magazine are happy with 'The Correct Use Of Soap' but I think it's a work of genius. If you're a music freak, as I was at 17 with my girlfriend, and one of your favourite bands puts that out and it really delivers every song, both musically and lyrically, you really appreciate it. It sounded like nothing else.'[513]

'The Correct Use Of Soap' peaked at 28 in the UK charts and the band released one non-album single in March 1980, a cover of Sly Stone's 'Thank You (Falettinme Be Mice Elf Agin)', with the B-side 'The Book'.

Reflecting the eclecticism of musical styles and genres emerging during the tail end of the 1970s and into the early

1980s, coupled with a high love of clubbing, McGeoch encountered Rusty Egan (formerly Rich Kids and Skids), who was DJing at the Blitz Club[514] in 1979, while McGeoch was still a member of Magazine.

Egan had been 'Blown away'[515] by 'Shot By Both Sides' and hatched the idea for a band that would be led by Egan and Midge Ure (formerly Rich Kids; latterly Ultravox vocalist and guitarist). The initial incarnation of Visage included three Magazine members: McGeoch, keyboard player Dave Formula and bass guitarist Barry Adamson, as well as Ultravox keyboard, violin and viola player Billy Currie.

McGeoch recorded one album with the band, the self-titled 'Visage', released in 1980 on Polydor Records. The album reached 13 in the UK album charts and number one in the German charts. Four singles were released from the album: 'Tar', released on 2 November 1979; 'Fade To Grey', released on 14 November 1980; 'Mind Of A Toy', released on 6 March 1981, and 'Visage', released on 3 July 1981. Visage gave McGeoch the opportunity to extend his musical range and, even though it wasn't ever going to be a permanent arrangement, it proved a welcome sojourn.

Getting The Band Back Together — 'Happy House'
Holding out for the best fit for Siouxsie and The Banshees would prove profitable for Sioux and Severin, Steve Severin recollects in Mark Paytress' biography: 'I'd seen John McGeoch on TV playing with Magazine and was really impressed. They were doing 'The Light Pours Out Of Me', and while I was a massive fan of the band's stuff, I thought his guitar playing was wonderful, very inventive.'[516]

This was around the same time that McGeoch was moonlighting from Magazine to play in Visage. It was not the only side project that the guitarist was involved in as McGeoch was also one of the additional players, along with ex-Sex Pistol Steve Jones, ex-Clash drummer Terry Chimes and ex-Rich Kids' Steve New, to appear on Generation X's 'Kiss Me Deadly', released on 23 January 1981.

McGeoch plays on eight of the album's ten tracks, stretching out, experimenting with an array of sounds and ways of playing, adding light, shade and texture, especially on 'Heaven's Inside', 'Stars Look Down' and 'What Do You Want', giving the songs a sense of the epic and raising the bar beyond straightforward power chords and thrash.

McGeoch remembers, 'Like everybody, I thought 'Hong Kong Garden' was a stunning song, and I'd seen the Banshees several times. I was surprised when I got the call, but I said "Okay." Steve Strange told me to wear black — though Budgie was a bit shy in those days — and invited me along to their rehearsal studio in Camden. Within two days, we'd routined 'Happy House'.[517]

'McGeoch was a better guitarist... Before they were really good, but now they were professional.'[518] Ray Stevenson.

When McGeoch was introduced to the rest of the band at the Camden recording studio, he arrived with a copy of 'The Correct Use Of Soap', proudly showing the Malcolm Garrett-designed album cover and, with regard to the music, 'A Song From Under The Floorboards' with its use of 'picking' the strings instead of strumming: the direction he wanted to head in as a guitarist.

This was to prove perfect for 'Happy House', which was being used as the Banshees' 'audition song' to ascertain how guitarists would approach it. McGeoch recalls the band being keen on the 'guitar top line'[519] but McGeoch didn't see it as a single.

Sioux and Severin weren't entirely sure if the band was going to be a set cohesive group of personnel, and there was some discussion about bringing in different musicians for recording subsequent albums.

Steve Jones recorded three tracks with the band for 'Kaleidoscope': 'Clockface', 'Paradise Place' and 'Skin'. Jones acknowledges his contribution to 'Kaleidoscope' in his 2016 biography 'Lonely Boy: Tales from a Sex Pistol': 'I hadn't paid that much attention when Siouxsie played her first gig at the 100 Club with Vicious drumming, because they were shit. But I appreciated the way she looked — she really went for it — and she obviously had some talent because the Banshees turned into a decent band in the end... 'Hong Kong Garden' is still a pretty cool tune — they probably have a blue plaque outside the Chinese takeaway that was about — and I played on a few tracks on 'Kaleidoscope', their album where the writing goes round in a circle on the back sleeve.'[520]

Around the time of recording 'Kaleidoscope', there was talk of employing the services of Pink Floyd 'Relics'[521] producer Hurricane Smith to produce the first single, as well as the possibility of covering 'Arnold Layne'. Sioux and Severin had been listening a lot to 'Relics', as well as The Rolling Stones' Their Satanic Majesties Request'.[522]

Bowie producer Tony Visconti was also in the frame, although this was jeopardised when Severin, attending a party at Visconti's Good Earth Studios in Dean Street, Soho, decided to steal the tape of the American version of David Bowie's 'John, I'm Only Dancing' as it was almost impossible to obtain a copy in the UK. Severin's zeal to acquire the song resulted in a portion of the equipment being taken with it, so Visconti was, by this point, unlikely to want anything to do with the Banshees.

In the end, the band went with The Police producer Nigel Gray, who had collaborated with the band on the first two albums 'Outlandos d'Amour' (1978) and 'Regatta de Blanc'

(1979). The demo for 'Happy House' was recorded on 16 January 1980 at Polydor Studios and the single was recorded on 23 February 1980 at Phil Manzanera's Gallery Studio in Chertsey in Surrey, but it was beset with technical problems so was subsequently recorded and mixed at Nigel Gray's Surrey Sound Studios in Leatherhead on 4, 5 and 7 February, where the majority of tracks on 'Kaleidoscope' were subsequently recorded.

The single 'Happy House' was also the chance for Sioux to exorcise a few demons, with the B-side, 'Drop Dead/ Celebration', a direct attack on the two previous members of the band Kenny Morris and John McKay. Billy Chainsaw recalls: 'The B-side 'Drop Dead' was aimed at John and Kenny. I remember Sioux and Severin adapting some stupid nursery rhyme and carving it in the run-out groove: "Bye Blackheads"! It was like "Fuck You!" They proved they didn't fuckin' need them.'[523] A rather more friendly message appears in the A-side run-out groove of 'Hello Budgie'.

Recorded between January and May 1980, 'Kaleidoscope' reflects a veritable revolution in the Banshees' camp. Reflecting the seriousness which the nucleus of Sioux and Severin were taking with the 'new' Banshees, they started to write at Chappell of Bond Street; a demarcation between their professional lives and social lives, culminating in renewed and reinvigorated confidence in songwriting due largely to the addition of two capable new band members.

John McGeoch played his last gig with Magazine at the 'Festival Of Fools' on 8 June 1980, by which time he had already played six gigs with Siouxsie and The Banshees between 21 March and 28 March, to support the release of 'Happy House', as well as three low-key gigs under the band's pseudonym 'Janet And The Icebergs' on 9,10 and 11 September, which afforded the band an opportunity to try several new songs live, including 'Happy House', 'Tenant', 'Paradise Place', 'Skin' and 'Eve White/Eve Black'.

The Banshees also played the two-day Futurama Festival at the Queen's Hall in Leeds, which was John McGeoch's '... official live debut as a full time Banshee...'[524] on Saturday 13 September, among a bill which included Soft Cell, U2, Clock DVA and Echo And The Bunnymen.

"Happy House', with its nagging riff and liquid guitar, was great pop as well, everything moving together to form its own distinctive sound and tension.'[525] Paolo Hewitt.

Musically, 'Happy House' represents quite an experimental departure for the band. The song still reflects the band's skill in understanding the 'negative' space between the notes but, with the addition of Budgie and John McGeoch, there seems to be more scope for experimentation and layering.

'Happy House' is driven by the polyrhythmic drumming of Budgie, and the effective, pounding bass of Severin. McGeoch demonstrates maestro-like versatility with regard to picking and playing chords, lending the song its air of cinematic menace. There is also the addition of harmonica, played by Budgie. 'Happy House' is more than reflective of Sioux and Severin's fascination with the macabre, lending the song an otherness that keeps it deliciously out of step with the pop charts, despite its increasing eclecticism.

Clearly determined to dust the cobwebs off incarnations past, the video for 'Happy House' enlisted the services of director Piers Bedford, instead of Clive Richardson. Filmed on 15–16 March 1980, the video is both promo and historical document in terms of the absence of McGeoch, not as yet signed to Polydor, and shows the band ostensibly as a three piece, despite McGeoch's playing on the single.

The video is stripped to its bare essentials: Sioux, Severin and Budgie in a Giorgio de Chirico-meets-Alice In Wonderland interior, with Sioux dressed as a harlequin or *saltimbanque* as painted by Picasso in the early 20th century. Sioux knows her role is to entertain so adopts the persona adeptly.

The distorted perspective of the room's interior is reflective of Sioux's lyrics, intended to be an acerbic observation about media portrayal of the perfect family 'It is sarcastic. In a way, like television, all the media, it is like adverts, the perfect family, whereas it is more common that husbands beat their wives. They are mental families really, but the projection is everyone smiling, blond hair, sunshine, eating butter without being fat and everyone perfect.'[526]

The video starts with Sioux looking through the distorted window, a casual voyeur as the trio appear one by one in the room. First Severin, then Budgie and finally Sioux. The video direction and the band's involvement in the video is not ostentatious and not entirely without humour, as Budgie sits in the corner playing a child's tin drum at one point during the song, and Sioux, in the absence of a guitarist, also sits on the floor strumming a ukulele.

As the song approaches its climax, Sioux, Severin and Budgie mime the chorus to 'Happy House' together under two multicoloured umbrellas. The artwork for the sleeve of 'Happy House' was designed by Polydor in-house designer Rob O'Connor. When asked why the image only contains a solo shot of Sioux, O'Connor remarked, 'It was one of a handful of ideas that I put forward. The solo shot of Siouxsie had a deranged look about it and seemed to suit the feeling of incarceration. I don't remember the other members of the band having a problem with the cover. The only single format was 7" vinyl and a group shot wouldn't have had the same impact. Usually, we would avoid having any shot of the band anyway... this one slipped through.'[527] O'Connor also mentions that 'One of the objectives was to avoid the sleeves looking like so many other 'post-punk' sleeves of the time.'[528]

The band's Top Of The Pops performance on 10 April 1980 sees them as a four piece, with McGeoch taking up guitar duties, albeit mimed, with the band, who look nonchalant and super cool, Sioux cracking a smile as she throws handfuls of confetti from her jacket pocket into the air on the cue of the second 'Fun' of the lyric.

Both Severin and McGeoch, flanking Sioux, bounce and move with zeal. The final refrain of the song sees Sioux, Severin and McGeoch gather around Sioux's microphone to mime the remainder of the lyric.

Budgie wields two timpani mallets as he mimes the drumming. Somehow, despite the artificiality of the situation, Siouxsie and The Banshees rise to the occasion, looking for all intents and purposes like they are not only stars but stars from the future, dress code: jackets required.

The band also performed as a three piece on the Netherlands' Top Of The Pops equivalent 'Top Pop',[529] with Sioux miming with the aid of a Gibson-looking Les Paul electric guitar. 'Happy House' peaked at 17 on the UK singles chart.

'Christine'

'I demoed 'Christine'… using a drum machine and bass. The piano element was me tinkering with ideas for a melody.'[530] Steve Severin.

'Christine' was the second single the band released, from what was to become 'Kaleidoscope', on 30 May 1980, with the B-side 'Eve White/Eve Black'. The song, Sioux said, is 'about Christine Sizemore… She's got twenty-two personalities! She don't know who to play with!'[531]

BothChristin andEve White/Eve Black' were 'inspired by a book called The Three Faces Of Eve,[532] about Christine

192

Sizemore, who boasted 22 personalities, each with different names like the Strawberry Girl and Banana-Split Lady.[533] One of the reasons Sioux was fascinated by Sizemore was because of 'the traumas she'd been through as a child. She witnessed many violent acts.'[534]

Sonically, 'Christine' reflects further experimental forays, not least because the guitar part is all acoustic. The drama of the song is immediate, introduced by a single acoustic guitar chord, then building with the snap of Budgie's metronomic snare strikes. The addition of Sioux's low vocal subsumes the listener into an unlit world of subterranean jeopardy.

The Banshees could always tell a good story but 'Christine', through the stealthy, skillful playing of Budgie and McGeoch, add further light and shade. Severin's bass playing leads and underpins the ominous texture of the song through the adoption of chords and could be said to lead the narrative.

The bridge of the song offers temporary respite and relief from the maelstrom, driven with urgency by McGeoch's expeditious playing during the chorus. The addition of Farfisa organ, played by McGeoch, furnishes 'Christine' with a sense of the supernatural.

The song's expedience is its undoubted strength and again demonstrates how Siouxsie and The Banshees have an absolutely innate understanding and genius about letting the music breathe.

For the promo video, filmed in June 1980, the band returned to director Clive Richardson. Sioux appears again with two rather than three Banshees, denoting the absence of McGeoch, with mimed acoustic guitar duties incumbent on Sioux, dressed in yellow and red colours that match the lyrics of the song — the 'Strawberry Girl' and 'Banana Split Lady' — with the slightly incongruous addition of a Scala hat covered in Budweiser motifs.

Budgie, looking a little more at ease than in the video for 'Happy House', is dressed in an unbuttoned military jacket while Severin opts for a unbuttoned patterned shirt and black jeans. The video adopts a myriad different effects, one of which is the colossal face of Sioux behind the band's backdrop of silhouetted Venetian blind, a motif also used on the 'Kaleidoscope' album sleeve, reflected in the highly polished black studio floor.

Richardson adopts numerous visually disorienting devices including the juxtaposition of band members, using colour negatives and filters and disconcerting camera angles. It is another video reflecting the band's acute understanding of the purpose of the pop promo as a medium that synergises the audio with the visual, and never settling for less than immaculate production values.

The Rob O'Connor-designed single sleeve was, he describes, '...a simple 'trick' photograph really, shot and assembled in an early 20th-century European kind of way. It's a single girl, cast from a model agency, shot in two positions and composited in the darkroom (no computers then). The look of the sleeve conveyed the band's interest in German film and photography. The hand-painted type and purple turtles hopefully added a sense of personality and naivety.'[535] 'Christine' peaked at 22 in the UK singles chart, the band's second-highest charting single after 'Hong Kong Garden'.

The B-side, 'Eve White/Eve Black', also centred around the story of Christine Sizemore, is an instrumental, a compositional triptych utilising both bass guitar and keyboard, conceivably a Fender Rhodes piano, which, exactly a minute into the song, is overtaken by the unexpected incongruity of looped analogue white noise, the calm replaced by the storm, before returning to the bass and keyboard again, more ominously haunting than before.

'Whereas 'Christine' relates to the entire 22 personalities that had emerged during her life (so far), 'Eve White/Eve Black' is representative of a confrontation between the two major personalities known to the doctor who initially made her case famous (though she remained unknown), and around which the film 'The Three Face Of Eve' was based, and of the battle for possession of Christine's body.[536]

Chapter 7
'Kaleidoscope'

K aleidoscope: 'an optical device consisting of mirrors that reflect images of bits of coloured glass in a symmetrical geometric design through a viewer. The name kaleidoscope comes from three Greek words 'kalos' meaning beautiful, 'eidos' meaning form and 'scopos' meaning watcher.'[537]

'Kaleidoscope' was released on 1 August 1980.

'We chose Kaleidoscope as a title as we were discovering that we had a lot of sides to ourselves and because we were multifaceted in our approach to making the album.'[538] Siouxsie Sioux.

There is no doubt about the elevated level of musicality the playing of Budgie and John McGeoch added to Siouxsie and The Banshees and, while neither would ever quite have complete autonomy — this was the established role of Sioux and Severin — they would definitely be able to have a degree of creative input, as Severin recalls when discussing McGeoch's role with Mark Paytress: 'He wasn't going to be able to run anything, but he would be able to interpret the ideas we had, which was a role he was comfortable with. He knew it was the right thing for him to do.'[539]

Comprising 11 tracks, 'Kaleidoscope' takes the band into a whole other sonic realm. The cohesion of the album replaces the schismatic unevenness of 'Join Hands', embracing a whole realm of possibilities afforded by two new, incredibly proficient and creative musicians. Opening with the haunting strains of

'Happy House', it was an incredibly assured and confident statement of intent, perhaps addressing and exorcising the ghosts of Banshees past, while embodying all constituent elements of tension, menace and phantasmagorical aberration the band were striving for.

'Tenant'

Looped feedback accompanied by furtive hi-hat and bass drum leads the way into 'Tenant', with phased bass guitar, this time played by Budgie, reflecting the mood of experimentation in the Banshees' camp. Sioux plays both acoustic and electric guitar on 'Tenant' and Severin plays electric sitar. Overlayed with the distant strains of acoustic guitar, Sioux's vocal moves, snake like, through the song. 'Tenant' was apparently inspired by the 1976 horror film 'The Tenant',[540] directed by Roman Polanski and based on the 1964 book of the same name by author Roland Topor, the synopsis of which centres around Trelkovsky, who rents an apartment in Paris where the previous inhabitant attempted to commit suicide.

Trelkovsky's increasingly strained relationships with his neighbours, who choose to complain about him, coupled with the discovery of a human tooth in a hole in the apartment wall, as well as his home being robbed, all contribute to his degenerating and delirious hallucinatory mental state, culminating in him waking up one morning after a night of feverish dreams. Realising his face has been made up and, after buying a wig and women's shoes and putting on a dress belonging to the previous tenant Simone Shoule, which he has found in a cupboard, Trelovsky proceeds to throw himself out of the window in exactly the same way Shoule had previously. The mood of the song reflects the unravelling, spiralling mental state of Trelovsky. 'Tenant' was first played live on 19 March 1980 at the Osborne Club in Manchester.

'Trophy'

In an interview with Rosalind Russell for Record Mirror, published on 23 February 1980, 'Siouxsie & The Banshees: Siouxsie And The Bitter Pill', Russell discussed, among other band-related themes, '…John Corrie's Private Members Bill to amend the 1967 Abortion Act. Corrie and his supporters want to nobble the Act, making it virtually impossible for anyone without money to obtain a legal abortion in this country…'[541]

There was a huge rally in London to protest against the Bill and to lobby MPs. During the speeches in Parliament, letters were read out from those who couldn't be there but were vehemently opposed to reform the Act, among them Siouxsie and The Banshees, whose message was acknowledged with much affirmation.

Sioux wasn't expecting the letter to be read out: 'I wasn't doing it to make a speech, I feel strongly about the issue. I just can't believe that they (Parliament) would want to take this step back to the dark ages. Really, there's no debating it — it's a personal thing to do with a woman. Women have the right to decide about their future…'[542]

Throughout the interview, Sioux is articulate and measured, not preaching but rationalising the dilemmas faced by young women and the power of self-determination, independence and choice. 'Women want careers and that's difficult with children. If you've got money, you can do what you want. But backstreet abortions will just put the sharks back in business. Up to 1967, abortion was a twilight zone. How many battered babies were the result?'

Sioux also mentions the prevalent tyranny of stereotyping with '…some little girls… given dolls that wet their nappies, or ironing boards and toys that they have to work with. And that's when they are at their most imaginative stage. Little boys are given spaceships, adventurous things. I didn't have many toys anyway, but I was given the old dolly. I preferred going out to playing with things.'[543]

'John and Kenny are going to recognise a few of the titles of the new songs, I think. Old lyrics that they've seen and turned their noses up at.'[544] Steve Severin.

The third track, side one of 'Kaleidoscope' and one of the songs originally pencilled in for 'Join Hands', 'Trophy' is '...a McGeoch number with a recurring guitar motif and an exploration by Siouxsie's lyrics of the usefulness of remembering past triumphs... "Dust gathers on mementos, dust gathers on proud moments, young voices grow thick and old, the cheers are distant, wearing thin".'[545]

The lyric is also possible part exorcism as Siouxsie and The Banshees, whatever the fanfares and may have been, view the past as something to be kept in a museum and '...locked away or polished every day.'[546] 'Trophy' also has the air of the mausoleum about it; the past was great, it's respected, dead and buried now, the period of mourning has elapsed; time to move on.

'Trophy' is another cornucopia of musical richness and is a hybrid of adventures in sound, largely due to the contribution of saxophone by McGeoch, almost lending the song a big-band feel, mixed with a hint of glam à la Roxy Music with a call and response between reed and pickup, executed with sangfroid.

The military snap of Budgie's drum is again evidenced in the song, as is Severin's bass, which, throughout 'Kaleidoscope', demonstrates flair and proficiency and is in many ways the glue that holds the audacious experimentation of the songs together.

Sioux's vocal delivery blends the song perfectly; another beautiful instrument, creating the 'fourth wall', akin to the mirror in Jan Van Eyck's 'Arnolfini Portrait' (1434),[547] and completing the song.

'Hybrid'

'That's good. Got a good middle bit.'[548] Budgie.

'It's a love song really. You read about how love's supposed to be, but in the papers you see all these other things that people do to get their certain kicks. More people seem to have those sort of kicks than meeting the girl next door. It's an angle of looking at things and they are there — it's not purely fictional.'[549]

The intro to 'Hybrid' is almost casually jam-like, abstract and improvised, as though McGeoch is searching for the right notes, held steady by Budgie's solid, imaginative drumming and Severin's stalwart bass, as John McGeoch's saxophone wails expressively, evoking 'Subterraneans' on David Bowie's 'Low'.[550]

McGeoch's guitar playing is a perfect accompaniment to Sioux's nonchalant vocal, which in itself belies the surreal, cryptic nature of the lyrics, akin to the nightmarish, discordant vision conveyed in 'Un Chien Andalou',[551] a 1929 French film written by Spanish artist Salvador Dali and Spanish-Mexican filmmaker Luis Buñuel, who was also the film's director

'Hybrid' is one of the longer tracks on 'Kaleidoscope', affording the band scope to extend their forays into the realms of the experimental; the Velvet Underground-like looseness of the initial song tightened up as McGeoch's guitar playing finds its fullest expression, running in parallel with Sioux's vocal.

'Clockface'

Following the longest track on 'Kaleidoscope', 'Clockface', is conversely the shortest song, at one minute and 52 seconds. Introduced by Severin's bass playing, it is an attenuated, ritualistic, shamanistic incantation, with a chanted vocal from Sioux.

'Clockface' is further evidence of the band defying

categorisation regarding musical genre. Music is the platform from which they express ideas and 'Clockface' exemplifies this philosophy beautifully. It is one of the three songs on which Steve Jones plays: understated, melodious and atmospheric. Severin plays synthesizer. It is an efficacious, attenuated intermission.

'Lunar Camel'

'People who consider dreams to be nothing to do with reality are being narrow-minded. At least a quarter of your life is dreaming; how can you dismiss it? You're a fool not to be affected by it. It's usually quite harrowing, and it's usually telling you something...'[552] Siouxsie Sioux.

'Around the time of 'Kaleidoscope', Sioux had a period when she kept a' notebook by her bed and started writing things down.'[553]

'Lunar Camel', a further sonic escapade, includes Sioux on keyboard duties, described by Billy 'Chainsaw' Houlston[554] thus: 'Against a droning dromedarian backdrop, the hauntingly, melodious (lullaby) vocals, invite you to climb aboard, and travel up and beyond the realms of reality to participate in a gently sweeping night flight over a phantasmagoric fairy-tale world. All this courtesy of Steve's mystic rhythms, and Siouxsie's experiments with her new toy, the synthesiser.

No abrupt end to this one, just a gentle dispersion that leaves you wondering if it's really happened... or was it all a dream?'[555] The nature of the lyrics could be further evidence of a thumbing of the nose to the competition, as, when asked about the band's peers: '... bands like the Clash, Jam?'[556] Sioux answers, 'Look, if I had a good word to say about them I'd tell you but it's so stupid to go slagging off people or bands you don't particularly like. I do like the Cramps though. You can laugh at them, at their characters and they're enjoyable without being part of this movement or that movement.'[557]

The lyric of the song could also be construed as further exorcism of the thoughts and feelings Sioux had about Morris and McKay, with Sioux in the role of the indomitable Black Knight[558] in 'Monty Python And The Holy Grail'.[559]

'Lunar Camel' was conceived as the result of a one of Sioux's dreams: 'I think a lot of interesting things come out in your dreams and sometimes you don't fully understand them and it's just the imagery or the suggestion from them that can lead you down a very interesting path.'[560]

The paring down of the song paradoxically lends it a multi-textural richness, as though one is falling through space and time: the mesmeric, hypnotic digitally sounding drumbeat, mixed using subtly different changes in volume accompanying minimal bass. The filmic, pictorial and moody narrative of the song puts one in mind of a John Carpenter[561] soundtrack, especially the main theme to the film 'Assault on Precinct 13'[562] which, in essence, is the simple but effective multi-layering of a whole range of synthesizer effects set to a somniferous drumbeat.

'Desert Kisses'

'It's Banshee-ballad. Not wet. It's a romantic, lonely song. Casablanca…'[563] Siouxsie Sioux.

'We'll always have Paris.'[564] Rick Blane, 'Casablanca'.[565]

After 'Christine', the first track on side two of 'Kaleidoscope', 'Desert Kisses' is a fully blown, almost orchestrally epically overlayed in its composition. A smorgasbord of sounds, with Severin's bass set to 'full phaser' mode and the inclusion of the sitar playing of McGeoch, accompanied with multi-faceted lead and rhythm guitar, evoking the ghosts of 'Hong Kong

Garden' past.

There are violin-like synthesizer sounds and the hauntingly beautiful credited 'Sirens', a pseudonym for the voices of Sioux, Severin and Budgie. The song swelters and swoons, both lyrically and musically' as images of ocean and sand are conjured through the words of the song.

The instrumentation in the song, attributable partly to McGeoch's sitar playing, sees the band entering the realms of the sublime and it is, therefore, unsurprising, that Sioux, once dubbed 'Ice Queen'.[566] should, when the muse is upon her, deliquesce now and again.

Sioux also plays Zills,[567] which add to the wistful evocation of far-flung places. It is also, although perhaps a little fanciful, not inconceivable that Sioux held in her psyche a little romanticism about her parents' first meeting on the African continent. The lyrics also have a semblance of the Homeric[568] as channelled through the final two verses of the Thom Gunn[569] poem 'The Discovery of the Pacific':

> 'And now their skin is caked with road, the grime
> Merely reflecting sunlight as it fails.
> They leave their clothes among the rocks they climb,
> Blunt leaves of iceplant nuzzle at their soles.
>
> Now they stand chin-deep in the sway of ocean,
> Firm West, two stringy bodies face to face,
> And come, together, in the water's motion,
> The full caught pause of their embrace.'[570]

The song's wistful beauty is an uncynical pan, again confounding any notion of Siouxsie and The Banshees being anything other than kaleidoscopically multi-dimensional.

'Red Light'

A sordid state of affairs, with all the damp, bare basement evocation one might associate with a clandestine appetite for titillating photographs, the red light has an unsettling ambiguity: used in the analogue chemical photographic process inside the darkroom, or, outside the darkroom, denoting the activities within and keeping daylight and unwanted parties out, or the Red Light district, where neon red lights are used in the doorways of prostitutes in areas such as Pigalle in Paris, De Wallen in Amsterdam, Reeperbahn in Hamburg and Antwerp's Schipperskwartie. These red neon neighbourhoods entice and cajole; piquing curiosity, even if it's just to take a peek.

It would be surprising if neither Sioux or Severin had seen Michelangelo Antonioni's 1966 film 'Blow Up',[571] the storyline of which pertains to the film's protagonist, fashion photographer Thomas, played by the actor David Hemmings,[572] immersed in a world of 1960s London hedonism, takes a series of impromptu clandestine photographs of a tryst between two lovers, a male and a female, in Maryon Park.[573]

Enlarging the black and white photographs in his darkroom studio reveals a third, blurred figure lurking in the bushes with what appears to be a pistol pointed at the male. Intrigued, Thomas returns to the park the same evening to find the man's body. The film juxtaposes aspects of manipulation and exploitation in Thomas's relationship with the young models, which extends beyond taking photographs, and Thomas's search for something more viscerally tangible and meaningful beyond the cosmetically manufactured realms of the fashion industry.

Billy Chainsaw comments on 'Red Light': 'The repetitious, electronic precision of Steve's synthesiser, and the sound of the rhythm-box and drums, produce an appropriate and ominous glare, to accompany Siouxsie's vocals; until the listener is overpowered, and drawn into the very core of the camera, where the soul is stripped bare and the faults revealed — not a pretty picture.'[574]

The lyric, one of Sioux's withering best, pertains to all the sleaze and desperation one might associate with late-night salacious proclivities in both dark room and dark room, the drum beat suggesting a world of smoke-filled subterranean Epicureanism and red-telephone-box call girl 'tart cards.'[575]

As Billy Chainsaw suggests, this is not a decorous world, as illustrated by the phrases 'shutterslut' and 'Kodak whore', and any promises of transcendental, lustful gratification are soon vitiated through the reality of 'an ancient nipple shrinking.'

Sioux is responsible for the mesmeric sound of the camera shutter one can hear on the song.

Although not released as a single, a promo video was filmed at Battersea Studios in June 1980, again directed by Clive Richardson. The Venetian-blind motif appears again, as it does in 'Christine', as well as the Rob O'Connor-designed 'Kaleidoscope' album cover, with Sioux, Severin and Budgie on the front cover, using a motion-blur effect that makes the figures appear out of focus and Severin and Budgie seem conjoined-twin like as they appear in motion, not unlike the effect Francis Bacon gave his paintings when he wanted to complete them by adding a slash or smear of white oil paint.

Sioux squats, staring out at the viewer, wearing a painterly, primary-colour tee-shirt that matches the typesetting of the album on the top left-hand corner. The 'Red Light' video is a clever juxtaposition and synchronisation of various lyrical elements, both literal and metaphorical, aligned with the sound of the camera shutter, switching between stroboscopic images of Sioux and Severin (on synthesizer duties) and the scene, drenched with the red light of the song as myriad different, overlaid Siouxsies appear, one of which dances against the backdrop of the blind and others, with sunglasses both on and off, come into the frame.

The second half of the video sees the band appear as a three piece as with 'Happy House' and 'Christine', again with the absence of McGeoch, who was still fulfilling Magazine duties. The irregularity of camera angles adds to the unsettling atmosphere of the song.

'Paradise Place'

'One example was this woman who went to have her crows' feet done, and one of these surgeons cut her eyelid off. It's irreparable and now she's constantly got one eye open with no eyelid. There's nothing you can do. Lots of women have died from infection — breast enlargement is most popular and breast decreasing is next popular. A lot of women die from oozing blood and milk and puss!'[576] Siouxsie Sioux.

A song about the resulting travails of plastic surgery, especially, as Sioux alludes to, in 'Beverley Hills, that operate at a cut price (slice), very cheap, and they end up messing up someone's features at the cost of how cheap it is.'[577]

Expanding on this theme, Sioux comments on the 'gross abominations caused by these operators. In the States it's legal for plastic surgeons to advertise like in Yellow Pages. Liquor Mart is the cheapest place to get beer, this is the cheapest place to get your nose fixed. It's quite common for American women to spend a few hundred quid getting something done — wrinkles, nose, ears, thighs toned down — for a cut price slice. It's quite horrific the things that go on. They have to go to proper surgeons then and spend three times as much getting it put right. They call them the 'Cosmetic Cowboys', and there's this actual place called 'Paradise Place' in Beverley

Hills.'[578]

An article in the New York Times Magazine 'The Dark Side of Plastic Surgery'[579] discusses the case of Elaine Young, a Los Angeles realtor whose 'successes... never assuaged her feelings of emptiness and of "not being good enough".'

In the spring of 1977, an old acquaintance walked into her office. 'She looked gorgeous, with stunning high cheekbones. She told me she had had silicone injections in her face... The next day, I was in her doctor's office.' For the next year and a half, Dr Jack Startz injected silicone into Elaine Young's cheeks at least once a month for the purpose of creating the look of strong, high cheekbones. Immediately following the injections, her face would swell, but "the silicone would go down the next day and it looked good." Really good, Elaine thought. She sent her friends and many of her celebrity clients to Dr. Startz.

About three years later, Elaine noticed that the shape of her face was changing. The silicone seemed to be moving and growing. Initially, it was 'just around the cheekbones; then it started moving around and growing out of both sides of my face. I became ugly and grotesque...'[580]

'Paradise Place' is an example of what happens when Siouxsie and The Banshees throw everything at a song, resulting in a multi-layered montage or patchwork of delicious noise and experimentation. Steve Jones plays guitar on 'Paradise Place', as does Sioux, both electric and acoustic.

The ensemble is completed by the steady underpinning of rhythmic aces Severin and Budgie, whose snare drum is as sharp as the cosmetic surgeon's scalpel or chisel. The impression of the song reflects the connotations of Sioux's lyric, creating a sense of unreality, not altogether without humour, as she sings of eyes being in the right place, as though some sort of hybridised inverse Prometheus or mid-career Picasso portrait.

The Mantovani[581] reference puts one in mind of the

final scene of the 1975 Bryan Forbes-directed film 'The Stepford Wives', where all the replicant, replacement wives exchange perfunctory pleasantries with each other in the local supermarket set to the sentimental, string-laden Michael Small[582] film score.

'Skin'

'Fur will still be prone to zeitgeist vagaries. For centuries, it was subject to sumptuary laws: wearing fur was not only a sign of wealth but of status. In the cinema and in Tatler, people saw glamorous furs. But in the "modom" shops on the High Street, not so much. And now of course, fur or its usurper, faux fur, mostly appear as ratty bits of goodness knows what on cheap-as-chips parkas, or as vintage "fun fur".'[583]

Fittingly, after its predecessor 'Paradise Place', which dealt with the pitfalls of humans having bits chopped off, silicone filled or realigned for the vanity's sake, the eleventh track on 'Kaleidoscope' sees Siouxsie and The Banshees in acerbically observational mode with 'Skin', a song about the butchering of animals solely for their fur, so the supposedly surgically enhanced owner can drape themselves in the 'Mink, seal and ermine' of the song lyric. It's conceivable that Sioux might baulk at the prospect but 'Trophy', 'Red Light', 'Paradise Place' and 'Skin', as a group of songs, are perilously close to a 'concept', if one were to see them in terms of expendable commodification, as Siouxsie suggests, 'It sounds really wet when you talk about animals, but it's exactly the same sort of emotion that you feel when you read about... a really defenceless four-year-old kid and it's been battered to death. It's just unthinkable that they've been treated like a little doll and slung about. It builds up a real sense of 'how could they?"'[584]

Sioux also doesn't buy the counter argument that there is

too much a proliferation of these animal species, as alluded to in the lyric 'There's just too many of them,'[585] expanding, 'We're against their pathetic arguments about the culls, saying there are too many animals. The one thing there is too much of is people.'[586]

The initial softness of the song, beginning with the scuttling sound of electric guitar and bass, soon to be accompanied by the shotgun-like snare and the hand-held Melodia played by Sioux, all add to the tension of the song as it takes full flight in parallel with the lyric 'Just a bitch in the manger to the balances of nature',[587] and result in Dervish intensity, perhaps Budgie's finest three minutes and 46 seconds on the album. The intensity ratches as the song builds in its venomous tirade and what Billy Chainsaw describes as 'animalistic urgency.'[588]

Even as the song burns itself out after the intense conflagration, the embers continue to glow with dazzling potency. During the recording for 'Kaleidoscope', 'Sitting Room', a short (one minute 22 seconds), playful demo was recorded with the triumvirate of bass guitar, drum machine and keyboard. It is not inconceivable that 'Sitting Room' might have ended up as one of the tracks on the album.

Chapter 8
Hands Rejoined

'Kaleidoscope' peaked at number five in the UK album charts, a rather extraordinary achievement considering the travails the band had gone through a year previously with the deficit of a guitarist and drummer, with the remainder of a tour to fulfil. With McGeoch now a full time Banshee, the band embarked, after McGeoch's official debut at the Futurama Festival, on a 33-date tour that included stints in Paris, Berlin, Hamburg, Dublin, Philadelphia, New York, Toronto, Boston and Los Angeles (where they played early and late evening performances on 27 November to 30 November). They ended the year with a performance at the Hammersmith Palais in London on 30 December 1980.

Touring America was to prove a great adventure for the band, although rather curate's-egg-like in terms of audiences, with East Coast crowds tending to be more receptive than those on the West Coast, and with Budgie commenting, 'We had a few cool young things at our East Coast gigs, but once we got to California everyone looked terrible. Even the ones who were trying to be punks were just spoiled rich kids wearing bin liners and safety pins,'[589] and Siouxsie observing 'America was at least five years behind Britain in terms of its musical taste. You see pictures of our early gigs over there and almost the entire audience is wearing lumberjack shirts and sporting feather haircuts. It's a grotesque sight.'[590]

Siouxsie and The Banshees were entering a new phase of camaraderie and creativity, with bonds being formed between band members. McGeoch and Severin became particularly close, with Severin commenting, 'I clicked with John immediately. I know I have a spiritual bond with Scots in general but this was instantly easier than with either (former members) John McKay and Kenny Morris. We started to hang out together almost immediately.'[591]

With a top ten album, two virtuoso musicians in the Banshees' fold, and a new lease of confidence and experimental licence igniting the cumulative talent and unassailable ambition of Sioux and Severin, the band were at the point of something extraordinary.

The story continues…

Epilogue

I made a conscious decision to complete the Banshees' story before the mezzanine phase of the single 'Israel',[592] which was recorded and released between 'Kaleidoscope' and 'Juju'[593] in the hope that there might be further interest and appetite for a sequel to 'Siouxsie and The Banshees: The Early Years'. The years 1976 to 1980 are really quite remarkable in the band's history, not least because Sioux readily admits that she was 'taking a punt' when she and Severin initially went on stage at the 100 Club on 20 September 1976.

However, a mixture of tenacity, ambition, graft and defiance took the band all the way to the portals of Polydor when they signed to the record label on 9 June 1978, leading to one of the most memorable and wonderful pop singles ever recorded, 'Hong Kong Garden', and one of the most perfectly formed debut albums, 'The Scream', with its themes of suburban curtain-twitching dystopia, tabloid sleaze and filmic and literary allusions.

Then the conception of 1979's 'Join Hands', an intriguing, ambitious album in its scope, reflecting the band's questioning of what was possible for them musically, committing a 14 minute and eight seconds version of 'The Lord's Prayer' to vinyl and referencing a whole gamut of influences from Edgar Allan Poe to Canadian war poet John McCrae.

The disappearance of established Banshees' members John McKay and Kenny Morris on 7 September 1979 did nothing to quell the defiance of Sioux and Severin as they set about finding a replacement guitarist and drummer, after, at unbelievably short notice, drafting in the services of a willing Robert Smith, and Budgie, to complete the remaining dates of the 1979 tour.

After inviting John McGeoch to audition/rehearse with Siouxsie and The Banshees in early January 1980, while McGeoch was still officially a member of Magazine, the band's synergy was resolutely complete and cemented with McGeoch's live debut with the Banshees on 13 September 1980 at the Futurama Festival at Queen's Hall in Leeds.

No one could have second guessed the sheer scope of 1980's polychromatic 'Kaleidoscope', which includes guitar playing by ex-Sex Pistol Steve Jones on three of the 11 tracks, with McGeoch playing on eight tracks. This was a band on a mission to rip up whatever rule book existed and, not only that, they would rewrite it, on their own terms, from beginning to end.

Acknowledgments

This book wouldn't exist without Jerry Bloom, Managing Director at Wymer Publishing, for which he has my wholehearted thanks and appreciation. I also thank my good friend Adrian Jarvis, whose books 'Chasing Shadows: The Search for Rod Evans' and 'Sculpting In Rock: Deep Purple 1968–70' are Wymer publications.

Huge thanks and appreciation go to Mike Stavrou, Steve Lillywhite, Ray Stevenson, Rob O'Connor, John Robb, Jill Mumford and Bertie Marshall for being so giving and generous with their time and answering my, often convoluted, questions with good humour and patience. I owe a debt of gratitude to Mark Paytress whose 'Siouxsie and The Banshees The Authorised Biography' proved invaluable in offering such a candid insight into the band's machinations and psyche, as well as such detailed chronology of events.

I thank the absolutely brilliant 'The Banshees and Other Creatures' website for a seemingly endless source of meticulously researched and collated Banshee's information. I am indebted to my brother Don for fostering my initial love of music. I also offer thanks to my friends Russell Wallace and Charles Taylor for their entertaining anecdotal observations about seeing Siouxsie and The Banshees playing live in a later incarnation with the introduction of the third John (Valentine Carruthers), as well as continuing to help me broaden my musical palate.

Most importantly, I reserve my greatest thanks for Catharine, Hermione, Cicely and Jude for their unwavering support and encouragement, not just in the instance of writing this book, but always.

Notes And References

1 'Bromley Bertie' Bertie Marshall SAF Publishing 2006.
2 Apocalyptic Consumerism: George Romero's 'Dawn of the Dead' 1978- A fortieth anniversary retrospective 2018.
3 'Siouxsie and The Banshees The Authorised Biography' Mark Paytress Sanctuary Publishing 2003.
4 Record Collector Suburban Relapse: The Birth of The Banshees June 2009.
5 Interview with Ray Stevenson 18 September 2022.
6 Siouxsie and The Banshees 'The Authorised Biography' Mark Paytress Sanctuary Publishing 2003.
7 Michael Bracewell 'Her Dark Materials' The Guardian Newspaper 24 September 2005.
8 ibid.
9 ibid.
10 Paytress.
11 Paytress.
12 Paytress.
13 'Anarchy in the Year Zero The Sex Pistols, The Clash and the Class of '76' Clinton Heylin Route 2017.
14 'Anarchy in the Year Zero The Sex Pistols, The Clash and the Class of '76' Clinton Heylin Route 2017.
15 Leonard Naverez Musical Urbanism 'Whey we don't hear the city in Siouxsie and The Banshees' February 26 2012.
16 ibid.
17 Michael Bracewell 'Her Dark Materials' The Guardian Newspaper 24 September 2005.
18 'I swear I was there, Sex Pistols, Manchester and the gig that changed the world' David Nolan Music Press 2016.
19 Anarchy in the Year Zero The Sex Pistols, The Clash and the Class of '76' Clinton Heylin Route 2017.
20 Anarchy in the Year Zero The Sex Pistols, The Clash and the Class of '76' Clinton Heylin Route 2017.
21 Heylin.
22 Heylin.
23 Heylin.
24 Heylin.
25 Siouxsie and The Banshees 'The Authorised Biography' Mark Paytress Sanctuary Publishing 2003
26 Billboard Magazine Gustav Metzger, 'Auto-Destructive' Artist Who Inspired Pete Townshend, Dies at 90 3/2/2017.
27 ibid.
28 'Anarchy in the Year Zero The Sex Pistols, The Clash and the Class of '76' Clinton Heylin Route 2017.
29 Clinton Heylin Interview – Anarchy in the Year Zero Route Online 2017.
30 'Queens of British Pop' Diane Newton first aired April 2009.
31 Interview with Ray Stevenson 18 September 2022.
32 'I Swear I Was There - Sex Pistols, Manchester and the Gig that Changed the World' David Nolan.
33 '1988 The New Wave Punk Explosion' Caroline Coon 1983 Omnibus Press.
34 Listen to Siouxsie and The Banshees provocative debut at the 100 club, 1976 Jack Whatley Far Out Magazine May 2020.
35 Whatley.
36 Whatley.
37 Whatley.
38 Record Collector 04 October 2007 20 Minutes To 20 Years – The Banshees' Tale.
39 'That's me in the picture: Simon Wright remembers seeing the Sex Pistols at the 100 Club in September 1976' The Guardian Friday 14 October 2014.
40 '1988 The New Wave Punk Explosion' Caroline Coon 1983 Omnibus Press.
41 Interview with Ray Stevenson 18 September 2022.
42 '1988 The New Wave Punk Explosion' Caroline Coon 1983 Omnibus Press.
43 Whatley.
44 "Humourless, us"? Siouxsie & the Banshees Phil Sutcliffe, Sounds, 29 September 1979.
45 Coon.
46 Coon.
47 Coon.
48 Coon.
49 Siouxsie and The Banshees 'The Authorised Biography' Mark Paytress Sanctuary Publishing 2003.
50 Paytress.
51 Paytress.
52 Whatley.
53 Siouxsie and The Banshees first gig Paul Nicholas M Magazine 22 Jul 2011.
54 Kenny Morris (Siouxsie And The Banshees): The John Robb interview 25 December 2020.
55 Kenny Morris (Siouxsie And The Banshees): The John Robb interview 25 December 2020.
56 Robb.
57 Robb.
58 Robb.
59 There are several online sources attesting to Siouxsie and The Banshees playing on the same bill but most state the second gig is The Red Deer, Croydon on 24 February 1977.
60 Robb.

61 Robb.
62 Robb.
63 Paytress.
64 Paytress.
65 'Berlin Bromley' Bertie Berlin SAF Publishing 2006.
66 Paytress.
67 Today programme originally aired on ITV 1 December 1976.
68 Today.
69 Today.
70 Today.
71 Today.
72 Today.
73 Today.
74 Today.
75 Paytress.
76 Paytress.
77 What really happened when the Sex Pistols appeared on the Bill Grundy show, John Bennett Classic Rock 21 June 2022.
78 Bennett.
79 Paytress.
80 Paytress.
81 Paytress.
82 Paytress.
83 Paytress.
84 'Punk Rock' The London Weekend Show 28 November 1976.
85 'Punk Rock' The London Weekend Show 28 November 1976.
86 Paytress.
87 Paytress.
88 Paytress.
89 Robb.
90 Robb.
91 Paytress.
92 Paytress.
93 Paytress.
94 Paytress.
95 Interview with Ray Stevenson 18 September 2022.
96 Zoom interview with producer Steve Lillywhite 19 July 2022.
97 Interview with Ray Stevenson 18 September 2022.
98 Paytress.
99 Paytress.
100 Paytress.
101 Paytress.
102 Sounds interview with Vivien Goldman 3 December 1977.
103 'Berlin Bromley' Bertie Marshall SRF 2006.
104 Zigzag Magazine No 77 October 1977.
105 A series of 31 British comedy films released between 1958 and 1978, produced by Peter Rogers and directed by Gerald Thomas.
106 1976 American supernatural horror film directed by Brian De Palma from a screenplay written by Lawrence D. Cohen, adapted from Stephen King's 1974 novel of the same name. Sissy Spacek plays the lead role of Carrie.
107 1962 American psychological horror thriller film directed and produced by Robert Aldrich, from a screenplay by Lukas Heller, based on the 1960 novel of the same name by Henry Farrell. The film stars Bette Davis as Baby Jane Hudson and Joan Crawford as her older sister Blanche Hudson.
108 American sitcom depicting the home life of a family of various fictitious monsters.
109 1922 silent German Expressionist horror film directed by F. W. Murnau starring Max Schreck as Count Orlok.
110 Melody Maker 21 October 1978.
111 Paytress.
112 Paytress.
113 Paytress.
114 Paytress.
115 Radio London.
116 Interview with John Robb 16 August 2022.
117 Spare Rib Magazine Issue 083 pages 16-18 June 1979.
118 Spare Rib Magazine Issue 083 pages 16-18 June 1979.
119 Melody Maker 28 October 1978.
120 Sounds 3 December 1977.
121 Holly Williams (May 30, 2015). 'Patti Smith's Horses: Lenny Kaye, Viv Albertine and more pay homage to the iconic album' 30 May 2015 The Independent.
122 Spare Rib Archive Dr D-M Withers.

123 'Clothes Clothes Clothes Music Music Music Boys Boys Boys' Viv Albertine Faber and Faber 2014.
124 "Rebellious Jukebox" Melody Maker. London. August 15, 1992 p. 34.
125 Jack Whatley Far Out Magazine The Cover Uncovered: The purity of Patti Smith's pioneering punk album 'Horses' 13 December 2020.
126 'The 150 Greatest Albums Made By Women' NPR p15 24 July 2017.
127 Melody Maker 21 October 1978.
128 'The Stepford Wives' Ira Levin 1972 Random House.
129 'Berlin Bromley' Bertie Berlin SAF Publishing 2006.
130 The Living Jarboe 14 March 2014.
131 Sounds interview with Vivien Goldman 3 December 1977.
132 'Maxwell's Silver Hammer' Lennon-McCartney 1969 EMI Records.
133 'Butterflies' was a British sitcom series written by Carla Lane broadcast on BBC2 from 1978 to 1983.
134 'I miss him so much': why did a devoted wife kill the man she loved? Anna Moore The Guardian 29 September 2018.
135 Goldman.
136 Goldman.
137 Goldman.
138 Paytress.
139 NME Derek Johnson 29 October 1977.
140 Paytress.
141 Interview with Ray Stevenson 18 September 2022.
142 Paytress.
143 Sounds Pete Silverton 1977.
144 Sounds Pete Silverton 1977.
145 Silverton.
146 Silverton.
147 Paytress.
148 Paytress.
149 Paytress.
150 Interview with Steve Lillywhite 19 August 2022.
151 The Making Of 'Hong Kong Garden' by Siouxsie And The Banshees Michael Bonner Uncut Magazine 27 May 2016.
152 'Overground' 'Carcass' and 'Helter Skelter'.
153 The Making Of 'Hong Kong Garden' by Siouxsie And The Banshees Michael Bonner Uncut Magazine 27 May 2016.
154 Mojo Magazine September 2014.
155 The Banshees and Other Creatures website Punk Top Ten Interview 08/06/01.
156 Paytress.
157 Paytress.
158 Paytress.
159 Zoom interview with producer Steve Lillywhite 19 July 2022.
160 Steve Lillywhite 19 July 2022.
161 Steve Lillywhite 19 July 2022.
162 Paytress.
163 The Making Of 'Hong Kong Garden' by Siouxsie And The Banshees Michael Bonner Uncut Magazine 27 May 2016.
164 Bonner.
165 Paytress.
166 Paytress.
167 'The Poem of Hashish' Charles Baudelaire Translated by Aleister Crowley 1895.
168 Paytress.
169 Interview with Jill Mumford 26 August 2022.
170 P.T.Barnam promoted freakshow hoxes such as the Fiji Mermaid and Tom Thumb. Co-founded the Barnam and Bailey Circus in 1919.
171 'This is Spinal Tap' 1984 Director Rob Reiner.
172 NME Paul Rambali 19 August 1978.
173 Record Mirror Mike Gardner 19 August 1978.
174 Sounds David Lewis 19 August 1978.
175 Ian Birch Melody Maker 19 August 1978.
176 Of course it wasn't the same band that played The 100 Club with Marco Pirroni on guitar and Sid Vicious on drums.
177 Steve Lillywhite 19 July 2022.
178 Steve Lillywhite 19 July 2022.
179 Steve Lillywhite 19 July 2022.
180 Melody Maker 21 October 1978.
181 Steve Lillywhite 19 July 2022.
182 Melody Maker 21 October 1978.
183 Kenny Morris (Siouxsie And The Banshees) : The John Robb interview 25 December 2020.
184 'Jigsaw Feeling' Siouxsie Sioux Kenny Morris Steve Severin John McKay.
185 The full quotation is 'If you have one ounce of hatred like we had for those two arty ones, you can kill them in my name' when, at short notice, Siouxsie and Steve Severin had to draft in Robert Smith on guitar and the band played an extemporised version of 'The Lord's Prayer'.
186 Record Mirror 9 December 1978.

187 Melody Maker 9 December 1978.
188 Siouxsie Sioux Sounds 24 June 1978.
189 Zigzag October 1977.
190 'The Story of Little Suck-a-Thumb' Henrich Hoffmann 1845.
191 'The Gift' Recorded September 1967 Released January 1968 John Cale Lou Reed Stirling Morrison Mo Tucker.
192 Steve Lillywhite 19 July 2022.
193 Sounds 24 June 1978.
194 'Charles Manson: How Cult Leader's Twisted Beatles Obsession Inspired Family Murders' Kory Grow Rolling Stone 9 August 2019.
195 'Charles Manson: How Cult Leader's Twisted Beatles Obsession Inspired Family Murders' Kory Grow Rolling Stone 9 August 2019.
196 Steve Lillywhite 19 July 2022.
197 Steve Lillywhite 19 July 2022.
198 Melody Maker 21 October 1978.
199 A British cultural movement that was prevalent in the late 1950s and early 1960s in theatre, art, novels, film and television plays.
200 Melody Maker 21 October 1978.
201 'The Hollow Men' TS Eliot publisher Faber and Faber 1925.
202 Steve Severin Melody Maker 21 October 1978.
203 Paul Morley, New Musical Express, 23 December 1978.
205 Morley.
206 Morley.
207 Morley.
208 Morley.
209 Morley.
210 Morley.
211 Morley.
212 Morley.
213 Morley.
214 Morley.
215 Morley.
216 Morley.
217 Morley.
218 Morley.
219 Morley.
220 Morley.
221 Morley.
222 Morley.
223 Morley.
224 Paytress.
225 Morley.
226 Siouxsie & The Banshees: 'The Scream' Peter Silverton, Sounds, 14 October 1978.
227 Silverton.
228 Silverton.
229 Silverton.
230 Silverton.
231 Silverton.
232 Silverton.
233 Silverton.
234 Silverton.
235 William Blake 'Engraving of the Lacoon' 1826-1827.
236 'Siouxsie and the Banshees: The Scream' Kris Needs, ZigZag, November 1978.
237 Needs.
238 Needs.
239 Needs.
240 Needs.
241 Needs.
242 Needs.
243 Needs.
244 Needs.
245 Needs.
246 Needs.
247 Needs.
248 Needs.
249 Needs.
250 Needs.
251 Needs.
252 Needs.

253 'Fame is a fickle Food' Emily Dickinson 1702 The Belknap Press of Harvard University Press 1999.
254 Paytress.
255 Paytress.
256 Paytress.
257 Paytress.
258 'Siouxsie and The Banshees' Kris Needs ZigZag magazine December 1978.
260 Needs.
261 Needs.
262 Needs.
263 Needs.
264 Needs.
265 Needs.
266 Needs.
267 Needs.
268 Paytress.
269 Paytress.
270 Siouxsie and The Banshees Kris Needs November 1978.
271 Siouxsie and The Banshees Kris Needs November 1978.
272 Sounds 7 April 1979.
273 Lennon- McCartney, released 26 May 1967.
274 One of the earliest forms of rock and roll which has its roots in western swing and rhythm and blues music.
275 Origins in punk rock and garage rock which started in the 1970s in California, New York and London.
276 Kenny Morris (Siouxsie And The Banshees): The John Robb interview 25 December 2020.
277 The Banshees and Other Creatures website.
278 Twelfth and final studio album by T. Rex. Released on 11 March 1977 on EMI Records.
279 The Banshees and Other Creatures websiteSource: Mark Paytress Liner Notes for Join Hands 2006 digital remaster.
280 The Banshees and Other Creatures websiteSource: Mark Paytress Liner Notes for Join Hands 2006 digital remaster.
281 The Banshees and Other Creatures websiteSource: Mark Paytress Liner Notes for Join Hands 2006 digital remaster.
282 1960 British science fiction horror film by Anglo-German director Wolf Rilla.
283 Paytress.
285 Post-Punk online journal March 2015.
286 Post-Punk online journal March 2015.
287 The Banshees and Other Creatures websiteSource: Mark Paytress Liner Notes for Join Hands 2006 digital remaster.
288 World War One Poem first published in England's Punch magazine in December 1915.
289 Max Kay Interviews Geordie Music UK June 1984.
290 "Humourless, us"? Siouxsie & the Banshees Phil Sutcliffe, Sounds, 29 September 1979.
291 'Regal Zone' Sioux Severin McKay Morris. Lyrics by Severin.
292 Isiah 1:19 King James Bible 1611.
293 The Banshees and Other Creatures website Source: Sounds 29 September 1979.
294 'Alice's Adventures In Wonderland' Chapter One Down The Rabbit Hole Lewis Caroll Macmillan publishing 1865.
295 The Banshees and Other Creatures website Source: Melody Maker 17 February Source 1979.
296 Icons Siouxsie Severin McKay Morris.
297 The Banshees and Other Creatures websiteSource: Sounds 7 March 1981.
298 French television serial made in the late 1960s directed by Yannick Andrei. Shown on the BBC in the 1970s.
300 Paytress.
302 Siouxsie and The Banshees Join Hands review Jon Savage, Melody Maker, 1 September 1979.
303 'The Premature Burial' Edgar Allan Poe 1844 The Philadelphia Dollar Newspaper.
304 Interview with Mike Stavrou 31 October 2022.
305 The Banshees and Other Creatures websiteSource: Sounds 29 September 1979.
306 'The Premature Burial' 1844 Edgar Allan Poe The Philadelphia Dollar Newspaper.
307 'The Premature Burial' 1844 Edgar Allan Poe The Philadelphia Dollar Newspaper.
308 'The Premature Burial' 1844 Edgar Allan Poe The Philadelphia Dollar Newspaper.
309 'The Premature Burial' 1844 Edgar Allan Poe The Philadelphia Dollar Newspaper.
311 The Premature Burial' 1844 Edgar Allan Poe The Philadelphia Dollar Newspaper.
313 'The Exorcist' 1973 Directed by William Friedkin.
314 Interview with Mike Stavrou 31 October 2022.
315 Siouxsie And The Banshees: Join Hands Jon Savage, Melody Maker, 1 September 1979.
316 Released March 28 1963, directed by Alfred Hitchcock, based on Daphne du Maurier's short story 'The Birds published 1952.
317 American folk song, originally adapted from Wee Cooper O'Fife in the late 1900s.
318 Scottish folk song with its origins in the late 1880s.
319 Interview with Mike Stavrou 31 October 2022.
320 Paytress.
321 The Lord's Prayer, also called the Our Father or Pater Noster, a central Christian prayer which Jesus instructed as the way to pray. 1662 Book of Common Prayer.
322 English-language nursery rhyme and musical round, composed by Thomas Ravenscroft, published in 1609.
323 Deuteromelia: or The Second Part of Musick's Melody, or Melodious Musick of Pleasant Roundelaies, K. H. mirth, or Freemen's Songs, and Such Delightful Catches Composer: Thomas Ravenscroft 1609.

324 Early in March 1554 the three English reformers and later Oxford martyrs, the archbishop of Canterbury, Thomas Cranmer, the former bishop of Worcester, Hugh Latimer, and the bishop of London, Nicholas Ridley, were transported to the supposedly safe location of Oxford to expedite their trials. Their stay in Oxford, however, turned out to be a long one, lasting until their execution by burning outside the Northgate there: Latimer and Ridley on 16 October 1555; Cranmer on 21 March 1556. Source: The Oxford Martyrs in Oxford: The Local History of their Confinements and their Keepers. Published online by Cambridge University Press: 01 April 1999.

325 Catching Fog http://nettelhorst.com/blog1/2013/05/04/three-blind-mice/ 'Three Blind Mice' Posted 4 May 2013 by R.P. Nettelhorst.

326 W. S. Baring-Gould and C. Baring-Gould, The Annotated Mother Goose: Nursery Rhymes Old and New (Bramhall House, 1962) .

327 Founded in 1960, became The Delga Group - encompassing design, origination, print, finishing and fulfilment - located in Rochester. Formerly address was located in Bromley, Kent.

328 Interview with Mike Stavrou 31 October 2022.

330 'The Banshees and other creatures. Source: Sounds 29 September 1979.

331 Australian Fairlight Computer Music Instrument (CMI), a vintage but state-of-the-art Synthesizer/Sampler workstation. .

332 Modular synthesizer developed by the American engineer Robert Moog.

333 Stavrou.

334 Neil Gaiman 'Coraline' 2002 Bloomsbury Publishing.

335 Songwriters: Susan Ballion Mother / Oh mein Papa lyrics © BMG Rights Management. Source: LyricFind.

336 Kate Bush 'Hounds of Love' EMI Released June 1985.

337 Richard Skinner 'Classic Albums' Interview: Hounds of Love BBC Radio 1, 26 January 1992.

338 A group of female and partly human creatures in Greek mythology that lured mariners to their death by their singing.

339 Writer of operas, oratorios and operettas, wrote 'O Mein Papa' which premiered in 1939, 21 December 1911 to 6 September 1977.

340 'Der Schwarze Hecht' (The Black Pike) was a musical comedy that premiered at The Playhouse, Zurich 1 April 1939.

341 'Das Feuerwerk' (The Firework), based on 'Der Schwarze Hecht' premiered at the Staatstheater am Gärtnerplatz 16 May 1950.

342 German theatre and film director, dancer and actor 8 April 8 1894 to 15 July 15 1974.

343 Writer and composer, 1916 to 1988.

344 German composer, lyricist, singer, and actor 29 September 1899 to 20 March 1978.

345 Swiss singer 3 March 1924 – 24 March 2018, won the first Eurovision Song Contest in 1956, released 'O Mein Papa' in 1953.

346 Björk Guðmundsdóttir Born 21 November 1965, recorded 'Pabbi Minn', a version of 'O Mein Papa' on the 1990 album 'Gling-Glo' in collaboration with Trió Guðmundar Ingólfssonar, released October 1990, Bad Taste Records.

347 Albert Edward "Eddie" Calvert 15 March 1922 – 7 August 1978, released Oh Mein Papa on Columbia Records in the UK, 1953

348 Original name Geoffrey Parsons, worked for the Peter Maurice Music Company, specialising in adapting songs originally in foreign languages into the English language. 7 July 1902 to 14 April 1982.

349 Kris Needs 'Siouxsie & The Banshees: Nigh t Of The Long Knives' New Musical Express, 22 September 1979.

350 'The Benefactor' Walter Winward 'The Eighth Pan Book of Horror Stories' 1967 edited by Herbert Van Thal.

351 The Banshees And Other Creatures. Source: Zigzag Magazine May 1980.

352 The Banshees And Other Creatures. Source: Sounds 5 April 1980.

353 Sixth studio album by English progressive rock band Yes, released as a double album on 7 December 1973, Atlantic Records.

354 Anderson Howe.

355 Musical genre characterised by loose, lengthy song structures centered around instrumental layers to produced otherworldly and ethereal sounds.

356 Rock band fusing elements of jazz and Space Rock into their metier, formed in Paris in 1967 by Australian musician Daevid Allen and English vocalist Gilli Smyth.

357 English rock band known as one of the pioneers of Space Rock. Formed in November 1969, Hawkwind have gone through many incarnations and have incorporated many different styles into their music, including hard rock, progressive rock and psychedelic rock.

358 William Claude Dukenfield 29 January 29, 1880 to 25 December 1946, known as W. C. Fields. American comedian, actor, writer and juggler.

359 activist.

360 Superhero in American comic books published by DC Comics. Created by artist Bob Kane and writer Bill Finger, debuted in the 27th issue of the comic book Detective Comics on 30 March 1939.

361 Lester Bullock born 25 June 1953, known by the stage name Dillinger. Jamaican Reggae artist.

362 Born Robert Allen Zimmerman 24 May 24, 1941. American singer-songwriter.

363 Written by David Bowie, originally released 24 November 1972. Lead single from the 1973 album Aladdin Sane.

364 Kenny Morris (Siouxsie And The Banshees) : The John Robb interview 25 December 2020.

365 Stavrou.

366 'Siouxsie And The Banshees: Join Hands' (Polydor) Jon Savage, Melody Maker, 1 September 1979.

367 'Siouxsie And The Banshees: Join Hands' (Polydor) Jon Savage, Melody Maker, 1 September 1979.

368 'Siouxsie And The Banshees: Join Hands' (Polydor) Jon Savage, Melody Maker, 1 September 1979.

369 Savage.

370 Savage.

371 Savage.
372 Savage.
373 Savage.
374 Savage.
375 Siouxsie And The Banshees: 'Join Hands 'Review by Peter Silverton, Sounds, 1 September 1979.
376 Silverton.
377 Silverton.
378 Silverton.
379 Silverton.
380 Silverton.
381 Silverton.
382 Silverton.
383 Silverton.
384 Silverton.
385 Silverton.
386 Silverton.
387 Paul Morley 'The Slits: Cut (Island); Siouxsie & The Banshees: Join Hands (Polydor)' New Musical Express, 1 September 1979.
388 Morley.
389 Morley.
390 Morley.
391 Morley.
392 Morley.
393 Morley.
394 Morley.
395 Morley.
396 Morley.
397 Morley.
398 Morley.
399 Kenny Morris (Siouxsie And The Banshees): The John Robb interview 25 December 2020.
400 Paytress.
401 Paytress.
402 Brand New Retro website.
403 Kris Needs 'Siouxsie & The Banshees: Night Of The Long Knives' New Musical Express, 22 September 1979.
404 Paytress.
405 Kenny Morris (Siouxsie And The Banshees): The John Robb interview 25 December 2020.
406 Paytress.
407 Paytress.
408 Paytress.
409 Paytress.
410 Paytress.
411 'Cured - The Tale Of Two Imaginary Boys' Lol Tolhurst Publisher: Da Capo Press 11 Oct. 2016.
413 Paytress.
414 Paytress.
415 Paytress.
416 1979 American prison thriller film directed by Don Siegel.
417 Paytress.
418 Kris Needs 'Siouxsie & The Banshees: Night Of The Long Knives' New Musical Express, 22 September 1979.
419 Paytress.
420 Needs.
421 Needs.
422 Needs.
423 Interview with Ray Stevenson 18 September 2022.
424 There Was I Waiting At The Church Siouxsie and The Banshees interview with Nick Kent published in New Musical Express, 22 September 1979.
425 Nick Kent.
426 Nick Kent.
427 Nick Kent.
428 Nick Kent.
429 Nick Kent.
430 Nick Kent.
431 Nick Kent.
432 Nick Kent.
433 Nick Kent.
434 Nick Kent.
435 Nick Kent.
436 Nick Kent.
437 Nick Kent.

438 'Cured- The Tale Of Two Imaginary Boys' Lol Tolhurst Publisher: Da Capo Press 11 Oct. 2016.
439 Paytress.
440 1964 film directed by Cy Enfield about outnumbered British soldiers battling with Zulu warriors at Rourke's Drift.
441 https://curiouscreaturespodcast.com/ Episode 10: Kate Schellenbach Pt 2: Los Angeles December 2021.
442 https://curiouscreaturespodcast.com/ Origins Part 1: Rogues And Ruffians November 2021.
443 Paytress.
444 Paytress.
445 https://curiouscreaturespodcast.com/ Bonus Episode 1: Fashion Faux Pas October 2021.
446 Paytress.
447 Paytress.
448 A nine-hour cycle of five plays staged by Ken Campbell and Chris Langham, based on the cult trilogy of anarchist science fantasy novels of the same name written by Robert Shea and Robert Anton Wilson.
449 UK label that was a subsidiary of the club of the same name.
450 Paytress.
451 http://www.philjens.plus.com/rattle/glen_beyond.html Beyond The Valley Of The Sex Pistols Part 2 '79-'81.
452 https://curiouscreaturespodcast.com/ Episode 1: James Murphy: Sex & Drugs & Northern Soul October 2001.
453 'Clothes Clothes Clothes Music Music Music Boys Boys Boys' Viv Albertine Faber and Faber 2014.
454 Released on Island Records in 1979, the album has Johnson's most memorable songs/poems, including 'Sonny's Lettah' and 'Fite Dem Back'.
455 https://curiouscreaturespodcast.com/ Episode 2: James Murphy: The Weird Kid In My Town October 2021.
456 https://curiouscreaturespodcast.com/ Episode 10: Kate Schellenbach Pt 2: Los Angeles December 2021.
457 Paul Morley 'The Slits: Cut (Island); Siouxsie & The Banshees: Join Hands (Polydor)' New Musical Express, 1 September 1979.
458 Musical reference book written by Robert Dimmery first published in 2005 by Universe Publishing.
459 Born 10 January 1956. British film director, DJ and musician.
460 Paytress.
461 https://curiouscreaturespodcast.com/ Episode 10: Kate Schellenbach Pt 1: New York December 2021.
462 Paytress.
463 Paytress.
464 Paytress.
465 Paytress.
466 'Humourless? Us?' - Siouxsie & the Banshees Phil Sutcliffe, Sounds, 29 September 1979.
467 Sutcliffe.
468 Paytress.
469 Siouxsie & the Banshees: De Montfort Hall', Leicester Kris Needs, New Musical Express, 29 September 1979.
470 'Siouxsie & the Banshees: De Montfort Hall', Leicester Kris Needs, New Musical Express, 29 September 1979.
471 https://www.youtube.com/@UntergrundTube Siouxsie And The Banshees - Live in Leicester 1979 [Full Concert].
472 'Siouxsie & the Banshees: De Montfort Hall', Leicester Kris Needs, New Musical Express, 29 September 1979.
473 'Siouxsie & the Banshees: De Montfort Hall', Leicester Kris Needs, New Musical Express, 29 September 1979.
474 Needs.
475 Needs.
476 Paytress.
477 Paytress.
478 'Siouxsie & The Banshees: Siouxsie And The Bitter Pill' Rosalind Russell, Record Mirror, 23 February 1980.
479 'The Light Pours Out Of Me - The Authorised Biography of John McGeoch' Rory Sullivan Burke Omnibus Press 28 April 2022.
480 Sullivan Burke.
481 Sullivan Burke.
482 Sullivan Burke.
484 Sullivan Burke.
485 Sullivan Burke.
486 Sullivan Burke.
487 Sullivan Burke.
488 'Buzzcocks/Magazine/John Cooper Clarke/The Worst/The Fall/The Prefects/The Negatives/Warsaw: Electric Circus, Manchester' Jon Savage, Sounds, 15 October 1977.
489 'Magazine' Peter Silverton, Sounds, 10 June 1978.
490 'Magazine: Real Life' Jon Savage, Sounds, 3 June 1978.
491 Painting by Pablo Picasso, 1907 MoMA.
492 'Magazine: Real Life' Jon Savage, Sounds, 3 June 1978.
493 https://www.theguardian.com/uk/2008/dec/29/nationalarchives-past Key Events Of 1978 Sam Jones 30 December 2008.
494 https://www.theguardian.com/uk/2008/dec/29/nationalarchives-past Key Events Of 1978 Sam Jones 30 December 2008.
495 https://www.theguardian.com/uk/2008/dec/29/nationalarchives-past Key Events Of 1978 Sam Jones 30 December 2008.
496 'Magazine: Real Life' Jon Savage, Sounds, 3 June 1978.
497 'Magazine: Real Life' Jon Savage, Sounds, 3 June 1978.
498 Musical reference book written by Robert Dimmery first published in 2005 by Universe Publishing.
499 https://www.rocklistmusic.co.uk/Uncut_P2.htm#Debut_Albums 'Uncut - 100 Greatest Debut Albums' August 2006.

500 'Magazine: 100 Club, London' Peter Silverton, Sounds, 4 February 1978.
501 'Magazine: The Lyceum, London' Ian Penman, New Musical Express, 5 August 1978.
502 Eleventh studio album by The Beach Boys, released 16 May 1966, on Capitol Records.
503 Written by Dave Formula. Appears on Magazine's 'Secondhand Daylight', Virgin Records, released 30 March 1979.
504 Famous recording studio located in the Kreuzberg district of Berlin, Germany.
505 'Howard Devoto: Shot By Both Sides' Paul Morley, Uncut, November 2000.
506 Written by Howard Devoto. Appears on Magazine's 'Secondhand Daylight', Virgin Records, released 30 March 1979.
507 'Magazine: Second-Hand Daylight' Nick Kent, New Musical Express, 31 March 1979.
508 Sullivan Burke.
509 Sullivan Burke.
510 Sullivan Burke.
511 Debut studio album by Joy Division, released on 15 June 1979 on Factory Records.
512 Sullivan Burke.
513 Sullivan Burke.
514 Club in Covent Garden, London 1979-80, credited with launching the New Romantic movement.
515 Sullivan Burke.
516 Paytress.
517 Paytress.
518 Interview with Ray Stevenson 18 September 2022.
519 Paytress.
520 'Lonely Boy: Tales From A Sex Pistol' Steve Jones. Publisher William Heinemann. First Edition 17 Nov 2016.
521 1971 compilation album by Pink Floyd. Released in the UK on 14 May 1971.
522 Sixth British (Eighth American) studio album by the Rolling Stones. Released December 1967 by Decca Records in the UK. London Records in the US.
523 Paytress.
524 Sullivan-Burke.
525 'Siouxsie & The Banshees: Kaleidoscope (Polydor)' Paolo Hewitt, Melody Maker, 26 July 1980.
526 Original Source 'Siouxsie interview'. Elektron (dutch television). December 1982.
527 Rob O'Connor interview The Banshees and Other Creatures website5 August 2004.
528 Rob O'Connor interview The Banshees and Other Creatures website5 August 2004.
529 The first regular Dutch pop music television series, broadcast by Netherlands AVRO and aired weekly from 22 September 1970 to 27 June 1988.
530 Paytress.
531 'Siouxsie & The Banshees: Haul Of Mirrors' Kris Needs, ZigZag Magazine, May 1980.
532 'The Three Faces of Eve: A Case of Multiple Personality' Corbett H. Thigpen, Hervey M. Cleckley First published 1 January 1957.
533 https://recordcollectormag.com/articles/20-minutes-to-20-years-the-banshees-tale Record Collector '20 Minutes To 20 Years – The Banshees' Tale' October 2007.
534 The Banshees and Other Creatures websitewebsite. Source Sounds 28 February 1980.
535 Rob O'Connor interview The Banshees and Other Creatures website5 August 2004.
536 The Banshees And Other Creatures. Source: 'CHRISTINE/EVE WHITE/EVE BLACK' Billy 'Chainsaw' Houlston.
537 https://www.camera-obscura.co.uk/article/a-brief-history-of-kaleidoscopes.
538 Paytress.
539 Paytress.
540 1976 horror film set in Paris, France, starring Roman Polanski, Isabelle Adjani, Melvyn Douglas, and Shelley Winters
541 'Siouxsie & The Banshees: Siouxsie And The Bitter Pill' Rosalind Russell, Record Mirror, 23 February 1980
542 'Siouxsie & The Banshees: Siouxsie And The Bitter Pill' Rosalind Russell, Record Mirror, 23 February 1980
543 'Siouxsie & The Banshees: Siouxsie And The Bitter Pill' Rosalind Russell, Record Mirror, 23 February 1980
544 'Siouxsie & The Banshees: Haul Of Mirrors' Kris Needs, ZigZag Magazine, May 1980.
545 'Siouxsie & The Banshees: Kaleidoscope (Polydor)' Paolo Hewitt, Melody Maker, 26 July 1980. Songwriters: Susan Janet Ballion/John Alexander McGeoch/Steven John Bailey. Trophy lyrics © Domino Publishing Co. Ltd.
546 Songwriters: Susan Janet Ballion/John Alexander McGeoch/Steven John Bailey. Trophy lyrics © Domino Publishing Co. Ltd.
547 1422 to 1441 Oil On Oak. Collection National Gallery, London.
548 'Siouxsie & The Banshees: Kaleidoscope (Polydor)' Paolo Hewitt, Melody Maker, 26 July 1980.
549Seventh studio album by David Bowie. Released 14 January 1977. RCA Records.
551 Un Chien Andalou (An Andalusian Dog). 1929 French silent film directed by Luis Buñuel, and written by Buñuel and Salvador Dalí.
552 The Banshees and Other Creatures websitewebsite. Source: Melody Maker 10 January 1987.
553 The Banshees and Other Creatures websitewebsite. Source: Deadline August 1980.
554 Billy 'Chainsaw' Houlston ran the Siouxsie & The Banshees 'File' fan club with close involvement from the band from 1979 to 1995. Source: Record Collector 20 Minutes To 20 Years – The Banshees' Tale 4 October 2007 and The Banshees and Other Creatures websitewebsite.
555 The Banshees and Other Creatures websitewebsite Kaleidoscope Billy 'Chainsaw' Houston.
556 The Banshees And Other Creatures. Source: Sounds interview with Robbie Miller 5 April 1980.
557 The Banshees And Other Creatures. Source: Sounds interview with Robbie Miller 5 April 1980.
558 Monty Python And The Holy Grail's most famous scene involves King Arthur (Graham Chapman) and his servant

223

Patsy (Terry Gilliam) encountering the Black Knight (John Cleese) whilst trying to cross a stream which results in the dismembering of all four of the Black Knight's limbs. Source: The Vintage News 9 Nov 2018 written by Steve Palace.
559 1975 British comedy directed by Terry Gilliam and Terry Jones.
560 The Banshees and Other Creatures websitewebsite. Source: The Sun Webchat 2003.
56176 Action Film written, directed and scored by Carpenter.
563 'Siouxsie & The Banshees: Haul Of Mirrors' Kris Needs, ZigZag Magazine, May 1980.
564 Line from Casablanca when Rick Blane tells Ilsa Lund he forgives her for leaving.
565 1942 American romantic film directed by Michael Curtiz.
566 Michael Bracewell 'Her Dark Materials' The Guardian Newspaper 24 September 2005.
567 Turkish finger cymbals.
568 Of, relating to, or resembling Homer or his poems. Source: collinsdictionary.com. Homer was an 8 century BC poet credited with writing epic poems the Iliad and the Odyssey.
569 English poet 1929 – 2004.
570 'The Discovery Of The Pacific' 1970 by Tom Gun poetryblogroll.blogspot.com
571 Film drama and thriller directed by Michelangelo Antonioni 29 September 1912 to 30 July 2007, starring David Hemmings, Vanessa Redgrave and Sarah Miles.
572 8 November 1941 to 3 December 2003. English actor and director.
573 Public park in Charlton, Greenwich, London.
574 The Banshees and Other Creatures websitewebsite Kaleidoscope Billy 'Chainsaw' Houston.
575 Originating in the 1960s, these cards, advertising prostitutes' services, were placed in newsagents' windows or telephone boxes.
576 Siouxsie & The Banshees: Haul Of Mirrors' Kris Needs, ZigZag Magazine, May 1980.
577 Siouxsie & The Banshees: Haul Of Mirrors' Kris Needs, ZigZag Magazine, May 1980.
578 Siouxsie & The Banshees: Haul Of Mirrors' Kris Needs, ZigZag Magazine, May 1980.
579 nytimes.com The Dark Side Of Plastic Surgery By Ann Louise Bardach 17 April 1988
580 nytimes.com The Dark Side Of Plastic Surgery By Ann Louise Bardach 17 April 1988.
581 Annunzio Paolo Mantovani, 15 November 15 1905 to 29 March 29, 1980, Italian-born British conductor and musician .
582 American film score composer May 30 May 1939 to 24 November 24 2003.
583 https://thecritic.co.uk/ 'The end of the skin game' Richard D. North November 2020.
584 The Banshees and Other Creatures websitewebsite. Source: NME 15 August 1981.
585 Songwriters: Susan Janet Ballion / Steven John Bailey Skin lyrics © Wb Music Corp., Webo Girl Publishing Inc., Domino Publishing Co. Ltd., Dreamhouse Music, Lemonjello Music, Webo Girl Publishing, Inc. Source: Musixmatch
586 The Banshees and Other Creatures websitewebsite. Source: 'New Women In Rock' Lisa Thompson 1982 Omnibus Press
587 Songwriters: Susan Janet Ballion / Steven John Bailey Skin lyrics © Wb Music Corp., Webo Girl Publishing Inc., Domino Publishing Co. Ltd., Dreamhouse Music, Lemonjello Music, Webo Girl Publishing, Inc. Source: Musixmatch
588 The Banshees and Other Creatures websitewebsite Kaleidoscope Billy 'Chainsaw' Houston.
589 Paytress.
590 Paytress.
591 'The Light Pours Out Of Me - The Authorised Biography of John McGeoch' Rory Sullivan Burke Omnibus Press 28 April 2022.
592 Siouxsie and The Banshees stand alone single released 28 November 1980.
593 Siouxsie and The Banshees fourth album released 19 June 1981.